AMULETS

AMULETS

SIR W. M. FLINDERS PETRIE

Introduction by Dr Geoffrey T. Martin

OXBOW | books
Oxford & Philadelphia

This edition published in the United Kingdom in 2023 by
OXBOW BOOKS
The Old Music Hall, 106–108 Cowley Road, Oxford, OX4 1JE

and in the United States by
OXBOW BOOKS
1950 Lawrence Road, Havertown, PA 19083

Paperback Edition: ISBN 979-8-88857-000-5
Digital Edition: ISBN 979-8-88857-001-2 (epub)

First published by Constable & Company Ltd, 1914
Facsimile edition published in 1972 by Aris & Phillips Ltd

Oxbow Books is grateful to the Petrie Museum for their collaboration in bringing out these new editions

Printed in the United Kingdom by CMP Digital Print Solutions

For a complete list of Oxbow titles, please contact:

UNITED KINGDOM
Oxbow Books
Telephone (0)1226 734350
Email: oxbow@oxbowbooks.com
www.oxbowbooks.com

UNITED STATES OF AMERICA
Oxbow Books
Telephone (610) 853-9131, Fax (610) 853-9146
Email: queries@casemateacademic.com
www.casemateacademic.com/oxbow

Oxbow Books is part of the Casemate Group

Front cover: String of beads, scarabs, scaraboids and a scorpion amulet. From Gurob, Egypt, Dynasty 18 (*c.* 1550–1069BC). Petrie Museum UC45602. Image © Mary Hinkley, UCL Educational Media.

CONTENTS

CONTENTS

CHAPTER VI.

PROTECTIVE AMULETS. (350)

CHAPTER VII.

HUMAN-HEADED GODS. (448)

CHAPTER VIII.

ANIMAL-HEADED GODS. (260)

CONTENTS

LIST OF PLATES

INTRODUCTION

It is a pleasure to welcome this reprint of Petrie's *Amulets*, which has been unobtainable for many years and which, even after more than half a century, is still a fundamental work of reference.

Petrie, with his usual discernment, recognized the importance of classified catalogues of Egyptian artifacts (of which *Amulets* was the first in a distinguished series written by him), the raw material upon which future archaeologists could base their more detailed analyses of selected objects or groups of objects.

Much of the material in *Amulets* was bought in Egypt by Petrie with a view to assembling a representative collection of Egyptian amulets; only a small proportion came from controlled excavations. It may well be asked therefore—particularly by scholars in other fields of Near Eastern and Aegean archaeology who refer to Petrie's catalogues for dating Egyptian objects from excavations outside Egypt—how Petrie arrived at his dating criteria. From the point of view of modern scholarship the absence of reasoned argument from the chronological standpoint is perhaps the weakest point in Petrie's catalogues. Yet Petrie's vast experience in handling material of every period of Egyptian history in the field enabled him to assign dates, sometimes intuitively, to great numbers of unprovenanced objects in museums and private collections. But Petrie himself realized that his work was only a starting-point, and expected others to build on his foundations, though this hope has seldom been realized. His *Amulets*, in the light of almost sixty years of Egyptological scholarship can be criticized in points of detail. Nonetheless his book is still the first one to which we turn for information on one of the commonest classes of Ancient Egyptian objects. Much more work remains to be done on objects of amuletic use—as on many classes of small artifacts from Egypt—from the point of view of typology and dating.

Petrie somewhat wryly remarks that the use of amulets was still widespread when he wrote in 1914. The situation has hardly changed in 1972. The manufacture and marketing of charms and talismans is a profitable business, and how many of us would deny ever having attributed 'luck' to the possession of some inanimate object? We all know that there are travellers who will never board aircraft unless they are under the 'protection' of a lucky charm. Certain athletes in the recent Olympic Games were seen to be the trusting possessors of lucky 'mascots'.

The belief in the efficacy of amulets, though totally illogical is very deeply ingrained in human nature, and harks back to remote antiquity. The difficulty in getting inside the minds of the ancients and understanding the real meaning of the different kinds of amulets lies mainly in the absence of explanatory texts. With regard to Egypt we are fortunate because many of the amulets have proven religious and other connotations, so that we are not entirely reduced to speculation. Religious papyri lay down instructions for the employment of amulets, and even specify the materials of which ideally they should be made. Excavations have revealed mummies with a whole range of amulets still in position, sometimes mounted on specially-designed frames[1].

Yet there remain many amulets whose meaning is obscure. The value of Petrie's book lies in the fact that it illustrates examples of a wide range of the known types of amulet from Ancient Egypt.

For reference a brief bibliography[2] of important studies on amulets which supplement Petrie's book is here appended for reference:

REISNER, G. A. *Amulets.* Cairo, 2 vols. 1907, 1958 [=Service des Antiquités de l'Égypte. Catalogue général des antiquités égyptiennes du Musée du Caire, Nos. 5218-6000 and 12001-13595].

BUDGE, *Sir* E. A. W. "Amulets", in id., *The mummy: a handbook of Egyptian funerary archaeology.* 2nd. ed. Cambridge, 1925, pp. 306ff.

id., *Amulets and superstitions.* London, 1930.

BONNER, C. *Studies in magical amulets, chiefly Graeco-Egyptian.* Ann Arbor, 1950 [=University of Michigan studies, humanistic series—49]. For supplement and corrections see id., "Amulets chiefly in the British Museum". *Hesperia* XX (1951), 301-45.

GEOFFREY T. MARTIN

August 1972

1. Cf. for example, GRAY, P. H. K., *and* SLOW, D. "Egyptian mummies in the City of Liverpool Museums". *Liverpool Bulletin, Museums Number* 15 (1968), esp. pp. 10–12 (framework for amulets, Roman Period), 50–52, 55 (amulets from a mummy of the Ptolemaic Period).

2. A more complete bibliography will be found in PRATT, I. A., *Ancient Egypt: sources of information in the New York Public Library* (*New York*, 1925), 49, and id., *Ancient Egypt, 1925–1941* (New York, 1942), 44–45.

PREFACE TO THE 2023 EDITION

In the 1970s, a much-anticipated new series of publications illustrated objects and themes related to the excavations of the archaeologist William Matthew Flinders Petrie (1853–1942) in Egypt, and aspects of the collection of University College London's Petrie Museum of Egyptian and Sudanese Archaeology. A young couple setting up in business in the early 1970s, Aris and Phillips published these works, written by members of the UCL Egyptology Department, in their *Modern Egyptology* series. Building on Petrie's own observations, the authors of these volumes aimed to complete the great task of publishing the Petrie Museum of Egyptian and Sudanese Archaeology's vast collection, and to present some of the research that Petrie himself was not able to address in his own published works during his lifetime. As the current Curator of the Petrie Museum, it is a great privilege for me to support Oxbow Books in their mission to republish the series, which remains a key source of information for all those interested in object-based approaches to the study of the ancient world.

The Petrie Museum, part of University College London (UCL), is home to one of the largest and most significant collections of Egyptian and Sudanese archaeology in the world. Free to visit, this extraordinary collection tells stories about the lives of ordinary people who lived along the Nile Valley thousands of years ago. Originally set up as a teaching collection, the Petrie Museum comprises over 80,000 objects housed together with an internationally important archaeological archive. It is a collection of world firsts and 'oldests': the oldest woven garment; the oldest worked iron objects; the first known depiction of loom weaving; the oldest known written document about women's health; the earliest veterinary treatise; the oldest will on paper. The Museum has Designated Status from Arts Council England, meaning that it is considered to have outstanding resonance and national cultural significance. The collection has a substantial, visible international reputation for research, supporting hundreds of researchers every year, both remotely and in person.

The Petrie Museum is named after Flinders Petrie, who was appointed in 1892 as the first Professor of Egyptian Archaeology and Philology in the UK at UCL. Over three-quarters of the material in the Museum comes from excavations directed or funded by Petrie, or from purchases he made for university teaching. In 1880 at the age of 26, Petrie travelled to Egypt to survey the Great Pyramid. For the next five decades he was at the forefront of the development of archaeology in Egypt and later in Palestine, and his detailed methodological approach continues to shape the discipline today.

Petrie worked at more sites, with greater speed, than any modern archaeologist: seeing his life as a mission of rescue archaeology, Petrie aimed to retrieve as much information as possible from sites that were shrinking dramatically in size as Egypt modernised during the late 19th and early 20th centuries. He published a large part, but not all, of the finds from his excavations in his illustrated typological volumes, arranged according to object types and themes. Today, much of the Petrie Museum's collection is displayed and stored in a way which reflects these publications: for example, several storage cupboards are dedicated to the material illustrated in the 'Objects of Daily Use' volume, and objects in the drawers are arranged according to the order of the published plates. This offers a unique opportunity for researchers to engage with Petrie's typological and methodical approach to archaeology, as well as with the history of museum collections.

The first catalogue to be published in the *Modern Egyptology* series was *Amarna: City of Akhenaten and Nefertiti* in 1972 by Julia Samson, Petrie Museum Honorary Research Assistant. As official publishers to the UCL Egyptology Department the series went on to produce facsimile reprints of eight of Flinders Petrie's most important site reports and many of his object catalogues, originally published through the British

PREFACE TO THE 2023 EDITION

School of Archaeology in Egypt. The substantial annual royalties from these reprints were paid into the 'Petrie Fund' at the time, which provided special grants to students in financial need.

In many ways, the new reprints of this classic series can be seen as the latest layer in a vast 'publication stratigraphy' of the thousands of finds from Flinders Petrie's excavations, which now live in museum collections around the world. On reading these volumes, I hope that readers will also be inspired to learn more about the Petrie Museum collection and its fascinating history.

Dr Anna Garnett
Petrie Museum of Egyptian and Sudanese Archaeology,
University College London
January 2023

PUBLISHER'S PREFACE

Oxbow Books is pleased to present this title in our *Classics in Egyptology* series. This series of facsimile re-issues is comprised of two sub-series. The first consists of 16 typological catalogues produced by W.M. Flinders Petrie based on his massive collection of Egyptian artefacts. Mostly excavated by Petrie during many seasons of campaign in the last years of the 19th and early decades of the 20th century, they now reside in the Petrie Museum at University College London. Published between 1898 and 1937 and long out of print, the catalogues were re-issued in facsimile by publishers Aris and Phillips in the 1970s. These were followed in the next 15 years or so by publication of a number of newly commissioned titles, based on more recent examination of elements of the Petrie Collection by contemporary experts, under the name *Modern Egyptology*. A selection of these additional titles forms the second component of our own series.

The archaeology of Egypt continues to fascinate. Multi-disciplinary investigation and research continues unabated, encompassing methodologies, scientific and data processing techniques, theoretical approaches, and even whole paradigms that were unheard of in the 1970s and undreamt of when Petrie was working in Egypt. Yet all the titles included in this series continue to be invaluable sources of basic data, providing an unparalleled resource that can easily be cross-referenced with the actual materials they describe and discuss. They remain within the Petrie Collection where they may be accessed and re-examined as new research flourishes. As historic documents, the Petrie catalogues stand as exemplars of the craft of typological classification, the backbone of modern archaeology – much of which, though refined by absolute dating and another 100 years of research, still stands the test of time.

A note on presentation

The facsimile titles of Petrie's catalogues re-issued in the 1970s were produced from scans of the original publications. Scanning technology at that time was not of the standard or resolution of today. The scans are no longer available, nor has it been possible to obtain, and in doing so destroy, original copies of the Petrie catalogues. These titles have therefore, of necessity, been rescanned from the 1970s re-issues. Where necessary the pages have been digitally enhanced for clarity of reading and to ensure the good quality of the plates, though inevitably a few are not of the standard we might wish, because of the quality of the previous scan, and occasional blocks of text are not precisely 'straight' or evenly situated on the page. However, some pages in the 1970s re-issues had been inserted in the wrong order and this has been corrected. The originals were produced at a folio size. The pages have been reduced slightly to standard A4 for ease of shelving and because this has the effect of slightly improving the scanned images. In some cases, illustrations were presented to scale and the original scale is given on the plate. There were also no digital files available for titles included in the *Modern Egyptology* series, so these too have been scanned from printed copies.

AMULETS

CHAPTER I

THE PRINCIPLES OF AMULETS

1. The present study of Egyptian amulets is based upon the University College collection, which I have tried to make as varied as possible; some two hundred and seventy different kinds of amulets are here described, together with a summary of those in some other collections, in order to show the numbers and the materials of which amulets were usually made. To understand the purpose of these amulets, it is needful to gain some general ideas from the use of amulets in other lands. The belief in the magic effect of inanimate objects on the course of events is one of the lower stages of the human mind in seeking for principles of natural action; it belongs to a condition of the intellect so low as to be incapable of clear reason about cause and effect. Yet it has become so ingrained a habit of thought during the vast ages before observation and induction were developed, that it survives the rise of knowledge and reasoning among most people. The use of amulets is by no means equally general in all races; the lowest of mankind—the Tasmanians—had great confidence in the power of amulets, the Shilluks of the Sudan wear them in a bunch, the Arabs have great faith in charms which are worn, and Southern Italy—in our own, as in Pliny's time—abounds in amulets. Strange to say, a large part of the children of the lower classes in England wear them; and the extent to which persons of supposed education will wear charms and mascots is an extraordinary revelation of the real fatuity and savagery of the mind of modern man. Yet other races seem early to have abandoned such thoughtless beliefs. The Veddahs and the Algerians—apart from Arab influence—avoid amulets, and there is no allusion to amulets in the minute personal details of the Icelandic and Norse Sagas. What is now required is an ethnological study of diffusion of amulets, which might throw light on the connections of various peoples.

2. What is an amulet, and why is it used? The name still defines it very well after two thousand years, and shows one line of diffusion of the idea. The Arabic *hamūlet*, a freight, burden, or thing carried, has passed in ancient times into the west, as it had originated the Latin *amuletus* as early as the time of Pliny. It seems most likely that the name had travelled with the Phoenicians, as they were the only source of Semitic words in the western seas before the Roman age; perhaps Carthage was the intermediary. The amulet therefore means something carried about by the wearer, in order to get some magical benefits from it, apart from any material use. In Egypt such amulets were also put upon the dead for benefiting them in a future existence; and we can hardly deny the name to some kinds of objects copied from personal amulets, and set up stationary in the house. In the records of amulets there is a great confusion with actual medicines, which we should nowadays recognise as acting by natural causes. The line between Nature and magic has been but very slowly defined; and what we look on as mere superstitions were regarded as soundly logical remedies two thousand, or even two hundred, years ago. In extracting ideas from ancient writers it is therefore needful to set aside all internal remedies, and some external ones which might be actually medicinal.

3. The meaning of each of the amulets, and the purpose for which it was carried, is here considered, as that is the real spirit and essence of the subject. Merely to catalogue amulets without any regard to their meaning, is much like collecting pretty shells without knowing anything of the creatures which produce them. The recent works of Prof. Bellucci, of Perugia, on the Italian amulets—ancient and modern—have set an excellent example of the intelligent study of the subject. A paper by Comm. Boni should be noted for its wide view (*Nuova Antologia*, October 1st, 1912). Various general principles of the purpose of amulets have been proposed, or might be considered. But, so far, the different theories have not been weeded by means of the test of actual instances. There may have been several different principles or starting points for the adoption of amulets, or possibly only one broad idea has developed in various ways. To get some insight upon this, it is necessary to try how far different instances can be explained by each view.

4. The explanations that are the more obvious are five:—

(A) The psychic effect of giving confidence and self-reliance, and the intent to live; with the result that the wearer would be thus fortified to steer through dangers without faltering, or would be saved from that terrible weakening due to fear, which often kills men as surely as knife or poison kills. To possess a charm which would defy *tabu* would be a vast advantage in lower forms of culture.

(B) The direction of thought to any physical weakness or disease, may have a very beneficial effect on illness; and the possession of an amulet supposed to benefit the patient, may easily act as a faith-healer and promote real recovery.

(C) The idea of a double or *alter ego* of different organs, connected with them in a mystic way, may be a purpose of amulets. In the tale of Anpu and Bata, the heart of Bata is set in a tree, and anything that happens to it happens also to him. So it might be imagined that a kidney-stone, a blood-stone, an eye-stone, or various other objects supposed to be connected with different organs, would by the care and attention paid to them have a reflex action in strengthening the organ involved.

(D) The provision of a vicarious double, to which evils and diseases may be transferred from the body. An object resembling the disease, or a model of the organ, might be supposed to receive the attacks of the malignant spirits to whom diseases are usually credited, and so save the real person.

(E) The influence often called "sympathetic magic" which might perhaps best be named "the doctrine of similars." Objects which have a similarity one to another, are supposed to be necessarily connected; they are in touch with the abstract quality or influence which has to be evoked: they generally act by producing a similarity in the person, but otherwise by averting a similarity, on the plea that the event has already taken place, and cannot therefore happen again.

No doubt the great majority of charms and amulets recorded by writers, have merely been selected by reason of casual connection. When any unusual event happened—good or bad—the person looked for some cause in his own surroundings; and if he carried, or did, anything unusual, it was naturally connected with the event. Then, no doubt, there was much theorizing from very mixed assumptions, in order to construct a charm for a given purpose. How far human folly can go in such a way anyone may see in the tangible field of medicine by referring to ancient prescriptions.

When we look at the various possible motives for the use of amulets stated above, we may doubt whether any one motive can account for the whole system, or whether several different motives have not been followed. Can all examples come under one explanation? or how many explanations are needful?

5. The only way to study this is to select test instances, and see whether there be cases which can be explained by only one motive, or only by another. To this we proceed.

(A) The Confidence theory will explain such cases as the wearing of part of a bear in order to give strength (Eskimo), a leopard's claw to protect from wild beasts (Central Africa), dog's teeth to protect from a mad dog (Italy), a figure of a siren for security (It.), a lizard with a forked tail to get luck (It.), and the wearing of written charms. But each of these examples can equally be explained by (E), the effect of similars.

Other examples, such as a serpent's skin worn to guard against the bite of reptiles, might be explained by (C), (D) or (E). Further examples are the figure of a heart worn for heart disease (It.), a lump of red coral for menstruation (It.), concretions and inclusions in stone for pregnancy (It.), which might be equally well explained on any of the five theories.

(B) The Faith theory, or the effect of thought-directing, will explain cases such as the fish worn for fecundity (It.), or the bat's head worn to prevent sleep (PLINY, xxx, 48); but these may equally be explained by (E), as cases of the effect of similars. The use of galactitis, a soft white stone worked up into a milky diffusion in water, and taken internally for lactation (PLINY, xxxvii, 59), might be explained by (D) or (E). Other cases which might equally be explained by (C), (D) or (E) are the wearing of a red stone of any kind against bleeding; a milk-white stone for lactation; the Dentalium shell for teething; the nephrite stone for the kidneys; the operculum of a shell ("eye of S. Lucia") for the eyes; an ivory ball like a breast, for lactation; a white and cold ivory tablet for fever (all in Italy); the bones of animals' heads for headache (PLINY, xxix, 36); the wearing of the yellow *Lyncurion* stone for jaundice (PLINY, xxxvii, 13), or a tooth for toothache (PLINY, xxviii, 27).

There is another kind of thought-directing, which must not be confounded with the above. Not only may the patient's thoughts be usefully directed, but also the dangerous thoughts of another person may be diverted away from the person who dreads them, by his wearing some object to distract the attention. In prehistoric times this was done in Egypt by a bright white piece of shell hung on the forehead; in one case a bright piece of sheet copper was used. In modern times women wear in Egypt a bright gilt tubular ornament down the middle of the forehead; and in Damaraland a chief's daughter wore a disc of shell, hung so that she could swing it over either eye (GALTON, *Travels in South Africa*, ed. 1890, p. 63). For the same purpose are the principal amulets against the evil eye in Italy. A facetted rock crystal, or even a bottle stopper, serves to catch the eye and thought of an observer and divert them from the wearer. Similarly the attention is easily diverted to sexual models, both kinds of which are reputed to be powerful protectors. The unquestionable truth of this thought-directing away from the patient has no bearing upon the reality of the beneficial direction of the patient's own thoughts, or the Faith theory.

(C) The Double theory, or *alter ego*, according to which an external double of an organ is so bound up with it that benefits to one are conferred on both, will account for most of the cases named. But where the wearer is unconscious of the amulet, as a tooth worn for teething (Italy, PLINY, xxviii, 78), the foregoing theories, (A), (B), could not hold good, but only the following, (D), (E).

(D) The Vicarious theory supposes that a model worn will receive the attacks of spirits and ward them off the actual person. This—as we have noticed—will account for most of the preceding cases. There are, however, some amulets which are specially to be thus explained, such as the placing of lead amulets on swine to avert suppuration and vermin, the dull, sluggish metal hindering the sluggish evils (It.); the use of amber which has motes in it, or a white opacity, for the benefit of the eyes (It.); the wearing of a tongue of a hyaena or a dog in the shoe to prevent dogs barking (PLINY, xxvii, 42; xxix, 32); the use of a chilly frog against the chill of fever (PLINY, xxxii, 38); the well-known heart or image pricked with pins or stabbed: all of these may be looked on as vicarious, or else as (E), similars.

Somewhat like this is the scape-goat idea of a victim to carry away the evil, as in the transfer of scorpion poison by speaking in an ass's ear (PLINY, xxviii, 42), or the spitting on a frog which is liberated to remove a cough (PLINY, xxxii, 29).

6. All of the examples of the above theories of amulets we have seen to be equally compatible with

(E) The doctrine of Similars, according to which objects which are closely alike have such a connection that power over one, or possession of one, enables the wearer to influence the other or to command like qualities. Here we at once find many cases which are explained by this belief, but which are not touched by any of the four preceding explanations or theories. One of the most instructive accounts of amulets is that by RASMUSSEN, describing the Eskimo in *The People of the Polar North*. The extreme simplicity and directness of the ideas, and the absence of any magical or theistic complication renders this a classical example of the doctrine of Similars. The amulet confers qualities or protects from danger; and—excepting the first case which might be explained on the Confidence theory (A) —these examples can only be reasonably accounted for as Similars. The amulets are: the skin from the roof of the mouth of a BEAR, worn in a child's cap in order to be *strong in danger;* the head or feet of a HAWK, sewn in a boy's clothes in order that he may become *a great hunter;* a black GUILLEMOT's foot, worn to become great *whalers;* a RAVEN's foot, worn to be *satisfied with little;* a head of a FOX, worn to be *cunning and guarded;* the head of a KITTIWAKE (which lays small eggs) put in a girl's clothes that she may give birth to *small children;* a piece of a HEARTHSTONE, which is durable and stronger than fire, worn to give *long life and strength;* a PEBBLE, which drops swiftly from a high rock, put on the necks of puppies that they may be *fleet and strong;* the skin of a LITTLE AUK caught fighting put on a dog that he may be a *fighter*.

In the *Heimskringla* (MAGNUSSON and MORRIS, i, 55—6), there is one of the nearest instances to an amulet in Norse writing: "Swipdag let take the heart out of a wolf, and roast it on a spit, and gave it thereafter to Ingiald, the king's son, to eat; and thenceforth became he the grimmest of all men, and the evillest hearted." This is essentially an instance of Similars.

In Italy the very common use of flint arrowheads or fossil teeth called "thunderstones" to protect from lightning, or serpentine to protect from serpents (also PLINY, xxxvi, 11), can only be explained by Similars. The same idea is shown by putting a dragon's head under the door-sill for good fortune (PLINY, xxix, 20), *i.e.*, trampling on evil influences; also by the frog, transfixed so that it cannot move away, to ensure faithfulness (PLINY, xxxii, 18); while the effect of opposites is shown by the hairs of a she-mule worn for fertility (PLINY, xxx, 49). A complex amulet of watchful animals is that of the eyes of river crabs, wrapped with the flesh of a nightingale in a deer's skin, to give watchfulness (PLINY, xxxii, 38).

From these various examples of charms and amulets, which are compatible with the different theories that we have considered, it appears that though some are consistent with each of the theories, yet no theory will explain all of them excepting the theory of Similars, otherwise called Sympathetic Magic. Other theories may give the explanation of some cases; they cannot be disproved as modes of thought. But every case which we have recounted as critical evidence can be the result of beliefs in Similars; and until some different class of beliefs can be proved to have existed, it is only legitimate to accept that belief as the underlying cause of all the uses of amulets which are generally recognised.

7. There is also another class of amulets, which the wearer regards as entirely individual, and which result from a casual observation of what happens to the person when certain objects are present. This is a lower form of belief than that in the general applicability of an amulet; it presupposes no law, but a chance connection which is wholly unaccountable. Yet—strange to say—this least intellectual form of belief is that which appears commonest at present in "mascots," carried by various classes of illogical persons. When we try to see some underlying cause for such a savage survival we may observe that the occupations of the wearers are those which seem most to depend on chance, and least on continuous will. Actors, gamesters and aviators, as well as motor racers, cling to amulets, and all are dependent upon conditions which are not obviously in their own control. We may smile at the use of basilisk blood to gain success in petitions (PLINY,

xxix, 19,); but it was more reasonable to believe in some general law on the matter than to believe in the effect of a man smoking a cigar opposite a theatre door to gain a profitable audience for the play. We may not believe in a star-fish smeared with foxes' blood, and nailed with copper nails over a door to repel evil (PLINY, xxxii, 16); but we see an ex-prime minister wearing a swastika for luck, and talking heartily about it to uneducated boys. While no one now wears the right shoulder of a chamaeleon to ensure victory (PLINY, xxviii, 29), we yet read of aviators wearing particular trinkets for their safety. On the whole the power of irrational belief seems to have gained, rather than lost its hold in modern times.

8. The primitive mode of thought seems unchanged by all that has past. The untamed mind of man appears to be continually feeling vaguely for different avenues to success; reason is so little developed that benefit seems only to be reached by trying blindly in all directions. I have often been surprised at the helpless way in which Egyptians will do things on the chance of success. They will follow some vague rumour—perhaps at third-hand—of a benefit or a gain, merely to see if any good result comes. It seems like the white ants making tunnels in all directions, on the chance of hitting something to eat, without any guide from the senses. This incessant vague searching, whenever it succeeds, produces a belief that any casual connection with other incidents is a real cause of success; the least intelligent think that their success is only individual to them, and cling to any tangible link as a "mascot"; the more intelligent seek for some law, and frame one of the innumerable generalities about wolves' tongues, dragons' tails, or serpents' eggs, which choke the pages of Pliny and many other old writers.

This subject of individual amulets, or "mascots," does not belong to our present work; the distinction should however be observed between this and the general amulet, and we should regard the difference of the much lower grade of superstition from which it originates. The individual amulet regards only chance connection without any law or reason; the general amulet is in the first groping stage of the acquisition of general laws, which eventually lead to the orderly view of organic nature. Both are absurd to anyone with the least real knowledge; yet the one is hopelessly animistic, while the other shows the sense of law, even if entirely misapplied.

9. When we read the pages of Pliny regarding ancient Italy, or Bellucci about modern Italy, we perceive how largely organic objects are adopted as amulets. These, in the nature of things, have been but rarely preserved for long; and even when found their meaning is not easily recognised. A mere twig of a tree, or a scrap of fur might be casually left in a grave without a meaning; while a carefully wrought stone or pottery object is clearly intentional. Hence we find what is in any case but a small part of the whole mass of amulets that have been in use. The nature of the beliefs in such things is doubtless in continual flux like all matters which have not been fixed by reduction to a written form. We can hardly realise how the thoughts of early man must have been incessantly shifting and changing their form, like an *amoeba*. We are so accustomed to reduce ideas to a written definition, which perpetuates them unaltered until they are entirely out of date, and passed by in further growth, that we cannot feel the sense of all ideas fluctuating with the individual. A popular belief, such as that in amulets and charms is one of the last things to be fixed by writing, and hence it has been exposed longer to the waves of changing thoughts. Even Roman law was not crystallized into writing till well into the historic age; and at the other end of the scale of certainties such vague beliefs as those in amulets must have been continually shifting.

10. In Italy at present we see the result of a long course of decay of beliefs. Of all the purposes of amulets, very nearly half are against the evil eye, and these are most incongruous in their nature—shells, claws, horn, teeth, toads, crescents, crystal, agate, madrepore — everything seems equally applicable. This great variety must have originated in very different ideas of connection; the purposes must have been very diverse originally. But all have been blended into one general idea of averting the ill will of another person; and this has passed further into the stage of averting mere ill-luck brought by another person without any intention. Such a jumble of different beliefs into one generality shows that there has been a long time for the details to be forgotten, and for one vague idea to be substituted for the specific observations of chances, out of which a multitude of beliefs had arisen.

CHAPTER II

EGYPTIAN AMULETS

11. The subject of Egyptian amulets is one that appeals both to the reader of folk lore, as well as to the Egyptologist, and hence it is needful here to deal with some elementary details which may not be familiar to one side or to the other. The whole subject of amulets is an immense one, and there is no general work of reference giving the ideas of various lands. Nor is this intended to deal with other than Egyptian amulets, though many collateral examples

are here introduced in order to explain them, and to illustrate their use. Studying thus with a past civilisation we are almost cut off from the largest class of amulets, those of animal and vegetable nature, so that this point of view here is but a partial one. On the other hand the Egyptian was so industrious in imitation, and believed so completely in the virtue of models, that he carried out his ideas in imperishable material more widely than any other people. The great variety of over two hundred and seventy different amulets used in Egypt, and the amount of light thrown on them by statements of their properties, or descriptive names, renders Egypt one of the most favourable lands for a general study of the subject.

12. In handling a subject which ramifies so widely, we must begin by some definitions and limitations. The principle of amuletic virtue extends to most of the sepulchral remains of the Egyptians. The model offerings, pictorial scenes of life, and ushabti figures of slave workers, provided in the tomb, are all based on the principle of Similars; such necessarily differ from amulets worn by the living in their being more extensive, and not suspended from the person. As for the dead, so also for the living, there are some classes of amulets numerous enough to form whole subjects in themselves, apart from their amuletic aspect; such are the scarabs with royal names, with other personal names, with charms, and with devices of unknown purport; also the plaques with similar devices, and the foreign class of button seals. Each of these classes is so important and numerous that we cannot include them in a detailed account with other amulets. Nor is it possible to divide between amulets for the living and for the dead, though many kinds belong exclusively to one or other category.

In general any object with a means of suspension on the person, and not of immediate use or ornament, must be classed as an amulet. The figures of the gods with loops for suspension we include as amulets, while those which were stood on a base must be treated along with all other images of divinities. Unfortunately the detail of the suspending ring or hole is not noted in catalogues; where following descriptions, I have therefore accepted all figures under two inches high (·05 m.) as amulets, and left larger figures apart. The great development of amulets for the dead is peculiar to Egypt; elsewhere they are found, but not with such variety and detail. In China the substitutes of paper or pottery figures of slaves, and paper dollars, is of the same purpose; but the great extent of symbolic amulets in Egypt is unparalleled.

13. The stages of the growth of the amulet system in Egyptian burials can be historically traced more completely than elsewhere. (1) In the earliest graves, such as the prehistoric, whole objects were buried. (2) In the later prehistoric and early historic time, the objects were deliberately broken or "killed." (3) In the early dynasties models of objects appear; besides the jars of grain there are small model granaries; besides the jars of beer and joints of meat here are models of food; and, in the Xth—XIth dynasties, besides the tomb there is the model of a dwelling house and furniture. (4) Beginning in the early pyramid age there are the sculptured objects in relief, where the master is portrayed as "beholding" all his farm and servants in full activity, and hunting in the desert or on the river. (5) As the model was succeeded by the relief, so that was succeeded in turn by the painting, beginning in the VIth dynasty, and fully developed in the XIIth. (6) Symbols were then substituted for the objects such as the model altar, or vase, or food, placed as an amulet with the body. (7) Besides amuletic substitutions for real objects, amulets were adapted to confer powers, such as the crowns, or sceptres, or verbal charms stating that the deceased was a god and must be obeyed as such. The wish to have actual objects buried still lasts in Egypt where food and even a bed may be placed with the dead. In England the same feeling is by no means extinct, as in 1912 a boot maker ordered that there should be buried with him a last, hammer, nails, unfinished boots and a piece of leather.

It appears that we must define amulets broadly as objects worn by the living, without any physical use but for magical benefits, or placed with the dead, or set up in the house for its magical protection, apart from deities for household worship.

14. The material used for the present study is mainly the collection which I have made during the last thirty years in Egypt, now taken over by University College. At first a collection purchased by a visitor or worker in Egypt is naturally miscellaneous and casual; gradually certain lines claim more interest, and besides the main pursuit of scarabs, tools, technical work, weights, and pottery, the curious variety of out-of-the-way amulets has proved attractive. Further information was also obtained from the regular excavations as to the positions in which amulets are found upon the body, and the detailed accounts of such here recorded are almost the only observations yet published on this matter. The dates of various amulets were also obtained from excavations, and in this—as in other subjects—the miscellaneous material purchased is immensely enhanced in its meaning and interest by the precise information gathered in scientific work. While the commoner amulets are illustrated by splendid examples in the national collections, there is no series nearly as complete as the present one for the rarer and more obscure amulets, only ten being absent.

Besides this collection many early discoveries and purchases of mine went to Miss Edwards for her collection, bequeathed to University College; these, along with other objects from my excavations that have been presented to the college, are all included in the present catalogue. In order to preserve a record, the number of examples in the original Edwards collection is marked E, and those added by the Petrie collection and discoveries are marked P. Of course, nothing resembling finality is possible in this, or any other, branch of archaeology; but the time has come for taking stock of the subject, classifying the various details, and making a platform for planning further investigations and seeing clearly the value of any fresh information.

Other collections have been referred to, partly from catalogues published, such as the excellent ones of Turin, St. Petersburg, and Cairo. The difficulty in using such is the defect of some information; in the Turin and St. Petersburg catalogues the details of form are often vague; in the Cairo catalogue the drawings are ample, but the nature of the material is very imperfectly stated. Of the British Museum there is no detailed catalogue, and the excessive reflection from double glass often makes the material indistinguishable. It is hoped that the photographs here given of nearly all examples, and the definition of the material, will leave but few uncertainties. It should be noted that in many types this collection has been severely weeded, so as to omit duplicates where of no additional importance; whereas the national collections, by their conditions, are swelled by numerous duplicates, kept for their beauty and attractiveness, or obtained as part of large acquisitions. The scientific value of a collection depends upon the scope and variety of it, rather than on the brilliance of particular specimens.

15. In the treatment of this catalogue, the figures which may have diverse meanings—such as the vulture—are nevertheless classed together, as it would be difficult, or impossible, to determine in all cases which was the intended meaning. Such figures are therefore placed under the first important heading to which any of them may refer, with cross-references from other headings. It is needless to give minute verbal descriptions or dimensions, when the photographs are before the reader, and are of the actual size, except in a very few instances which are specially noted. The first principle of a modern catalogue is to have full and clear pictures of every object, and then to build upon that such description as is needful to supplement the picture. Unhappily all existing catalogues—including that of Cairo—have begun at the wrong end, with a verbal description supplemented by a picture. The modern conditions of illustrations developed in the last few years have completely reversed the old idea, and there is no excuse now for burdening a reader with a description of what can be grasped with a tenth of the time and thought in a picture.

The principle of the arrangement of this catalogue is that it should follow the real life of the subject—the meaning attached to each amulet—rather than any external feature of form or material. These meanings of the amulets are given by various sources; principally by (A) the chapters of the Book of the Dead which refer to the amulets; (B) the very full list of seventy-five amulets, with their explanatory names, in a papyrus of that Book, belonging to the Rev. William MacGregor, which is here transcribed from the photograph published by Dr. Capart (Z. A. S. xlv, 14); (C) the analysis of the objects represented upon coffins in Cairo, published by M. Lacau (*Sarcophages antérieurs au nouvel Empire*, 1904, Caire); (D) various scattered allusions and mythological references and figures; and (E) references from other countries, which may help us to understand the ideas when no explanation remains in Egypt.

16. The amulets named in the MacGregor papyrus are each stated to be of gold, which is omitted in the copy here given. There is also a list of amulets of Osiris given on the upper part of the temple of Dendereh, and copied here (pl. xlviii) from the publication by Mariette, *Dendereh*, iv, 87. They are there classed according to their material, and after each name of material a dividing line is here inserted. The materials named are *Uher* or *Heru*, which, by the nature of the amulets and coming first, is probably gold, perhaps a form of the Greek *Khrusos*. *An. en. deb*, probably "stone of Edfu"; the house sign in Mariette's copy is probably the square block of stone. *Mefkat*, *Mefkat Amen*, *Mefkat of Kharu* (Syria): this was a green mineral in general, including turquoise, malachite, and probably chrysocolla: that from Amen was probably western, from Kharu, Syrian. *Neshen* is green felspar. *Kartef?* of Rutennu (Syria), unknown. *Sef. s. tahen? Sef* is the name of white quartz (Kennard tablet), and *tahen* is amethyst; this is therefore amethystine quartz. *Shesteb*, a late form of *Khesdeb*, lazuli. *Kes. ankh*, alabaster. *Qo* or *Qedu* is unknown, another form is *Qy*; being used for the plummet and square which are usually of haematite, this was probably the material. *Seher*, the "charming" stone, is unknown. So also is *Behet*. *Khenem* is usually jasper, as it is the material of the girdle tie amulet, but it is sard on the Kennard tablet. The reference numbers of the amulets in this volume are put below each column.

17. On examining the two hundred and seventy different kinds of amulets found in Egypt, there are only about a dozen which remain unclassed, and without any known meaning; these are dealt with last of all. The various ascertained meanings may be completely put in order under five great classes, in which the amulets are here arranged. These are (I) the amulets of Similars, which are for influencing similar parts, or functions, or occurrences, for the wearer: (II) the amulets of Powers, for conferring powers and capacities, especially upon the dead: (III) the amulets of Property, which are entirely derived from the funeral offerings, and are thus peculiar to Egypt: (IV) the amulets for Protection, such as charms and curative amulets: (V) the figures of Gods, connected with the worship of the gods and their functions.

As international names are desirable in dealing with any scientific classification, and one word is preferable to a description when handling a subject, it is best to have a proper name for each class, independent of English. The Similars may be termed *Homopoeic* (from ὁμος, like, or same, and ποιεω, I do, or make); the amulets of Powers we call *Dynatic* (from δυνᾰτος, able, powerful, adequate); the Property amulets *Ktēmatic* (from κτῆμα, goods, possessions); the Protective amulets, *Phylactic* (from φυλακτῐκος, fitted to guard, familiar in the term "phylacteries"); and the amulets of Gods, *Theophoric* (from θεος, god, and φορεω, I bear, or wear).

Our classes then are called here amulets of

Similars, or Homopoeic.
Powers, or Dynatic.
Property, or Ktematic.
Protection, or Phylactic.
Gods, or Theophoric.

Of these classes the Similars are undoubtedly the most primitive, being found among races like the Eskimo who have no other amulets, and being the basis of the Italian ideas of amulet. The Powers and Property amulets are entirely Egyptian, and originate with the models of the funeral furniture, arising, therefore, after the development of the funeral system. The Protective amulets are a later class, depending on quasi-medical ideas, or verbal incantations or prayers written down. Lastly, the figures of Gods belong to the age of a developed theology. The list of all these amulets of each class is here given, in the Contents of this volume. For purpose of reference each kind of amulet has a number assigned to it, the same in the text and in the plates; each separate specimen shown has a letter added to the number as **6k**, **154c**, and duplicates which are here stated without illustration have a second number as **6**k2, or **154**c 3.

The transliteration of Egyptian is that followed in the Student's History, except that the arm, *àin* is rendered by its historical equivalent *o*. For the reed, *a* is continued, as its written equivalent is *aleph* whenever rendered in Semitic names, and the value *i* or *y* is a theoretical early stage, of which not a single transliteration is known. The golden-headed vulture is short ă. For very familar names the usual forms are retained, as Isis, Horus, Ra, etc.

In the record of specimens, groups are numbered which have been found together; a list of such groups is placed at the end of the volume.

SYSTEM OF THE CATALOGUE

Name, is the ancient Egyptian name, with reference when not in dictionaries.

Meaning, is the Egyptian meaning if known ; also that in other lands for comparison.

Period, is stated in dynasties, I to XXX.

Figures, describes the figures in the plates from amulets in University College. The number of the class of amulet is stated : the following letter refers to the specific example ; where a number follows the letter it refers to duplicates of the lettered examples, not usually figured in the plates.

Material, includes the total number of examples of each material in this collection and in others which have been published or noted. One new term is used for indurated mud or ash, which is of the composition of slate, but without a slatey fracture. As no usual word was available, it is here called Durite ; it has been usually confounded with the fused rock, basalt.

Collection, states the number of examples in each collection, to show how far common the amulet is. Univ. Coll. refers to the collection at University College, London, catalogued here; after it with P. is stated the number collected by Petrie, with E. the number by Miss Edwards, mainly also collected by Petrie.

The principal books referred to are:—

Bell. Bellucci, Dr. Giuseppe, *Catalogo . . . della Collezione inviata all' esposizione . . . di Torino.* 1898. 104 pp.

Am. Bellucci. *Gli Amuleti.* Perugia, 1908. 64 pp., 36 fig.

Fet. Bellucci. *Il Feticismo primitivo in Italia.* Perugia, 1907. 158 pp., 74 fig.

Lanz. Lanzone, R. V. *Dizionario di Mitologia Egizia.* 1312 pp., 408 pl.

Lacau. Lacau, *Sarcophages antérieurs au nouvel Empire.* 1904.

Alnwick. Birch, S., *Catalogue of Egyptian Antiquities at Alnwick.* 1880.

Cairo. Reisner, G., *Catalogue of Amulets. Cairo Museum.* 1908.

Edinburgh. Murray, M. A., *Catalogue of Egyptian Antiquities in National Museum.* 1900.

Price. Price, Hilton, *Catalogue of Egyptian Antiquities.* 1897.

St. Petersburg. Golenischeff, W. *Ermitage Impérial. Inventaire de la Collection Egyptienne.* 1891. 386 pp.

Turin. Lanzone, R. V. *Regio Museo di Torino. Antichita Egizie.* 1882. 484 pp.

The Athens collection is from my notes. The Murch collection (now in New York) is from the notes of Mr. A. C. Mace.

CHAPTER III

AMULETS OF SIMILARS

HOMOPOEIC AMULETS, 1—26.

THIS class of amulets is the most primitive in its nature, but in Egypt it was mainly adapted to the service of the dead. In order that the various functions of life should be continued, models of the different parts of the body were placed with the mummy. Thus the amulets would ensure the seeing, hearing, taste, force to act, use of the hands and the feet, and other functions. Other similars would ensure growth and flourishing, watchfulness, and protection from wild beasts. In this way the safety, well-being, and activity of the dead in a future life were secured by the appropriate similar placed with the body. These amulets are classed here as parts of the body, from the head downward (1—17), and then the animal figures which would ensure the welfare of the body (18—26).

1. HEAD BEARDED.

Name. *Tep* is the name of the bearded head from the earliest times. In the hieroglyph the beard is turned up at the end, like the beard of the men of Punt, and the hair is worn long; this seems to be an earlier type than that of the historic Egyptian.

Meaning. The chief or head-man, but possibly referring, as an amulet, to the power of the senses.

Varieties. A, single face. B, face front and back. C, head and shoulders.

Period. XXV—Ptolemaic (?).

Figures. **1**a, blue-green glaze, bluer in hollows, flat back, loop broken from top; **1**b, yellow green glaze, face front and back, notch between two beards; **1**c, amber head (of child?) and shoulders. See as **1**b from Saft, in *Hyksos and Israelite Cities*, xxxvii a.

Materials. Green glaze 2, **1**c Amber.

Collection. Univ. Coll. P. 3.

2. FACE.

Name. *Her* means the face, always figured front view, with a short, wide beard, different from that of *Tep*. See the foreign figure in *Hierakonpolis*, pl. i.

Meaning. While as a hieroglyph it means "facing" or "over-against," it is probably used as an amulet of the power of the senses.

Varieties and *Period.* In the Old Kingdom it is usually roughly cut in carnelian or sard. In Roman times it is made in black steatite without a neck.

Figures. **2**a, carnelian, group 1; **2**b, carnelian, group 2; **2**b 2, green felspar, group 9; **2**c, carnelian, group 3; **2**d, e, bone, group 5; **2**f, blue glaze, group 12; **2**f 2, carnelian, group 7 (2a to f about VIth dynasty); **2**g, blue glaze, black lines, XVIIIth dynasty; **2**h, onyx rudely cut as a face, Roman (?); **2**j, black steatite, Roman; **2**k, l, pl. xliv, black steatite, Roman.

Materials. Carnelian 10, Black steatite 3, Blue glaze 2, Bone 2, Green felspar 1, Onyx 1.

Collections. Univ. Coll. P. 23, Murch 6, British Museum 3.

3. UZAT EYE.

Name. The *uzat* eye is that of Horus, the markings below it being derived from the feather pattern on a hawk's cheeks.

Meaning. As the eye of Horus it will be dealt with under 138 to 142. Here it is to be included as being placed upon the left side of the coffin, opposite to the head, in order that the deceased might have the power of seeing out. The deceased being identified with Horus, he is able to see by means of the eye of the god.

Varieties. Sometimes inlaid with obsidian, white limestone, lazuli, blue glass, or copper, in the wood of the coffin. Otherwise painted on the coffin.

Period. Inlaid in XIIth dynasty, from Assyut 28,118 (Cairo), from Dahshur 28,100 (Cairo); painted in IVth, Tarkhan; and XIIth, Rifeh (Manchester) (Gizeh and Rifeh, pl. x a); and many in Cairo.

4. EYE.

Name. *Ari.*

Meaning. The power of sight.

Varieties. Single, or three together.

Period. XXIII (?), Roman.

Figures. **4**a, green glaze; **4**a 2, gold foil found at Hawara, Roman; **4**b, blue-green glaze; **4**b 2, same; **4**b 3, same, in a square.

Materials. Green glaze 4, Gold 1.

Collection. Univ. Coll. P. 3, E. 1.

5. EAR.

Name. *Mes-zer*, "Producing the distant," a functional name.

Meaning. The power of hearing; when a mummy amulet, for conferring hearing; when on a prayer tablet, for gaining the ear of the god.

Varieties. A, simple ear. B, ear incised on a tablet.

Period. XVIII.

Figures. **5**a, b, blue glaze, flat back, pierced with hole for suspension; **5**a 2, full blue glaze; **5**c, green glaze on schist. For tablets see *Memphis I.*

Materials. Blue glaze, 4.

Collection. Univ. Coll. P. 3, E. 1.

6. TONGUE.

Name. *Nes.*

Meaning. Power of speech.

Period. Roman.

Figures. See *Labyrinth*, xxxvi, p. 36.

Material. Gold.

Position. In mouth.

Collection. Univ. Coll. P. 2, Manchester 2, Oxford Anthrop., 2, 1 each in Brussels, Munich, Boston, Chicago, Glasgow, Leicester, Aberdeen, Bolton.

7. HEART.

Names. The physical heart is named *ab*, and also *hati*—the chief part—as referring to the will; but the amulet of the heart is named *opert* on the coffins, and in the title of the chapter (Lacau, p. 125). The chapters relating to the heart in the Book of the Dead are the 26th, to be engraved on lazuli, "Whereby the heart is given to a person in the underworld"; the 27th, to be engraved on green felspar, "Whereby the heart of a person is not taken from him in the underworld"; the 28th and 29th with the same title; the 29th B, "Another chapter of the heart upon carnelian. I am the Heron, the soul of Ra, who conducts the glorious ones to the Duat. It is granted to their *bas* to come forth upon the earth, to do whatsoever their *ka* willeth. It is granted to the *ba* of the Osiris *N* to come forth upon the earth to do whatsoever his *ka* willeth." This chapter is referred to by the figure of the heron or *akhet* bird upon the backs of some hearts and heart scarabs. The 30th chapter is that inscribed on the heart scarabs, and will be given under 90, the heart scarab.

Meaning. The power of living and will. In Italy a heart of bone is worn against the evil eye and heart disease (Bell., xii, 10; xiii, 11, 18).

Varieties. A, plain without side projections. B, with side projections of arteries. C, with marks on the front, as figs. **7**m, o. D, with the *akhet* bird, representing the spirit or illumination which resides in the heart, as fig. **7**n. E, with the sun's disc over it, as **7**g.

Period. In VIth, carnelian, but rare; in XVIIIth, of carnelian, gold or glass; very common in various materials in XXVIth. Ptolemaic.

Figures. Type A, **7**a, **7**b, **7**bb (pl. xlv), carnelian; **7**a 2, calcite; **7**a 3, green felspar; **7**c, clear green glass with yellow and white stripes, XVIII; **7**cc, gold (pl. xliii); **7**d, violet glaze, with wreath and lotus pendant upon it, possibly a vase model, XVIII; **7**e, red and white jasper; **7**f, red and white breccia; **7**f 2, red and white breccia burnt brown; **7**g, see type E; **7**g 2, blue paste; **7**h, light blue glass; **7**h 2, blue glass, Zuweleyn; **7**h 3, grey serpentine; **7**h 4, red glass; **7**j, lazuli; **7**j 2, green volcanic ash; **7**j 3, serpentine; **7**j 4, basalt Zuweleyn; **7**j 5, brown steatite; **7**j 6, black steatite; **7**j 7, green glaze; **7**j 8, bronze; **7**j 9, 10, white limestone (8, 9, 10, Nebesheh); **7**k, dark brown jasper; **7**k 2, black and green serpentine, **7**k 3, sard; **7**k 4, blue-green glaze; **7**l, blue glaze, trace of wreath round shoulder, XVIII; **7**ll (pl. xliv), green glaze, Illahun, XXII; **7**m, violet glaze, with bright blue inlay of crescent and heart sign; **7**p, rough blue glaze, Ptolemaic, Dendereh, group 21. Type C, **7**o, light green glaze, same marks on both side; **7**o 2, dark blue glaze, same marks. Type D, **7**n, blue glaze, Ptolemaic, Dendereh, group 26; **7**n 2, blue glass, burnt. This type appears also in the heart scarabs, where the *akhet* bird is figured on the back. Type E, **7**g, calcite.

Materials. Carnelian and sard **26**, Basalt 19, Blue glaze 16, Green glaze 15, Haematite 15, Variegated glass 9, Lazuli 8, Porphyry 8, Limestone 8, Green jasper 8, Steatite 6, Serpentine 6, Gold 5, Quartz 4, Beryl **4**, Red limestone 4, Red jasper 4, Obsidian 3, Prase 3, Agate 3, Blue glass 3, Amethyst 2, Red glass 2, Red and white breccia 2, 1 each of Brown jasper, Green felspar, Green volcanic ash, Pink granite, Granite, Calcite, Alabaster, Black glass, Bronze, Gilt wood.

Positions. 6 on neck; 2 on left breast; 15 from top down to low on chest.

Collections. Cairo 51, Univ. Coll. P. 27, E. 14, St. Petersburg 33, Turin 21, Athens 17, Alnwick 13, Price 9, Edinburgh 7, Murch 7.

8. BREAST.

Names. *Menz.*

Meaning. Power of lactation. An ivory ball is worn in Italy for the increase of milk (Bell., xii, 11).

Varieties. Flat to rounded.

Period. All Ptolemaic and Roman.

Figures. **8**a, wax gilt, Dendereh, Ptolemaic, group 20; **8**b, blue glaze with black nipple, Dendereh, Ptolemaic, group 21.

Materials. Blue-green glaze 1, Gold foil 1, Wax gilt 1, Wood gilt 1.

Position. On breast.

Collections. Univ. Coll. P. 3.

AMULETS OF SIMILARS

9. ARM.

Names. Bent *Qeb*; forearm *Remen.*

Meaning. Power of action.

Varieties. A, bent. B, straight.

Period. A VI.

Figures. Greenish-blue glaze. Type B, green glaze, Turin.

Materials. Green glaze 2.

Collections. Univ. Coll. P. 1, Turin 1.

10. TWO ARMS.

Name. *Ka,* from Ist dynasty onwards; implying the activities of the will.

Meaning. The power of will and intention.

Period. XVIII.

Figure. **10**a, blue glaze, flat back; **10**a 2, green glaze, Riqqeh, 257.

Material. Blue or green glaze.

Collections. Cairo 2, Univ. Coll. P. 2, Brit. Mus. 1.

11. HAND OPEN.

Name. *Det.*

Meaning. Power of action.

Varieties. Right and Left.

Period. VI.

Figures. **11**a, bone, group 6; **11**b, c, d, carnelian; **11**e, f, green glaze; **11**g, green glaze, Zaraby. See *Deshasheh,* xxvi, 4, 10, 13; 2 of carnelian; 1 grey agate.

Materials. Carnelian 29, Green glaze 3, Bone 2, Grey agate 1.

Position. Wrist.

Collections. Univ. Coll. P. 12, Brit. Mus. 5, Turin 4, Cairo 4, Murch 3, Price 3. Of those where the side is noted there are 12 right hands, 16 left hands.

12. FIST CLENCHED.

Name. *Khefo.*

Meaning. Vigorous action, as in the determinative hieroglyph of action.

Varieties. Right and Left.

Period. VI; **12**d, e, Roman.

Figures. **12**a, sard, group 3; **12**a 1—3, sard, group 1; **12**a 4—6, sard, groups 6, 7, 8; **12**b, sard, group 3; **12**b 2, 3, group 1; **12**b 4, green felspar, group 3; **12**c, bone, group 13; **12**c 2—4, sard, group 1; **12**c 5, group 3; **12**d, steatite, crescent and other signs on base; **12**d 2, steatite bird on base; **12**e (pl. xlvi), steatite, crescent. This type, **12**d, e, seems to be Roman, under Syrian or Asianic influence. See *Deshasheh,* xxvi, 17, 19, 20, 24; 3 of carnelian: 1 brown limestone.

Materials. Carnelian 23, Steatite 2, Blue glaze 2, Green felspar 1, Brown limestone 1, Bone 1.

Position. Wrist.

Collections. Univ. Coll. P. 17, Price 3, Brit. Mus. 2. Of those noted there are 15 right fists, 5 left fists.

13. FIST, THUMB BETWEEN FIRST AND SECOND FINGERS.

Name. Unknown.

Meaning. Sexual power (?). Against evil eye in Italy, Bell., xv, 11.

Varieties. Right and Left.

Period. Roman.

Figures. **13**a, dark blue glaze; **13**b, dark blue glaze with yellow points, group 22.

Materials. Blue glaze.

Collections. Cairo R. 4, L. 1, Turin 3, Univ. Coll. P. 2.

14. TWO HANDS SIDE BY SIDE.

Name. Unknown.

Meaning. United action (?)

Period. VI.

Figure. **14**, blue glaze, Mahasna, tomb 13.

Material. Blue glaze.

Collection. Univ. Coll. P. 1.

15. LEG.

Name. *Uort.*

Meaning. Power of walking. In Italy a leg carved in bone is an evil eye charm (Bell., xiii, 19).

Period. Vth and VIth dynasties.

Figures **15**a, carnelian whitened, showing ankle bone, left leg; **15**a 2, smaller, group 2; **15**b, carnelian; **15**b 2, light brown agate; **15**c, light red agate, showing heel; **15**c 2, similar, smaller; **15**c 3, sard, group 7; **15**d, milky and brown agate; **15**e, sard; also **15**e 2, 3; **15**e 4, group 1; **15**e 5, 6, group 2; **15**f, sard, group 14.

Materials. Sard or Carnelian 21, Glaze 1.

Collections. Univ. Coll. P. 15 (groups 1, 2, 7, 14), Murch 4, Brit. Mus. 3.

16. PHALLUS.

Name. *Moza, Moza-kherti* entire (MacG. 40).

Period. Only Roman.

Figures. **16**a, blue glaze with yellow; **16**b, red glass, and **16**b 2, group 23; **16**c, d, gold, Memphis, group 27.

Materials. Gold 2, Green glaze 4, Green glaze with yellow points 1, Red glass 2, Haematite 1.

Collections. Univ. Coll. P. 5 (groups 23, 27), E. 2, St. Petersburg 2. The whole figures (**16**e, green glaze) are entirely of Graeco-Roman age, and there is no trace of any such amulet in use by Egyptians. Univ. Coll. P. 1, E. 1, green glaze.

17. SMA.

Name. *Sma,* "union" (Lacau, 80); also *By,* "joy" or "ecstasy" (Lacau, 88); comp. French "fille de joie."

Meaning. Union, see earliest form Ist dynasty, *Royal Tombs,* ii, II.

Period. Form figured on VI—XIII coffins as an emblem; amulets all of XXVI.

Figures. **17**a, b, c, e, obsidian; **17**d, black porphyry.

Materials. Obsidian 25 (?), Haematite 2, Black porphyry 1, Yellow limestone 1.

Position. Base of stomach, umbilicus.

Collections. Cairo 16, Univ. Coll. P. 5, Turin 2, St. Petersburg 2, Alnwick 2, Price 2.

18. FROG AND TOAD.

Names. *Heqt=Rana,* Frog. *Abnekh* for *Ab-nekhekh,* "spotty old man"=*Bufo* (?) Toad.

Meaning. The tadpole is the hieroglyph for 100,000. The frog is the emblem of Heqt, the goddess of birth, and it would appear to symbolise fecundity. A bowl with frogs modelled all over the interior and round the edge, found at Tell Rotab (*Hyksos and Israelite Cities,* pls xxxii, xxxiv B), might well be for giving potions against sterility. There is, however, another meaning suggested by a frog-pattern lamp, with the quotation "I am the Resurrection" (LANZONE, *Diz. Mit.* 853), which has been accepted as indicating the meaning of the frog. As however the frog is one of the commonest types of lamps (*Roman Ehnasya,* pl. lxiii, lxiv), there may be no connection between it and a text quoted on the lamp.

Varieties. There appear to be two more species represented, a wide form, the toad, with the legs hidden by the body, *Bufo viridis;* and a slender form, the frog, with the legs outstanding, and often ribbed down the back, *Rana mascareniensis.* These are not however generally distinguished in collections. We may note separately

A. Single frog. B. Group of three frogs. C. Group of four frogs.

Period. Many examples are known from the prehistoric times, as **18**a, b; others in the Old Kingdom, as **18**l; many in the XVIIIth and XXIInd dynasties, as **18**j, k; and some in the XXVIth.

Figures. **18**a, *Bufo,* hard grey steatite; **18**b, *Rana* (?), greenish-grey serpentine; **18**c, *Bufo,* ivory, prehistoric; **18**d, cut on a *Nerita* shell; **18**e, limestone, Hawara, XII; **18**f, limestone, rude scrolls, and *uaz* pattern on base, Hawara, XII; **18**g, *Rana,* bronze; **18**h, *Rana,* bronze; **18**j, *Rana,* bright red glazed pottery, yellow eyes, late XVIII; **18**k, *Rana,* green glaze, XVIII; **18**k 2, *Rana,* violet glaze, *sa* sign on base, XVIII; **18**l, *Bufo,* calcite, group 13, VIth dynasty; **18**m, *Bufo,* black and yellow serpentine; **18**n, green felspar; **18**o, green glass, two latter for inlaying; **18**p, four frogs on base, blue glaze, black marks, two crocodiles, head to tail, incised on base.

Materials. Green—Glazed pottery 38, Glazed stone 3, Prase 3, Green felspar 4, Green jasper 2, Glass 2. Other colours are much less common; Lazuli 5, Carnelian 7, Bronze 4, Quartz crystal 2, Serpentine 3, Steatite 2, Limestone 3, Diorite 2, 1 each of Haematite, Chalcedony, Agate, Amethyst, Porphyry, Calcite, Violet glaze, Red glaze, Ivory, Shell. See *Deshasheh,* xxvi, 25.

Position. On neck (1); on chest (7); right arm (1); lower part of stomach (1).

Collections. Cairo A 33, B 1, C 1, Univ. Coll. P. 20, St. Petersburg 14, Murch 11, Turin 10, Alnwick 10, Price 9, Athens 4, Edinburgh 1.

19. FLY.

Name. *Ofef* (Z. A. S., 1883, 78).

Meaning. The collar of gold flies, given to a very active fighter in XVIIIth dynasty (BREASTED *Records,* ii, 23, 585, 587) suggests that the fly was an emblem of activity or swiftness; the manner in which the decoration is named almost indicates that there was a corps of *aides de camp* thus decorated. The great collar of gold flies found with the jewels of Aah-hotep and Kames is in Cairo.

Varieties. The fly with rounded wings appears distinct from a sharper-bodied form with pointed wings.

Period. Prehistoric, XII and XVIII.

Figures. **19**a, green serpentine; **19**b, c, pink limestone, prehistoric; **19**d, d 2, red jasper; **19**e, gold, XVIIIth dynasty; **19**f, black glaze; **19**f, 2—12, blue paste, Kahun, XII; **19**g, green glaze, Kahun, XII (pl. xliv); **19**h, green glaze (pl. xlvi); **19**j, string of yellow glaze, late XVIII. See also **131**e; **19**k, dragon fly, XII, Kahun (xlv).

Materials. Yellow glaze 30, Blue paste 13, Gold 4, Green glaze 3, Lazuli 3, Jasper 2, Pink limestone 2, Green porpyhry 1, Serpentine 1, Glazed steatite 1.

Position. Necklaces.

Collections. Univ. Coll. P. 52, Murch 6, Brit. Mus. 2. See *Naqada,* pl. lviii.

20. PAPYRUS SCEPTRE.

Name. *Uaz* (MacG. 50).

Meaning. Flourishing, as of green plants; youth. Chapter 159 of the Book of the Dead reads:—"The chapter of the column of green felspar put on the neck of the deceased. O thou who comest out every day, in the divine house, she who has a big voice, who goeth round . . . she takes hold of the potent formulae of her father, the mummy which is on the bull. She is Renent."

Period. XXVI—XXX, the age when the goddess Uazet was most worshipped.

Figures. **20**a, black and white glass, Tahutmes III; **20**b, black, white and yellow glass, XVIII; **20**c, c 2, green glaze; **20**d, d 2, d 3, green glaze faded; **20**e—e 10, green glaze; **20**f, green-gone-brown glaze; **20**f 2, haematite; **20**f 3—5, green felspar; **20**f 6, 7, green glaze; **20**g, brown limestone; **20**g 2, dull green calcite; **20**h, blue glaze, XVIII (?). A stem of the sceptre, like **20**c, green glaze, yellow leaves, is inscribed *Khonsu nefer hotep upt renpet nefer,* "Khonsu-nefer-hotep open a good year." See green felspar amulet of Khaemuas (MARIETTE, *Serapeum,* iii, xx).

Materials. Green glaze 38, Blue glaze 35, Green felspar 16, Beryl 4, Prase 2, Green diorite 2, Green calcite 1; thus more than two-thirds are green or blue. Of other colours there are Haematite 14, Lazuli 8, Carnelian 2, Basalt 2, Blue glass 2, Black and white glass 2, Gold 1, Serpentine 1, Schist 1, Steatite 1, Brown limestone 1.

Position. Forehead (1) ; throat (1); top and middle rows on chest (11) ; stomach (1, Dendereh), or low on stomach (2, Nebesheh, Abydos).

Collections. Cairo 45, Turin 34, Univ. Coll. P. 17, E. 9, St. Petersburg 18, Price 10, Alnwick 8, Athens 4, Murch 3, Edinburgh 2.

21. PAPYRUS ON A PLAQUE.

Name. *Uaz.*

Meaning. To be as durable as *neshem* stone—green felspar. Chapter 160 of the Book of the Dead is as follows: "Giving the column of green felspar. I am the column of green felspar, which cannot be crushed, and which is raised by the hand of Tahuti. Injury is an abomination to it. If it is safe, I am safe; if it is not injured, I am not injured; if it receives no cut, I receive no cut. Said by Tahuti, arise, come in peace, lord of Heliopolis, lord who resides in Pu. When Shu has arrived, he found the stone at Shenemu, as its name is *neshem.* He (deceased) makes his abode in the enclosure of the great god; whilst Tum resides in his dwelling, his limbs will never be crushed."

Period. As these are always of hard stone they probably belong entirely to the XXVIth dynasty, before glass became common for amulets.

Figures. **21a**, green felspar, fine colour, incised; **21b**, dull green felspar, in relief; **21c**, dull green felspar; **21c** 2, half as large again, dull green felspar.

Materials. Green felspar 21, Beryl 3, Serpentine 1, Sard 1.

Position. Throat (1); Middle of chest, and shoulders (5).

Collections. Cairo 10, Alnwick 5, Turin 4, Univ. Coll. P. 4, Price 3, St. Petersburg 3.

22. JACKAL HEAD.

Name. Unknown.

Meaning. To find the way in the future world, as the jackal was "the opener of ways" (*up-uatu*) in the desert: or perhaps for watchfulness.

Period. V.—VI.

Figures. **22a**, bone, group 8; **22b**, yellow sard, group 3; **22c**, calcite, group 13; **22c** 2, carnelian, group 7; **22d**, pink steatite. **22d** 2, minute carnelian, group 10; **22e**, bone; **22e** 2, carnelian, group 7; **22f**, carnelian; **22f** 2, same, ruder, group 1; **22g**, green felspar; **22g** 2, green felspar, group 30; **22h**, j, green limestone; **22** k, carnelian; **22** l, m, n, o, blue glaze, Zaraby, VIth dynasty; **22**p, ebony, pl. xlv.

Materials. Sard and carnelian 16, Blue glaze 8, Green felspar 2, Green limestone 2, Lazuli 1, Bone 1, Wood 1.

Position. Wrist.

Collection. Univ. Coll. P. 27.

23. LEOPARD HEAD.

Name. *Peh.*

Meaning. *Valour*, as in the title *ao pehti,* "great and valorous." Possibly used for protection from wild beasts.

Period. V.—VI.

Figures. **23**, blue paste, Mahasna, tomb 461. *Deshasheh,* xxvi, 1 lazuli.

Materials. Lazuli 1, Blue paste 1, Greenglaze 1.

Position. Wrist.

Collections. Univ. Coll. P. 1, Turin 1.

24. CLAW.

Name. *Ogăt.*

Meaning. Leopard's claw used for protection from wild beasts, Central Africa (Leicester Museum). Cray fish claw against evil eye (BELL., xi, 3). Elk's claw (BELL., xiv, 3).

Period. Prehistoric, Roman.

Figures. **24**a, red porphyry; **24**b, c, green serpentine; **24**d, e, f, green serpentine, probably claws; all the previous, prehistoric; **24**g, sard, Mahasna, tomb 386; **24**h, j, bronze, Illahun, Roman. Natural claw, Shurafa, Roman, pl. xiv, **24**k.

Materials. Red porphyry 1, Green serpentine 5, Sard 1, Bronze 2, Actual claw of large bird, vulture (?) 1.

Collection. Univ. Coll. P. 10.

25. TOOTH.

Name. *Nazhi.*

Meanings. Human tooth, for toothache (PLINY, xxviii, 11). Child's, first shed, for pains (P. xxviii, 9). Lion's, for gaining favour (P. xxviii, 25). Leopard's, to gain aid of friend's spirit, Central Africa (Leicester Museum). Hyaena, toothache (P. xxviii, 27); of left side, pain in stomach, nightmare (P. xxviii, 27); of right upper, to strike animals in hunting (P. xxviii, 27). Wolf's, for dentition (P. xxviii, 28). Dog's, quartan fever (P. xxx, 30), evil eye, hydrophobia (BELL., xii, 9, 15; xiii, 1). Horse's, evil eye (BELL., xii, 8). Deer's, repels serpents (P. xxviii, 42). Wild boar's, evil eye (BELL., xii, 5). Pig's, dentition (BELL., xii, 3). Boar's tusk, evil eye (BELL., *Am.* 58, *Fet.* 35). Dolphin's, infant's fright (P. xxxii, 48). Fossil shark's, dentition and lightning, (BELL., xi, 29). Crocodile's right tooth, aphrodisiac; eye teeth, for periodic fevers and aphrodisiac (PLINY, xxviii, 28; xxxii, 50).

Varieties. Crocodile teeth. Fossil shark teeth. Glazed pottery figure.

Period. XXII to Roman.

Figures. **25a**, tooth of shark, fossil, one of the *Lamnidae*, set in copper; **25b**, tooth of crocodile set in silver; **25c**, tooth of crocodile set in gold; **25d**, figure of a tooth carved in bone; **25e**, blue-green glaze, Roman; **25f**, blue-green glaze; **25g**, tusk carved from shell, prehistoric; **25h**, tooth of hyæna—tied to knotted cord, pl. xviii, **131f**.

Materials. Actual teeth 4, Green glazed pottery 2, Bone 1, Shell 1, Carnelian 1.

Position. On neck cord knotted.
Collections. Univ. Coll. P. 8, Murch 1.

26. LOCUST.

Name. *Si-nehem*, possibly "son of Nehemat," a goddess.
Meaning. Protection from locusts (?).
Period. Prehistoric, XVIII, Roman.
Figures. **26**a, b, grass-green and yellow glazes. XVIII.
Materials. Limestone 1, Yellow glaze 2, Green glaze 1.
Collections. Univ. Coll. P. 2, Turin 1, Murch 1.

CHAPTER IV

AMULETS OF POWERS

DYNATIC AMULETS, 27—61.

THE idea of conferring powers upon the dead by means of amulets, is a logical development of the previous idea of continuance of the faculties. If the hand amulet could give the power of action, so the amulet of the sceptre which the hand held, could confer the power connected with the sceptre in real life. When once this idea was grasped, the various kinds of powers could be conferred. This was carried out by means of hieroglyphs of the ideas, as the wagtail or duckling; by emblems, as the head-rest or plummet; or by models of objects, as the stairs or the crown. Each of these kinds of amulets gave the powers of qualities, or of conditions, or of authority. In this class of amulets they act by symbolism of some kind, and not as direct similars like the previous class.

27. WAGTAIL.

Name. Sign for "great," *ur*.
Meaning. Conferring greatness (?).
Period. VI.
Figures. **27**a, b, bone, group 5; **27**b 2, smaller, carnelian, group 10.
Materials. Bone 2, Carnelian 1.
Position. Necklace.
Collection. Univ. Coll. P. 3.

28. HUMAN-HEADED BIRD.

Name. *Ba. Ha-ran-herot* (MacG. 49, for *Haru-neher*, full of face?).
Meaning. Human soul, probably derived from large-faced owl living in tombs.
Varieties. A, plain. B, double. C, crowned. D, spread wings.
Period. XXVI to Ptolemaic.
Figures. **28**a, violet glass, white head; **28**a 2, violet glass; **28**b, double, side by side, green and black glaze; **28**c, green and black glaze; **28**d, blue and black glaze, Ptolemaic, group 21.
Materials. Green glaze 3, Blue glaze 8, Grey glaze 1, Red glass 2, Lazuli 2, White glass 1, Blue and white glass 3, Blue glass 7, Green glass 1, Black glass 1: D, Gold inlaid (Hor-uza, Hawara).
Position. Throat (1); breast (5).
Collections. Athens 13, Alnwick 8, Univ. Coll. P. 4, E. 1, St. Petersburg 2, Murch 2.

29. DUCKLING.

Name. *Za.*
Meaning. Virility.
Period. VI.
Figures. **29**a, sard, group 7; **29**b, bone, group 6.
Materials. Sard 1, Bone 1.
Position. Necklace.
Collection. Univ. Coll. P. 2.

30. MAN'S GIRDLE TIE.

Name. *Onkh, Onkh-er-ta kher-redui-f* (LACAU, 113).
Meaning. Life. "Many lives (*pl.*) upon the earth that is beneath his feet" (L. 113): the plural of life may imply a belief in reincarnation.
Varieties. A, pendant. B, on open-work ball bead. C, between two *uas*.
Period. XIX to Ptolemaic.
Figures. **30**a, blue glaze, Dendereh, Ptolemaic, group 21; **30**b, light blue glaze, Memphis; **30**b 2, green glaze; **30**c, green glaze, Sams collection; **30**d, blue glaze, XIX dynasty (?) (pl. xliv); **30**e, wax, gilt, Dendereh, Ptolemaic, group 20; **30**f, dark blue glass, type C; **30**g, dull blue glazed ball, alternate with rams' heads bearing disc, XXV; **30**h, red jasper (pl. xlvi). See *Mahasna*, xxxiv, tomb 435, gold.
Materials. Gold 1, Green glaze 12, Blue glaze 8, B 1, Purple glaze 1, Black glaze 1, Dark blue glass, C 1, Red jasper 1.
Position. Chest (Hawara); on feet (Dendereh).
Collections. Turin 8, Cairo 8, Univ. Coll. P. 6, E. 1, Price 1, St. Petersburg 1.

31. NEFER.

Name. *Nefer*, supposed to be derived from the heart and windpipe, as the markings are similar to those upon the *ab* sign.
Meaning. Beauty or excellence.
Period. XVIII.

Figures. **31**a, blue glaze; **31**a 2, obsidian; **31**b (pl. xliv), gold, XVIIIth dynasty.

Materials. Gold 6, Haematite 2, Obsidian 1, Blue glaze 1.

Position. Necklace.

Collections. Univ. Coll. P. 7, E. 1, St. Petersburg 2.

32. SISTRUM.

Name. *Sesh-shet* (MacG. 16).

Meaning. Joy, especially in the dance. Emblem of Hathor.

Period. XXVI.

Figures. **32**a, green felspar, Meroe; **32**a 2, small, blue glaze; **32**b, green glaze, Hathor head with wig.

Materials. Green felspar 1, green glaze, 3, blue glaze, 1.

Collections. Univ. Coll. P. 2, E. 1, Price 1, Athens 1.

33. COUNTERPOISE OF COLLAR.

Name. *Menat.* With a fringe, *Menkhet* (LACAU, 441—3; MacG. 37).

Meaning. Joy, health.

Varieties. A, plain. B. inscribed.

Period. XXVI.

Figures. **33**a, light green glaze, "says Bastet, give life to Pedu-heb-bast eternally"; the name shows the person was begotten at the great festival of Bubastis. Head and arms of Hathor; **33**a **2**, light green glaze, "Hapi born of Pedu-ast, son of Zed-nebt-amu-auf-red"; **33**b, light green glaze, plain; **33**c, c 2, blue glaze, plain; **33**d, dark green glaze, three cats on the top, Bast on the stem, Nehebka (?) on the disc, reverse "says Bast of (pa) Bast"; **33**e, pl. xliv, light green glaze, group 16.

Materials. Blue glaze 13, Green glaze 11, Green felspar 2, Bronze 1, Gilt wood 1.

Position. Back of neck (4 at Nebesheh), lower chest (Abydos).

Collections. Price 11, Turin 7, Univ. Coll. P. 4, E. 2, St. Petersburg 2.

34. HEAD-REST.

Name. *Urs,* of various woods, cedar (LACAU, 110), *shen* (L. 105), and *mer* (L. 105).

Meaning. Restoration of the head, after primitive preparation of the corpse. The 166th chap. B.D. reads "Chapter of the Headrest. Awake! thy sufferings are allayed, *N.* Thou art awaked when thy head is above the horizon. Stand up, thou art triumphant by means of what has been done to thee. Ptah has struck down thine enemies. It has been ordered what should be done to thee. Thou art Horus, the son of Hathor, the flame born of a flame, to whom his head has been restored after it had been cut off. Thy head will never be taken from thee henceforth. Thy head will never be carried away."

Varieties. On coffins are named the *shen* head-rest (LACAU, 105), the *mer* head-rest (L. 105) and the head-rest of *osh,* cedar wood (L. 110). Solid block head-rests were copied in Ptolemaic time.

Period. First in tombs of IInd dynasty, full size; continued to the XIIth, and then also painted on coffins; as small amulets, XXVI—Ptolemaic.

Figures. **34**a, b, b 2, c, c 2, c 3, d, haematite; d 2, large and rough; **34**e (pl. iv), blue glaze, Dendereh, Ptolemaic, group 21; **34**e 2, green glaze, Ptolemaic; **34**f, blue glaze (xlvi); **34**g, apple-green glaze (xlvi).

Materials. Haematite 70, Blue glaze 6, Green glaze 3, Basalt 2, 1 each of Red glaze, Dark glaze, Diorite, Wood, "Brown stone."

Position. Left breast, left foot, low on stomach (Dendereh), neck (Abydos).

Collections. Cairo 34, Alnwick 15, Univ. Coll. P. 3, E. 4, St. Petersburg 11, Edinburgh 5, Turin 4, Price 4, Murch 1.

35. ZAD.

Name. *Zad* (MacG. 43). Probably the four columns which supported the heaven (*Medum,* 31, xiii); later mistaken by the Egyptians for the backbone of Osiris. The name of Nilometer is only a modern guess.

Meaning. Stability or duration. The 155th chapter of the Book of the Dead reads: "Here is thy backbone thou still-heart! here is thy spine thou still-heart. Put it close to thee. I have given thee the water thou needest. Here it is. I have brought to thee the *zad,* in which thy heart rejoiceth. Said on a *zad* of gold inlaid into the substance of sycomore wood, and dipped into the juice of *ankhamu.* It is put on the neck of this *Khu,* he arrives at the doors of the Duat, and he comes forth by day, even though he be silent. This *zad* is put in its place on the first day of the year, as is done to the followers of Osiris."

Varieties. A, plain. B, crowned with feathers and horns. C, double. D, with two apes (MacG. 74). E, with Hathor.

Period. VI to Roman.

Figures. **35**a, sard, VIth dynasty (?); **35**b, blue glaze, XVIII; **35**c, c 2—c 12, pale green, Hawara, XXVI; **35**c 13, 14, red glass; **35**c 15, yellow steatite; **35**c 16, white limestone; **35**c 17—22, green glaze; **35**d, pale green; **35**e, pale green, Hawara; **35**f, green, the top peg of the column much developed; **35**g, green and brown glaze, crowned, and with two arms holding *uas* sceptres; **35**h, blue-green glaze, with *ankh* and *uas* on *neb* sign; **35**j, micaceous steatite; **35k**, blue glass; **35**l, blue glass, three double capitals; **35**m, yellow glass, Anpu holding the *zad*; **35**n, green glass, *zad* crowned with *sma* feathers; **35**o (xliv), blue glaze faded, XIX, with **30**d. See **39**, b, c, d, on pl. iv.

Materials. Green glaze 191, Blue glaze 56, Lazuli 37, Carnelian 37, Grey glaze 6, Red glass 2, Gold 2, Obsidian 1, Blue glass 4, Yellow steatite 1.

Position. Throat (2); top of chest and base of chest (17); across stomach (8).

Collections. Cairo 64, St. Petersburg 53, Turin 40, Univ. Coll. P. 23, E. 11, Alnwick 8, Price 10, Edinburgh 9, Athens 8, Murch 2.

36. SQUARE.

Name. *Kheses*, square, connected with *Seqeq*, the plummet (see next); a play of words similar to the variation of two Arab words for glass, *Qizaz* and *Zigag*.

Meaning. Rectitude (?). It is not the *hap* sign, carried by kings in festival, as that is acute-angled and equal-sided, whereas this is right-angled and unequal, and is always associated with the plummet.

Period. XXVI to Ptolemaic.

Figures. **36**a, b, b 2, c, d, e, e 2, f, haematite ; **36**g, blue glaze, Dendereh, Ptolemaic, group 21 ; **36**g 2, green glaze ; **36**h, pale green glaze, fine work.

Materials. Haematite 46, Yellow limestone 4, Basalt 3, Green glaze 4, Blue glaze 2, Lazuli 1.

Position. Top row on chest, or left breast (6), with plummet; stomach.

Collections. Univ. Coll. P. 10, E. 2, St. Petersburg 9, Alnwick 6, Turin 4, Edinburgh 3, Athens 3, Price 1, Murch 1.

37. PLUMMET.

Name. *Seqeq* (see previous).

Meaning. Making equilibrium. *Qeqt*, determined by a plummet, is the name of Aswan, where the sun is in equilibrium between north and south at midsummer. Probably worn to impart an evenly-balanced mind, which is held up as a great virtue of character in the Proverbs.

Period. XXVI to Roman.

Figures. **37**a, b, b 2, c, c 2, d, e, e 2, haematite ; **37**f, blue and black glaze, Dendereh, Ptolemaic, group 21 ; **37**g, green glaze, Ptolemaic, showing the plummet cord.

Materials. Haematite 3, Slate 4, Blue glaze 4, Basalt 2, "Brown marble" 1, "Dark marble" 1, Green glaze 1.

Position. Top and middle of chest or left breast (7), low on stomach (2).

Collections. Univ. Coll. P. 8, E. 2, Alnwick 10, Cairo 9, St. Petersburg 9, Turin 6, Price 2, Athens 2, Edinburgh 1, Murch 1.

38. FORKED LANCE.

Name. *Peseshkef*, from *pesesh* to divide, the forked flint lance being used to divide the mouth of the mummy in the ceremony of "opening the mouth."

Meaning. To confer the power of speaking and feeding, as described in Chapter 23 of the Book of the Dead, on the opening of the mouth.

Varieties. The different forms descend as follows :—

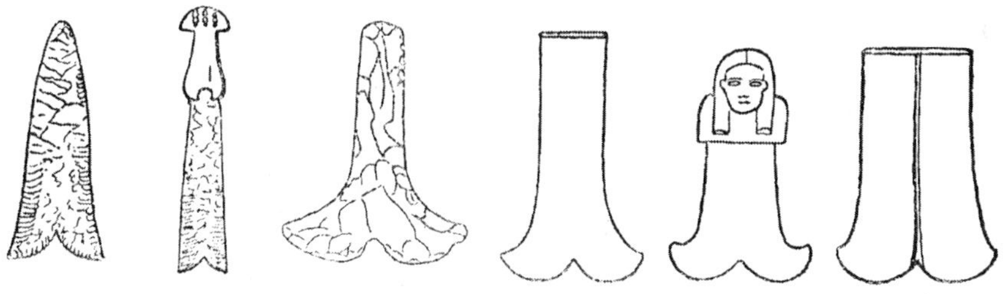

1 : 6 6500 B.C. | 1 : 10 6000 B.C. | 1 : 2 5500 B.C. | 1 : 2 4000 B.C. | 1 : 1 3000 B.C. | 1 : 1 500 B.C.

Figures. **38**a, b, black jasper; **38**c, black steatite ; **38**d, e, f, obsidian ; **38**g, bronze ; **38**h, green glass. These last two may, perhaps, be intended for a clothing amulet surmounted by feathers; or if the flint forked lance was wrapped with cloth for a handle, it might then start this form. A similar form in carnelian is of prince Khaemuas (MARIETTE, *Serapeum*, iii, xi).

Materials. Obsidian 4, Black jasper 2, Black steatite 1, Bronze 1, Green glass 1.

Position. Throat (1); chest (6); stomach (1).

Collection. Univ. Coll. P. 9, E. 1.

Owing to the resemblance to the Plumes (39) and Feathers (41) following, these three amulets are confused in catalogues, and were probably not truly distinguished by the Egyptians. The Materials and Collections stated here are therefore restricted to those which can be verified.

39. OSTRICH PLUMES.

Names. *Shuti*, the two plumes ; or *Shed-shed*.

Meaning. The two ostrich plumes were supposed to fly away in the wind, bearing the king's soul (*Sethe* in *Mahasna*, 19), and the pair of plumes therefore were provided as a vehicle for the soul of the deceased. The single plume is probably the emblem of Maat.

Varieties. Double plume. Single plume.

Period. XIX to Ptolemaic.

Figures. **39**a, b, obsidian ; **39**a 2, obsidian ; **39**a 3, 4, white limestone ; **39**b 2, slate ; **39**b 3, b 4, serpentine ; **39**c, gilt wax ; **39**d (pl. xliv) green glass ; **39**e (pl. xlvi) basalt ; inscribed "Osiris lord of Restau. The high priest, King's son, Khaemuas," son of Ramessu II ; **39**f, green glaze (xlvi).

Materials. Obsidian 3, Serpentine 3, Basalt 2, 1 each of Alabaster, White limestone, Blackened limestone, Green glaze, Gilt wax.

Positions. Throat (1) ; chest (6) ; stomach (2).

Collections. Univ. Coll. P. 5, E. 6, Athens 4, Edinburgh 3, Murch 2.

40. TWO PLUMES, DISC, AND TWO HORNS.

Name. *Sma.*

Meaning. The union of different powers.

Varieties. A, complete. B, disc and horns only.

Period. Ptolemaic.

Figures. **40**a, white glass plumes, red glass disc, purple-black glass horns. Upon the *zad*, **40**b, green and black glaze, Dendereh, Ptolemaic, group 21; **40**c, d, dark blue and black glaze, Dendereh, group 26. See also **35**n, green glass; C. Abydos, group 10 (pl. l).

Materials. Blue glaze 3, Coloured glass 1.

Position. Chest.

Collection. Univ. Coll. P. 4.

41. PAIR OF FEATHERS.

Name. *Qa.*

Meaning. Elevation.

Varieties. A, plain. B, with horns.

Period. XXVI (?).

Figure. **41**, hard brown limestone, Univ. Coll. E.

Materials. Serpentine 17, Basalt 4, Obsidian 4, Green felspar 4, "Yellow stone" 4, Brown limestone 4, Haematite 3, Lazuli 1, Black limestone 1, Beryl 1, Green slate 1, Green diorite 1.

Position. Top of chest (3); middle row (1); low on stomach (2).

Collections. Cairo 24, Athens 6, St. Petersburg 4, Alnwick 3, Price 2, Univ. Coll. E. 1, Edinburgh 1. Perhaps some of these really refer to the previous classes 38—39.

42. RISING SUN.

Name. *Aăkhet.*

Meaning. Power "to behold Ra at his coming forth in the horizon" (*Labyrinth*, 36).

Period. XXVI to Ptolemaic.

Figures. **42**a, red jasper; **42**a 2, light green serpentine.

Materials. "Red sandstone" (? Jasper) 9, Red jasper 7, Blue glaze 4, Red glass 2, Red granite 1, Green glaze 1, "Green stone" (Murch), Light green serpentine 1. Thus nearly all are red.

Position. Low on chest.

Collections. Cairo 11, Turin 4, Univ. Coll. P. 1, E. 2, Alnwick 3, St. Petersburg 3, Price 2, Murch 1.

43. DISC OF SUN.

Name. *Ro*; pronounced *Ria* XVIII dynasty, *Ra* or *Re* Greek.

Meaning. To see the sun.

Period. XXVI to Ptolemaic.

Figures. **43**a, glaze faded white; **43**b, steatite.

Materials. Lazuli 8, "Black stone" 3, Yellow limestone 2, Green felspar 1, Beryl 1, Agate 1, Granite 1, White glaze 2, Steatite 1.

Position. Top of chest (1); middle of stomach (4); left hand (2).

Collections. Cairo 12, Turin 3, Edinburgh 2, Univ. Coll. P. 2, St. Petersburg 1.

44. CROWNED SUN.

Name. ?

Meaning. To see the sun ruling.

Period. XXX (?).

Figure. **44**, Steatite.

Materials. Steatite 1, Obsidian 1.

Collections. Univ. Coll. P. 1, Alnwick 1.

45. BARK OF THE MOON.

Name. *Aoh* (LANZONE, *Diz. Mit.*, xxxvii).

Meaning. To voyage in the sky after the sun.

Period. XVIII—

Figures. **45** (and **45** 2) carnelian, Hawara, XVIII.

Materials. Carnelian 4, Green glaze 1.

Position. Necklace.

Collections. Univ. Coll. P. 4, Kennard 1, Cairo 1, Brit. Mus. 1.

46. STAIRS.

Name. *Khet.*

Meaning. Ascent to sky. In the Book of the Dead, Chapter 22, the dead says: "I am Osiris the lord of Restau, the same who is at the head of the staircase," up which the dead are shown mounting to the judgment. In Chapter 149, in the eleventh domain the dead says: "I raise my ladder up to the sky to see the gods," with a vignette showing a flight of stairs. This form may have become confused with that of a throne (suggested by SCHÄFER in *Z. A. S.* xliii, 66) as the stairs are shown in a boat in the vignette of Chapter 110.

Varieties. 6 to 9 steps.

Period. XXVI to XXX.

Figure. **46**, green glaze.

Materials. Blue glaze 4, Green glaze 2.

Collections. Turin 3 of 7 steps, 1 of 9 steps, Univ. Coll. E. 1 of 6 steps, Price 2.

47. HORNET.

Name. *Bat.*

Meaning. Royal power of Lower Egypt.

Period. VI to XII.

Figures. **47**a, yellow sard, group 3; **47**b, orange sard; **47**c, blue paste, Mahasna, tomb 386; **47**d, blue glaze, XII dynasty.

Materials. Sard and carnelian 9, Blue glaze 1, Black limestone 1, Brown agate 1.

Position. Wrist, 2 (*Deshasheh*, xxvi, 3, 21).

Collections. British Museum 6, Univ. Coll. P. 4 (groups 3, 9).

48. WHITE CROWN.

Name. *Hezt* (LACAU, 486).

Meaning. Royal power of Upper Egypt.

Period. XXVI.

Figures. **48**a, green glass (?) burnt; **48**b, **48**b 2, light green glaze; **48**c, **48**c 2, **48**c 3, light green glaze; **48** d, d 2, green glaze.

Materials. Green glaze 26, Blue glaze 12, Green glass **1**, Black glaze 1, White glaze (faded ?) 1.

Collections. Cairo 14, Univ. Coll. P. 6, E. 3, Turin 6, St. Petersburg 5, Price 3, Alnwick 3, Murch 1.

49. RED CROWN.

Name. *Deshert;* or *Sekhemti* (LACAU, 481), probably confused with the double crown of that name (L. 483).

Meaning. Royal power in Lower Egypt.

Varieties. Crown alone. Crown on *neb.*

Period. XXVI.

Figures. **49**a, a 2, green glaze; **49**b, c, c 2, d 2, green glaze, Memphis; **49**b 2, green glaze; **49**d, blue glazed stoneware, group 28; **49**e to e 8, pl. xliv, green glaze, crown on *neb.*

Materials. Green glaze 30, Blue glaze 9.

Collections. Univ. Coll. P. 14, E. 3, Cairo 12, St. Petersburg 6, Turin 5, Price 4, Murch 1.

50. DOUBLE CROWN ON NEB.

Name. *Sekhemti.*

Meanimg. Royal power in Upper and Lower Egypt.

Period. VI.

Figures. *Mahasna*, xxxiv, xliii, tomb 87.

Material. Gold.

Position. Necklace.

51. VULTURE AND URAEUS.

Name. *Smauti.*

Meaning. Royal power in Upper and Lower Egypt.

Period. VI.

Figures. *Mahasna*, xxxiv, xliii, tomb 87.

Material. Gold.

Position. Necklace.

52. ROYAL CROOK.

Name. *Heqt* (MacG. 54); *Heqt Out*, "Crook of the flocks," used by shepherds (LACAU, 317).

Meaning. Rule in Heliopolis.

Period. XXVI (?).

Figure. Not here.

Material. Grey glaze 1.

Collection. Turin 1.

53. ROYAL SCOURGE.

Name. *Nekhekh* (MacG. 54).

Meaning. Rule in Heliopolis.

Figure. MacG. papyrus 54. Found broken up in tombs of the XIIth dynasty, full-sized, in limestone (*Riqqeh*).

Collection. Portions in Univ. Coll. P.

54. SHEPHERD'S STICK.

Name. *Uas* (MacG. 28; LACAU, 315). *Zom* (LACAU, 314), with wavy stem.

Meaning. Guidance of the flock. Such a form is regularly used by the eastern Bedawy at present. Secondary sense, Rule at Thebes.

Varieties. A, alone. B, with *Zad* and *Onkh.*

Periods. XXVI to XXX (?).

Figures. **54**a, gold; **54**b, blue glass, burnt; **54**c to c 8, pl. xliv, blue glaze, faded, with **30**d, **35**o. See **35h** with *Zad* and *Onkh.*

Materials. Gold 1, Blue glass 1, Blue-green glaze B 1.

Collection. Univ. Coll. P. 2, and 8 of type B.

55. DISC MACE.

Name. *Men* (MacG. 27).

Meaning. Fighting power.

Period. Prehistoric.

Figure. **55**a, pl. xliv, white limestone with black spots, prehistoric; **55**a 2, plain limestone (*Tarkhan II*).

Material. Painted limestone.

Collection. Univ. Coll. P. 5.

56. PEAR MACE.

Name. *Hez* (MacG. 27).

Meaning. Fighting power.

Period. Prehistoric, IV, XII.

Figure. No models, only actual maces buried.

Material. White limestone, Red granite in XII (*Riqqeh*).

Collection. Univ. Coll. P. many.

57. FEATHERS AND SCOURGE.

Name. *Ames* (MacG. 27).

Meaning. Ruling power.

No amulets known.

58. URAEUS SERPENT.

Names. *Aorot*, any goddess (MacG. 6, 30). *Merseger*, goddess (LANZ., *Diz. Mit.*, cxxviii). *Onkh-neter* (MacG. 8). *Rannut*, goddess (LANZ., *D. M.*, clxxxix). *Sat* (LACAU, 94). *Seqer* (MacG. 7; LACAU, 34, 91). *Shem-remtu* (MacG. 9; LACAU, 94). *Urt hekat*, goddess (MacG. 10). *Zet* (LACAU, 94). Also conferring qualities, "giving youth" (LACAU, 90); and with coiled body, "giving being" (?) (LACAU, 91). *Mehen*, uraeus on the crown.

Meanings. Goddesses above named; Knowledge; Divine life; Going among men; Royal power of judgment; Giving youth, and being.

Varieties. A, royal form. B, wavy. C, coiled. D, winged. E, double. F, lion head. G, cat head. H, human head. J, crowned.

Period. XXVI to Roman.

Figures. **58**a, green glass, crowned uraeus on column; **58**b, carnelian, with silver suspension loop; **58**c, branch of red coral, with silver uraeus twisted upon it; **58**d, bronze, tail coiled behind; **58**e, bronze, double crowned with sun discs inlaid; **58f**, bronze, crowned with discs; **58**g, pewter plate, incised; **58** h, green glaze, Memphis; **58**j, light blue glaze, Memphis; **58**k, green glaze, Memphis; **58**k, 2, 3, 4, 5, green glaze, Nebesheh; **58**l, faded green glaze, Memphis; **58**m, green glaze; **58**n, grey glaze; **58**o, green glaze, XVIII; **58**p, blue glass. Pl. xliv, **58**q, gold; **58**r, electrum; **58**s, silver; **58**t, u, blue glaze, Dendereh, Ptolemaic. See gold from Serapeum (Mariette, *Ser.*, iii, xi).

Materials. Green glaze 35, Blue glaze 26, Lazuli 4, Bronze 3, Gold 2, Yellow glaze 1, Grey glaze 1, Green glass 1, White agate 1, Pink limestone 1, Carnelian 2, Silver on red coral 1, Red glass 1.

Position. Forehead (2); necklace (1); chest (10); stomach (3); feet (1).

Collections. Univ. Coll. P. 15, E. 4, Cairo 15, St. Petersburg 8, F 1, G 1, Turin 8, Alnwick 7, Murch 6, Athens F 2, Edinburgh 1.

59. MAN KNEELING WITH PALM BRANCHES.

Name. *Heh.*

Meaning. Millions of Years. Duration.

Period. XII, Roman.

Figures. **59**a, gold; **59**b, gold, group 4; **59**c, lead; **59**d, apple-green glaze, Dendereh, Ptolemaic, group 21; **59**e, silver (pl. xlvi). And see *Mahasna*, xxxiv, xliii, tombs 87, 435.

Materials. Gold 2, Silver 1, Lead 1, Green glaze 1.

Collections. Univ. Coll. P. 5.

60. BOUND CAPTIVE.

Name. *Kheft.*

Meaning. Power over a slave.

Varieties. A, figure standing. B, kneeling. C, painted on soles of sandals.

Period. Prehistoric to Roman.

Figures. **60**a, red limestone, quartz crystal eyes inlaid, male, prehistoric; **60**b, light blue glaze, female, XXVI; **60**c, white limestone, male, XXVI; **60**c 2, similar figure found at Defenneh (*Tanis*, ii, xl); **60**d, lead, male, wrapped in sheet lead; **60**e (pl. xlv), wax, two figures standing, hands joined; **60**f, wax, perhaps a figure; see also figures on soles of sandals (Univ. Coll. E) of Roman mummies, Hawara, (*Roman Portraits*, x, 5), and mud figure of Hyksos age (*Hyksos and Israelite Cities*, vi, 8).

Materials. Lead 1, Red limestone 1, White limestone 2, Blue glaze 1, Wax 2, Cartonnage 1.

Collections. Univ. Coll. P. 6, E. 2, Price 1.

61. FIGURE WITH NECKLACES.

Name. *Shap* (?). See *shap*, to accept; *shapep*, rich; *shapt*, to adorn.

Meaning. From the stoutness, adornment, and easy posture, this seems intended to represent wealth. Compare the Chinese embodiment of wealth.

Period. Roman.

Figure. **61**, black steatite, Quft.

Material. Black steatite.

Collection. Univ. Coll. P. 1.

CHAPTER V

AMULETS OF PROPERTY

Ktematic Amulets, 62—82.

These amulets, representing the funeral offerings of food and drink, and the furniture of objects for the use of the dead, are peculiarly Egyptian. From very early times provision for the continued life of the deceased was placed in the grave, sometimes on an immense scale. As the belief in substitutes grew, so gradually models came to replace the real objects, and then small amulets were substituted for the models. It might seem doubtful where to divide between this class and the last. The mace heads are classed as amulets of power, as the mace is used symbolically by the king in all periods; but the spear head included as property, is never used symbolically. Again, the plummet and square are probably emblems of qualities, as the dead is never represented as building; but the writing tablet and seal are classed as property, as in the future life the deceased would require to write and seal orders. These are the means of writing rather than symbols of the power of writing. The border line of the two classes is seldom really in question.

The order followed here is, food, drink, clothing and objects used.

62. OX HEAD.

Name. Unknown.

Meaning. Food offering. An actual head is often found in graves, from the prehistoric down to the XIIth dynasty.

Period. Prehistoric to XVIII.

Figures. **62**a, calcite; **62**b, quartz, green-glazed; **62**c, carnelian; **62**c, 2, 3, 4, 5, 6, 7, carnelian; **62**d, clear green serpentine, prehistoric; **62**e, blue glaze, VI (?); **62**f, red glass, XVIII (?); **62**g (pl xliv), quartz, green-blue glaze; **62**h, carnelian.

Materials. Carnelian 9, Quartz, green-glazed 2, Noble

AMULETS OF PROPERTY

79. SEAL.

Meaning. Power over property.

Period. XXVI to Ptolemaic.

Figures. **79**a, white limestone; **79**b, brown limestone; **79**b 2, green felspar; **79**b 3, 4, lazuli; **79**b 5, basalt; **79**c (pl. xliv), blue glaze, Dendereh, Ptolemaic, group 21.

Materials. Lazuli 17, Green felspar 9, Green glaze 7, Basalt 7, Blue glaze 4, Limestone 4, Slate 2, Quartz 2, Prase 1, Agate 1.

Position. Right hand 5; left hand 5 (on 2nd finger, between 2nd and 3rd finger); low on stomach.

Collections. Cairo 18, St. Petersburg 12, Univ. Coll., P. 3, E. 3, Alnwick 5.

80. SEAL RING.

Name. Zebot.

Meaning. Power over property.

Period. XXVI to Ptolemaic.

Figures. **80**, Lazuli.

Materials. Gold 1, Lazuli 2, Green glaze 1 (Hor-uza, Hawara).

Position. Between 2nd and 3rd, between 3rd and 4th fingers right hand; on 3rd finger of left hand; in left hand; chest.

Collections. Cairo, Horuza 2, Univ. Coll. P. 1.

81. CIRCLE OF CORD.

Name. Shen, explained as *Onkh-shau* (Lacau, 112).

Meaning. "Benefits of life," as *shen* means "fulness, completion," this implies the fulness of the gains and rewards of life.

Period. XXVI.

Figures. **81**, broken away at sides of base, same both sides, light green glaze.

Materials. Basalt 5, Steatite 2, Lazuli 2, Green felspar 2, Quartz 1, Limestone 1, Green glaze 1.

Position. Top row, by cartouche.

Collections. St Petersburg 7, Alnwick 3, Univ. Coll. P. 1, E. 1, Price 1.

82. SLAVE FIGURE.

Name. Ushabti.

Meaning. To work for the deceased in the future life.

Varieties. Too extensive to state here. A breast-piece of pendant ushabtis occurs in the XIXth dynasty.

Period. XVIII to XXX. (The stone figures of the XIIth dynasty are really figures of the dead.)

Figures. **82**, One example of the XXIInd dynasty marks the place of this subject as an amulet; this ushabti is of Zed-tehuti-as-onkh.

Materials. Bronze, all available stones, all colours of Glaze, Pottery, Wood.

Position. A boxful of 200 was placed on each side of the mummy.

Collections. All. This subject is as extensive as all other amulets together.

CHAPTER VI

AMULETS FOR PROTECTION

Phylactic Amulets, 83—137.

In this class the amulets or charms for protection are what are more popularly regarded as amulets. The purpose of these is to call into account some external agency which is not as definite as a divinity. The most primitive means are preferred, such as wearing shells, bones, animals, cords, stones, etc. Doubtless a great number of vegetable and animal objects were also included in this class, though the great majority of such have naturally disappeared in the course of ages. The great popularity and literary importance of the inscribed charms, especially inscribed gem stones, has fixed more attention on this kind of amulet, almost to the exclusion of the various other classes.

83. SUN AND WINGS.

Meaning. Ra as protector.

Varieties. Seldom on the mummy, but usual over figures and entrances to temples.

Period. Ptolemaic, as an amulet.

Figures. **83**a, black steatite; **83**b, gilt wax, Dendereh, group 20.

Materials. Black steatite 1, Gilt wax 1.

Collection. Univ. Coll. P. 2.

84. SUN AND URAEI.

Meaning. Ra as ruler.

Varieties. Seldom on the mummy, but used as previous.

Period. Ptolemaic, as an amulet.

Figures. **84**a, wood with traces of stucco and gilding; **84**b, green glaze, Dendereh, Ptolemaic, group 21.

Materials. Green glaze 1, Wood 1.

Collection. Univ. Coll. P. 2.

85. CRESCENT.

Name. *Aoh.*

Meaning. The protection of the moon god. Against evil eye and witchery (Bell., xv, 26; xvi, 25). The emblem of patricians at Rome (Boni, *Nuov. Antol.*, 1 Oct., 1912).

Varieties. A, alone. B, with disc. C, with cross.

Period. XVIII to Roman. Specially worn in early part of 2nd cent. A.D. (*Roman Portraits*, 12, 14).

Figures. **85**a, b, pale blue glass, XVIII; **85**c, black glaze, XII or XVIII; **85**d, e, silver, Memphis, Roman, group 27; **85**f, gold, Memphis, group 27; **85**g, silver; **85**h, base silver; **85**j, j2, white glass on blue, with red spots around, Gurob, Roman. Type B, **85**k, electrum, XII dynasty (?); **85**l, blue glaze, XVIII; **85**m, black and yellow serpentine, Roman; **85**n, bronze, Shurafeh, Coptic period. See also plain bronze crescent, Roman age, Saft, in *Hyksos and Israelite Cities*, xxxvii a.

Materials. Gold 1, Electrum 1, Silver 4, Bronze 2, Glass 5, Blue glaze 1, Black glaze 1.

Position. Necklace.

Collection. Univ. Coll. P. 8.

86. MUMMY.

Name. *Sah* (MacG. 64). *Sokar khent oper*, "Sokar in clothing" (Lanz., *Diz., Mit.*, xvii).

Meaning. Preservation of the body in mummy form (?).

Period. Graeco-Roman.

Figures. **86**a, b, dark blue glass.

Materials. Green glaze 2, Blue glass 2.

Collections. Univ. Coll. P. 2, Turin 2.

87. MUMMY ON BIER.

Name. ?

Meaning. Preservation of the body (?).

Varieties. A, alone. B, with Anpu.

Period. Ptolemaic.

Figures. **87**a, green glaze; **87**b, glass, burnt. Type B, **87**c, blue glaze with black paint, Dendereh, Ptolemaic, group 21.

Materials. Blue glaze 4, B 1, Green glaze 1, Red glass B 1, Glass (burnt) 1, Painted pottery 1.

Position. Chest (2); stomach (2); knees (1).

Collections. Univ. Coll. P. 4, Athens 2, Edinburgh 2.

88. GIRDLE OF ISIS.

Name. *Thet.*

Meaning. Protection by the blood of Isis. Also the girdle of Nut (Lanz., *Diz. Mit.*, cli). This is the primitive women's girdle, fuller than the *onkh*, the men's girdle. The 156th chapter of the Book of the Dead reads: "Chapter of the tie of red jasper which is put on the neck of the deceased. The blood of Isis, the virtue of Isis; the magic power of Isis, the magic power of the Eye, are protecting this great one; they prevent any wrong being done to him This chapter is said on a tie of red jasper, dipped in the juice of *ankhamu*, inlaid into the substance of the sycomore wood, and put on the neck of the deceased. Whoever has this chapter read to him, the virtue of Isis protects him; Horus the son of Isis rejoices in seeing him, and no way is barred to him, unfailingly."

Varieties. A, alone. B, double. C, double with *zad* sign.

Period. XIX to Roman.

Figures. **88**a, red glass; **88**b, green glass; **88**c, green glaze; **88**c 2, blue glaze; **88**d, e, e 2, 3, green glaze, group 28, XXV dynasty (?); **88**f, faded green glaze; **88**g, dark blue glaze, XVIII or XIX; **88**h, h 2, j, j 2, j 3, red glass; **88**j 4, red limestone; **88**j 5, slate; **88**k, pewter, possibly a clothing sign **72**; **88**l, wax, gilt, Dendereh, group 20. See pl. xlvii, **88**m, carnelian of the royal scribe Paari; **88**n, jasper, of the chief archer Nekht-a-min; **88**o, jasper of Roi; **88**p, blue and black glaze, Dendereh, Ptolemaic, group 26. Type B, double, red glaze, XVIII (Ed). Also see 2 carnelian of Khaemuas and 1 of Hapi (Mariette, *Serapeum*, iii, xi, xx).

Materials. Red jasper 21, Carnelian 3, Red glass 18, Brown jasper 13, Blue glaze 27, Green glaze 18, Red glaze 1, Lazuli 2, Obsidian 1, Gold 1, Silver 1, Pewter plate 1, Brown paste 1, Green glass 1, Wax gilt 1.

Position. Neck (2); chest usual (11); stomach (2); toes (1).

Collections. Cairo 47, Univ. Coll. P. 16, E. 7, Turin 12, Price 12, Alnwick 11, St. Petersburg 7, Edinburgh 1, Murch 1.

89. SCARAB, FLAT BASE.

Name. *Kheper.*

Meaning. Heart of Isis given to the deceased. See Nos. **7** and **90** for the Book of the Dead.

Period. XVIII to XXX.

Figures. **89**a, grey steatite, Ramesseum; **89**b, lazuli, formerly set on a pectoral; **89**c, lazuli veneer on slate base, Ramesseum; **89**d, basalt, Ramesseum; **89**d 2, volcanic ash; **89**e, limestone, Ramesseum; **89**f, malachite; **89**g, slate; **89**g 2, slate; **89**g 3, steatite; **89**h, peridot; **89**j, k, indigo glaze, XXII dynasty; **89**l, blue-green glaze; **89**l 2, red glass; **89**m, blue paste, Saqqareh, pierced for stitching on mummy wrapping or network, as also the next; **89**n, deep blue paste; **89**o, red glass; **89**p, violet glass; **89**q, violet glass; **89**r, s, deep blue clear glass; **89**t, same, burnt; **89**u, deep blue clear glass; **89**uu (pl. xliv), same; **89**v, yellow glass; **89**w, x, amber; **89**x, 2, 3, durite; **89**y, green glaze with yellow points, Roman.

Materials (apart from Cairo catalogue which is uncertain). Basalt 17, Serpentine 15, Steatite 8, Green jasper 6, Porphyry 4, Green quartz 4, Schist 1, Blue glaze 5, Blue glass 4, Green glaze 4, Lazuli 3, Violet glass 2, Blue paste 2, Amber 2, Durite 1, Green felspar 1, Limestone 1, Malachite 1, Peridot 1, Red glass 1, Yellow glass 1.

Position. Inside the body.

Collections. Univ. Coll. P. 27, E. 5, Alnwick 28, St. Petersburg 66, Price 10.

90. SCARAB, INSCRIBED BASE.

Name. *Kheper.*

Meaning. Heart of Isis given to the deceased. The 30th chapter of the Book of the Dead appears in a slightly different form (version B) upon the heart scarab, reading: "My heart of my Mother, my heart of my Mother, my heart of my becoming (in future life). May nothing rise up against me in evidence; may no hindrance be made against me by the divine chiefs; may there be no enemy of thee against me in the presence of the Guardian of the Balance. Thou art my *ka* in my body, the creator making sound my limbs. Come forth to the bliss towards which we are bound. May our name not be in bad odour with the Ministrants, those who deal to men their course in life; and be there good for us, be there good to the hearer, be there joy of heart, by the Weighing of words. May not lies be uttered in the presence of the God, before the great God lord of Amenti. Behold thy uplifting is in the acquittal."

Varieties. A, various forms of this chapter are used, sometimes only omitting half a dozen words, as on **90l**, sometimes leaving only the opening invocation to the heart, as on **90c**. B, a *suten du hotep* formula is rarely used, as in **90**u, v, aa.

Period. XVIIIth to XXIIIrd dynasties.

Figures. The backs on pl. viii, the inscriptions on pl. ix; **90**a, black steatite, name Huy; **90**b, brown limestone, of Huria; **90**c, glazed steatite, of Set-mesu; **90**d, black steatite, of Tuaä; **90**e, black steatite, of Ma-nehes, "the alert lion"; **90f**, hard light brown limestone in silver mount, of Min-em-hat; **90**g, a metamorphic mud, similar in material to slate, usually mis-called "green basalt," here called *durite,* of Tet-bet, "nursing shepherd" (?); **90**h, durite, of Dudut; **90**j, durite, of Repen (?); **90**k, jade, called by the Egyptians *nenmehen,* as stated on the Kennard tablet (now in Berlin), of the singer, Thentamen; **90l**, durite (volcanic ash) of Pamoy (secondary use); **90**m, durite of Anefer; **90**n, durite, of Tetames; **90**o, green glaze in copper mount, of the scribe Nashuy; **90**p, durite, of Amen-mes; **90**q, limestone stained brown-black (XVIIIth dynasty, as kohl pots) of the overseer of the serfs of Min, Kanure, from Ekhmim; **90**r, durite, of the singer of Amen, Shab-mer-ast; **90**s, durite of Zed-ptah-a-onkh; **90**t, jade, name lost; **90**u, black steatite of Hor-se-ast; **90**v, blue paste, very illegibly cut, apparently of Peh-ne-kha-user; **90**w (pl. xlvi) lazuli, of the keeper of the cattle Tahutimes, XVIIIth dynasty. The following not in plates:—**90**x, violet glass plate, with hollow crystal back in which is painted the heron, backed with gold foil, for Auf-neren-neheh, Gurob, XVIIIth dynasty; **90**y, limestone, coloured brown, of the singer of Isis, Hatsheps, XVIIIth dynasty; **90**z, limestone, of Huy; **90**aa, lazuli, *nesut du hotep* formula without a name, group 31.

Materials (omitting Cairo as uncertain; the other collections as stated, but probably in error on basalt). Basalt (?) 18, Durite 9, Porphyry (?) 6, Limestone 5, Steatite 5, Serpentine 5, Green jasper (?) 4, Schist 4, Jade 2, Lazuli 2, Green felspar 1, Glazed steatite 1, Green glaze 1, Blue glaze 1, Blue paste 1, Violet glass 1.

Position. On the chest (?).

Collections. Univ. Coll. P. 26, Alnwick 17, Price 5.

91. PECTORAL.

Name. Unknown.

Meaning. Heart of Isis.

Varieties. A, in one piece. B, with separate scarab (see MacG. 68, 69, 70).

Period. XVIII to Ptolemaic.

Figures. **91**a, durite, filled in with yellow paste; upper side, scarab with *akhet* bird on back, Isis and Nebhat standing on a boat adoring it; under side, the scarab outline with the invocations of the beginning of the chapter, and figure of Unnefer adoring Osiris; **91**b, black steatite, Isis and Nebhat, winged, adoring, but the middle blank, probably a scarab has been attached; back, Osiris "lord of eternity, lord of Ta-zeser," adored by the deceased and Isis; on the top edge the name "Set-ha-em-tepy"; **91**c, gold, a woman Nefert-her adoring "Isis the great mother"; **91**d, electrum, figure of Tahuti, with altar of offerings. "The speech of Tahuti, lord of Khemenu, give life, health, and strength to the son of the high priest of Amen, Uasakauasa, acquitted, son of the high priest of Amen, Fu-ua-merth, acquitted"; **91**e, green glaze, *zad* between two *thet* girdles, back, jackal couchant on shrine, with right *uzat* eye above; **91**f, blue-green glaze, jackal couchant on shrine "Anpu in his bandages lord of the desert"; **91**g, shrine of black and yellow serpentine, apparently an inserted figure has been lost. See green-glazed pectoral of Pasar (Mariette, *Serapeum,* iii, xii).

Materials. Green glaze 13, Blue glaze 3, Glazed stone 8, Slate 6, Durite 1, Wood 8, Schist 2, Blue frit 2, Steatite 1, Serpentine 1, Red-brown glaze 1, Gold 1, Electrum 1.

Position. On breast (2); on stomach (1).

Collections. Cairo 35, Univ. Coll. P. 7, St. Petersburg 6, Price 2, Edinburgh 1, Alnwick 1.

92. SCARAB WITH LEGS.

Name. *Kheper* (MacG. 61).

Meaning. Protection against quartan fever (Pliny, xxx, 30). Snake bite (Africa). Agate scarab against evil eye (Bell., xiii, 27). Horns of scarab for children (Pliny, xxx, 47).

Varieties. Actual beetles were buried in jars in prehistoric graves. An alabaster case in the form of a scarab, to hang round the neck, hollow as a reliquary, of Ist dynasty, Cairo (*Tarkhan,* xiv). A, with legs, natural head. B, hawk-headed. C, with four rams' heads (Lanz., *Diz. Mit.,* 490). D, human headed (L., *Diz. Mit.,* ccl).

Period. Ist to XXXth dynasties.

Figures. **92**a, obsidian, of exquisitely detailed work (the wing cases being also delicately ribbed), and probably of the XIIth dynasty, when obsidian was a favourite material for the best inscribed scarabs; **92**b, diorite; b 2, 3, 4, Hawara, porphyry, hard steatite, brown limestone, XXVI; **92**c, green glaze; **92**d, greenish-blue glaze; **92**d 2, 3, white limestone; d 4, steatite; d 5, haematite; d 6, 7, green glaze; **92**e, f, f 2 f 3, green glaze faded, Hawara, XXVI; **92**e 2, brown basalt; **92**g (pl. xliv), green glaze, Dendereh, Ptolemaic; **92**h (pl. xlvi), green glaze; **92**j, blue and black glaze, Dendereh, Ptolemaic, group 26 (pl. xxxii).

Materials. Basalt (durite ?) 22, Porphyry 14, Lazuli 13, Green glaze 34, Blue glaze 8, Serpentine 8, Haematite 6, Carnelian 6, Brown steatite 7, Limestone 4, Prase 3, Black syenite 4, Green syenite 2, Green glass 3, Green felspar 2, Beryl 2, Obsidian 2, White glass 1, Bronze 1, Diorite 1.

Position. Throat (4); chest (23); stomach (5); left hand (2).

Collections. St. Petersburg 65, Univ. Coll. P. 35, E. 15, Price 22.

93. SCARAB WINGED.

Meaning. Protective power of the Creator (?).

Varieties. A, winged. B, winged, on legs walking Dendereh 15, pl. li). C, winged in boat.

Period. XXII to XXX.

Figures. **93**a, flame-coloured sard, XVIII(?); **93**b, pewter, group 18; **93**c, bronze with human head, crowned with disc, horns, and uraeus; **93**d, blue paste, with holes for stitching on to a mummy network; **93**e, f, blue glaze, with four genii, Dendereh, Ptolemaic, group 21; **93**g, green glaze with violet inlay in the hawk heads, and four genii. For other figures of the genii see **182**. Type C, **93**h, blue glaze (xlvii).

Materials. Green glaze 3, Sard 1, Blue paste 1, Pewter 1, Gold 1, Blue glass 2, Black glaze 1.

Position. Collar-bone (3); breast (3); stomach (1).

Collections. Univ. Coll. P. 8, Athens 3, St. Petersburg 1.

94. VULTURE STANDING.

Names. *Nert, Demzedet, Ament, Themt, Urtheka, Sebkhet Kherert* (MacG. 12, 13, 14, 15, 29, 45, 47, 66).

Meaning. Five different vultures confer Being, Divinity, Living with gods, Going among men, and Youth (Lacau, 99).

Period. VI to Roman.

Figures. **94**a, bone, VI, group 5; **94**a 2, carnelian, group 7; **94**a 3, 4, blue glaze, rude, VI, Zaraby; **94**b, bone, group 6; **94**c, bone, group 8; **94**d, gold. (See Mariette, *Serapeum*, iii, xi; *Naqada*, lviii, XIIth dynasty.)

Materials. Lazuli 4, Gold 2, Blue glaze 3, Bone 3, Carnelian 1, Syenite 1, Yellow glaze 1, Red glaze 1.

Position. Neck (2); base of chest (3).

Collections. Univ. Coll. P. 7, Turin 3, Murch 2, Cairo 2 (Horuza), St. Petersburg 1, Alnwick 1.

95. VULTURE WITH WINGS SPREAD.

Name. *Nert-hent-pet-er-remtu* (?), "The Vulture mistress of heaven over mankind." *Nert-her-ne-pot,* "The Vulture who is over men" (MacG. 34, 48).

Meaning. Protection. The 157th chapter of the Book of the Dead is as follows: "Chapter of the vulture of gold, put on the neck of the deceased. Isis has arrived; she hovers over the dwellings, and she searches all the hidden abodes of Horus when he comes out of the northern marshes knocking down him whose face is evil. She causes him (the deceased) to join the bark (of the sun), and grants him the sovreinty over the worlds. When he has fought a great fight, He (Horus) decrees what must be done in his honour; He causes fear of him to arise, and He creates terror. His mother, the Great One, uses her protective power, which she has handed over to Horus. Said on the vulture of gold. If this chapter is written on it, it protects the deceased, the powerful one, on the day of the funeral, and undeviatingly for times infinite."

Varieties. A, vulture head. B, ram head. C, curved wings.

Period. VI to Roman.

Figures. **95**a, gold; **95**b, gold; **95**c, pewter, group 18; **95**d, bronze. See type B, gold inlaid, in Mariette, *Serapeum*, iii, xii; also C, gold inlaid, in Mar., *Ser.*, iii, xx.

Materials. Gold 4, Pewter 1, Bronze 1.

Position. Neck 1; chest 1.

Collections. Univ. Coll. P. 4, Cairo, Horuza 1, St. Petersburg 1.

96. SERPENT (Not Uraeus, 57).

Name. *Zet* (MacG. 5).

Meaning. Preservation from serpents (?). Teeth for dentition (Pliny, xxx, 47).

Varieties. A, long. B, in tube. C, wavy. D, coiled. (screw). E, spiral (volute).

Period. Prehistoric to XXVI (?).

Figures. A, **96**a, dark wood, serpent of Mertseger (Lanz., *Diz. Mit.*, cxxvii); **96** b, flint, from Koptos, Ist dynasty (?). B, **96**c, red glass. C, two early dynastic house amulets in pottery. D, **96**d, yellow-brown limestone, prehistoric, apparently to be placed round a finger or staff, two and a half turns. E, **96**e, lazuli, prehistoric; **96**f (pl. xlvii), limestone, prehistoric, large amulet to hang in house, scale 2 : 5.

Materials. Pottery 2, Lazuli 1, Flint 1, Yellow limestone 1, Limestone 1, Red glass 1, Wood 1.

Collection. Univ. Coll. P. 7.

97. SERPENT HEAD, OR FOREPART.

Name. *Menqaryt, Menqabet* (Lacau, 82; MacG. 1).

Meaning. To avoid snake bite. Chapter 33 of the Book

of the Dead reads: "Chapter whereby all serpents are kept back"; Chapter 34: "Chapter whereby a person is not devoured by the dweller in the shrine"; Chapter 35: "Chapter whereby the person is not devoured by a serpent in the underworld." There is nothing in these chapters to explain the amulets further.

Varieties. A, half length. B, head only.

Period. Prehistoric to XXVI.

Figures. **97**a, red glass, of "the lady of the house Nefer-renpit"; **97**b, carnelian, of "the royal scribe Ptah-mes, keeper of the horses"; **97**c, d, carnelian; **97**e, sard; **97**e 2, yellow jasper; **97**f, f 2, green glaze; **97**g, carnelian; **97**h, haematite; **97**j, red limestone, prehistoric. Also see 2 carnelian of Hapi (MARIETTE, *Serapeum*, iii, xi).

Materials. Carnelian 50, Haematite 1, Red limestone 1, Ivory 3, Blue glass 2, Red jasper 1, Green glaze 5, Green glass 1, Brown glass 1, Gold 1, Agate 1, Yellow jasper 1.

Position. Throat (2); base of neck (1); base of chest (1).

Collections. Cairo A 28, B 14, Univ. Coll. P. 9, E. 3, St. Petersburg B 3, Murch 3, Alnwick 2, Turin 1.

98. COBRA ON CASE.

Name. Unknown.

Meaning. Snake's skin eases delivery (PLINY, xxx, 44). For malaria (BELL., xiii, 20).

Varieties. A, reared up. B, lying twisted on case.

Period. This class of reptiles on cases is shown by the inscribed names to be as early as the XXVth dynasty; and being mentioned by Pliny it probably extended to Ptolemaic times.

Figures. Type A, **98**a, bronze; **98**b, bronze, cornice to box; **98**c, bronze, upper part of hood broken away, inscribed "Atmu give life to Un-nefer, son of Khonsu-ardus, . . . life to Hapy, son of Shab-pa-hor"; right *uzat* eye on front. (This is classed by Daressy as a figure of Atmu, by the inscription (Cairo Cat. 38,704), but as Atmu never appears elsewhere as a serpent, the god is probably only invoked for the fever.) Type B, **98**d, d 2, d 3, bronze; **98**e, bronze. For shape of head see *Descrip. Eg.* Reptilia, Supplem. 3.

Material. Bronze.

Collections. Univ. Coll. P. 6, E. 2, St. Petersburg 1.

99. AMPHISBAENA ON CASE.

Meaning. Worn alive for pregnancy (PLINY, xxx, 43). Worn dead for rheumatism (P. xxx, 36).

Period. XXV to Ptolemaic.

Figures. **99**a, b, bronze.

Material. Bronze.

Collection. Univ. Coll. P. 2, St. Petersburg 2.

100. PHAGRUS EEL ON CASE.

Meaning. Tooth of phagrus worn for malaria (PLINY, xxxii, 38).

Period. XXV to Ptolemaic (?).

Figure. **100**a, b, c, bronze.

Material. Bronze.

Collection. Univ. Coll. P. 1, E. 2. See WILKINSON, *M. and C.*, iii, 342.

101. LIZARD ON CASE.

Meaning. Spotted lizard worn in case for quartan fever. (PLINY, xxx, 30). Green lizard in case for tertian fever (PLINY, xxx, 30).

Varieties. A, lizard. B, two lizards. C, lizard and cobra.

Period. XXV to Ptolemaic (?).

Figures. These vary somewhat, but different types of Gecko are not distinguishable. Type A, **101**a, b, c, bronze; **101**a 2, b 2, bronze. B, **101**, bronze. C, **101**d, bronze.

Material. Bronze.

Collection. Univ. Coll. P. 3, E. 4.

102. TAURT ON CASE.

Meaning. For pregnancy, as amphisbaena in PLINY, xxx, 43.

Period. XXV to Ptolemaic (?).

Figure. **102.**

Material. Bronze.

Collection. Univ. Coll. P. 1.

103. SHREW MOUSE ON CASE.

Meaning. Dead shrew mouse passed round boils (PLINY, xxx, 34).

Period. XXV to Ptolemaic (?).

Figure. **103.**

Material. Bronze.

Collections. St. Petersburg 2, Univ. Coll. P. 1.

104. HORN.

Name. *Ob.*

Meaning. For evil eye (BELL., xii, 12).

Period. Roman.

Figure. **104**, gazelle horn tip, Shurafeh, 1912.

Material. Horn.

Collection. Univ. Coll. P. 1.

105. BONE.

Meaning. Human, for ulcer (PLINY, xxviii, 11); human skull, epilepsy (BELL., xiv, 12); hare's pastern, bowel pains (P. xxviii, 56); pig's pastern promotes discord (P. xxxviii, 81); frog, fevers and aphrodisiac (P., xxxii, 18); perch vertebra, tertian fever (P., xxxii, 38).

Varieties. A, mammalian bone. B, crocodile plate.

Period. Roman.

Figures. A, **105a**, Shurafeh, 1912. B, **105b**, crocodile

plate: **150c**, crocodile plate with iron rings, and silvered mirror stuck on by resin.
Collection. Univ. Coll. P. 3.

106. CORAL.

Meaning. Worn in India for dangers (PLINY, xxxii, 11). Worn by infants (PLINY, xxviii, 7). In Italy worn against evil eye (BELL., ix).
Period. Graeco-Roman.
Figure. **106**, branch of coral with silver uraeus twisted upon it. (See figure **58c**, and Coral dog, **233c**.)
Collection. Univ. Coll. P. 1.

107. CYPRAEA SHELL.

Name. Unknown.
Meaning. Protection from evil eye and witchery, from resemblance to vulva; (BELL., *Am.*, 61; *Fet.*, 38). In tombs at Ascolano (BONI, *Nuov. Antol.*, 1 Oct., 1912).
Period. Prehistoric to Roman.
Figures. **107a**, *Cyp. pantherina*, prehistoric, south town, Naqadeh; **107b**, *Cyp. annulus*, prehistoric, 1625 Naqadeh; **107c**, d, same, Roman, Gheyta; **107e**, *Cyp. caurica*, Ballas; **107f**, silver gilt, same both sides; **107g**, silver sheet; **107h**, carnelian; **107h**, 2, dark blue glaze; **107j**, green glaze, Mahasna 448, VIth dynasty; **107k**, green glaze; **107l**, pl. xliv, black and white porphyry, XVIIIth dynasty; **107m**, green glaze (pl. xlvi).
Materials. Shell, Silver gilt 1, Silver 1, Carnelian 1, Green glaze 3, Blue glaze 1.
Position. Necklace, and bracelets.
Collection. Univ. Coll. P. 6, E. 1, and many shells.

108. NERITA CRASSILABRUM SHELL.

Period. XIIth dynasty.
Figures. **108a**, b, Sinai, Serabit temple; **108c**, carnelian, threaded with blue-glazed ball beads, XIIth dynasty.
Position. Necklace.
Collection. Univ. Coll. P., carnelian string, and many shells.

109. MITRA MACULOSA SHELL.

Period. Late prehistoric to XIIth dynasty.
Figures. **109a**, prehistoric, Ballas; **109b**, blue paste, Ballas 355, XIIth dynasty.
Position. Necklace.
Collection. Univ. Coll. P., string of beads, and many shells.

110. CONUS SHELL.

Period. Late prehistoric, XXIIIth dynasty.
Figures. **110a**, Zowaydeh; **110b**, c; **110d** (pl. xv), slice of top, Hawara, XXIIIrd dynasty.
Position. Necklaces.
Collection. Univ. Coll. P.

111. CARDIUM EDULE SHELL.

Meaning. Against evil eye and witchery (BELL., xi, 4; *Fet.* 47).
Period. Prehistoric to VIth dynasty.
Figures. **111a**, prehistoric, Ballas 225; **111b**, same (?); **111c**, carnelian, group 14; **111d**, carnelian, group 1; **111e**, carnelian, Mahasna, tomb 461; **111f**, g, h, carnelian, group 2; **111j**, carnelian, group 3.
Materials. Carnelian 8, many shells.
Position. Pectoral pendants.
Collection. Univ. Coll. P.

112. MELEAGRINA MARGARITIFERA SHELL (RED SEA PEARL).

Period. XII to XVIII.
Figures. **112a**—a 5 (pl. xliv), engraved with name of Senusert I; **112c**, electrum, with name of Amenemhat III; **112c**, 2, 3, 4, 5, 6, plain, of XIIth dynasty; **112d**, gold, pectoral of King Rasekenen; **112e**, carnelian; with glass beads, XVIIIth dynasty.
Materials. Shell 5, Gold 1, Electrum 4.
Position. Pectoral pendants.
Collection. Univ. Coll. P. 12.

113. CLEOPATRA BULIMOIDES SHELL.

Period. Late prehistoric to VIth dynasty.
Figures. **113a**, string of shells, Ballas; **113b**, bone, group 5; **113c**, green felspar, group 30; **113c**, c 2, sard, group 3; **113d**, sard, group 2.
Materials. Shells, Sard 2, Green felspar 1, Bone 1.
Position. Necklace.
Collection. Univ. Coll. P. 4, and shells.

(The following shells are found pierced for wearing, but no imitations are known.)

114. PECTUNCULUS VIOLACESCENS SHELL.

Meaning. Worn by Troglodyte women against witchery (STRABO, XVI, iv, 17); pierced, for evil eye and witchery (BELL., *Fet.*, 41). Worn in Rome, tombs in Forum (BONI, *Nuov. Antol.*, 1 Oct., 1912).
Period. Prehistoric.
Figure. **114**, Ballas 519, Naqadeh 1681.
Collection. Univ. Coll. P.

115. POLINICES MAMILLA SHELL.

Period. Prehistoric.
Figure. **115**, Ballas 572, Koptos.
Position. Necklace.
Collection. Univ. Coll. P.

116. CASSIS NODULOSA SHELL.

Period. Late prehistoric.
Figure. **116**, Ballas 207.

Position. Necklace.
Collection. Univ. Coll. P.

117. MUREX TERNISPINA SHELL.

Figure. **117.**
Collection. Univ. Coll. P.

118. HELIX DESERTORUM SHELL.

Figures. **118**a, b, c, prehistoric, Naqadeh 698; **118**d, e, f, XIIth dynasty, Hawara; **118**g, h, prehistoric, Naqadeh 1615.
Position. Necklaces.
Collection. Univ. Coll. P.

119. CLANCULUS PHARAONIS SHELL.

Period. XXVth dynasty.
Figure. **119.**
Collection. Univ. Coll. P.

120. TURBO, OPERCULUM

Period. Early.
Figure. **120**, Koptos.
Collection. Univ. Coll. P.

121. OLIVA SHELL.

Period. Early.
Figures. **121**a, b, Koptos, Naqadeh 1567.
Collection. Univ. Coll. P.

122. TEREBRA CONSOBRINA SHELL.

Period. Prehistoric.
Figure. **122**, Naqadeh 1567, Koptos.
Collection. Univ. Coll. P.

123. STONE IMPLEMENT.

Names. *Peseshkef*, and others.
Meaning. To open the mouth of the mummy (see **37**). Black round stones like axes are called *baetuli*, and longer ones *keraunia*e; they are sacred, and potent in taking cities and fleets (PLINY, xxxvii, 51). Called "thunderstones" in Italy and Northern Europe; worn as charms against lightning and evil actions (BELL., I—III; *Fet.*, 43; *Am.*, 14). Also regarded as thunderstones in China.
Period. Prehistoric to XXVIth dynasty.
Figures. **123**a, yellow steatite, VIth dynasty, group 13; **123**b, c, black jasper, the *baetuli* described by PLINY; **123**d, honey sard, Hawara; **123**e (pl. xliii), basalt; **123**f (xliii), slate; **123**g (xliii), green glaze, e, f, g, all from Ist dynasty town Abydos; **123**h (xliv), green glaze, VIth dynasty, Zaraby; **123**j (xv), green serpentine, prehistoric, Naqadeh 1567; **123**k, silver; **123**l, iron; **123**m (pl. xlv), alabaster, Illahun, XXIInd dynasty.
Materials. Black jasper 2, Green glaze 2, Alabaster 1, Green serpentine 1, Yellow steatite 1, Honey sard 1, Silver 1, Iron 1.
Collection. Univ. Coll. P. 12.

124. BELL.

Meaning. Worn by children against the evil eye (BELL., xv, 10). In Egypt probably worn by children, as it has a head of Bes on the earlier examples.
Period. XXVI (?) to Roman.
Figures. **124**a, iron, Illahun; **124**b, bronze, Gurob; **124**c, bronze, with head of Bes on each side (pl. xliv); **124**d, bronze (pl. xlvi).
Material. All Bronze and Iron.
Position. Bracelet.
Collection. Univ. Coll. P. 5.

125. DOOR BOLT.

Name. *Sest.*
Meaning. Security (?).
Period. VIth dynasty.
Figure. **125**a, b, green glaze, Mahasna, tomb 13.
Collection. Univ. Coll. P. 1.

126. SEATED PRINCE.

Name. *Repoti-hat.*
Meaning. Protector (?).
Period. XVIIIth to XIXth dynasty.
Figures. **126**a, blue glaze faded white; **126**a 2, red glaze, Rifeh.
Collection. Univ. Coll. P. 2.

127. PRINCESS.

Name. *Hent.*
Meaning. Protector (?).
Period. XVIIIth dynasty.
Figures. **127**a, bronze Tell el Amarna, perhaps a badge worn by the household of a princess; **127**b, blue glaze.
Material. Bronze 1, Blue glaze 1.
Collection. Univ. Coll. P. 2.

128. MEDUSA HEAD.

Meaning. To protect by repelling onlookers.
Period. Roman.
Figures. **128**a, b, green glaze; **128**c, green, yellow, and black glaze (xliii).
Collection. Univ. Coll. P. 3.

129. BULLA.

Meaning. Protection.
Period. I to Roman.
Figures. **129**a, b, b 2 (pl. xliii), carnelian, group 14; **129**c (xliii), green opaque serpentine, Ist dynasty town, Abydos;

129d, alabaster; **129**e, agate, XXIIIrd (?) dynasty, Ramesseum; **129**f, ivory; **129**g, jade, gilt resin attached to end for the suspension hole; **129**h, black steatite; **129**j, green glass in silver frame: **129**k, gold over a white paste body; **129**l, flint nodule set in bronze frame (pl. xlvi). See *Naqada*, lviii, lxiv, 97.

Materials. Carnelian 2, 1 each of Emery, Jade, Flint, Agate, Black steatite, Alabaster, Gold, Ivory, Green glass.

Collection. Univ. Coll. P. 12.

130. FOREHEAD PENDANT.

Meaning. To distract and avert the evil eye.

Varieties. A, plain. B, matwork. C, figures. D, gilt tube, modern.

Period. Prehistoric, Modern.

Figures. **130**a, shell, hook inside at lower end to hold up veil; **130**b, shell, Naqadeh, T. 16; **130**c, shell, Naqadeh 399; **130**d, shell, Naqadeh 1848; **130**e, shell, Naqadeh 1007; **130**f, shell; **130**g, shell, Naqadeh 1848; **130**h, shell, Naqadeh 1384; **130**h 2, shell, Naqadeh 144; **130**j, shell, Naqadeh, B. 323; **130**k, l, shell; **130**m, shell, Naqadeh 399; **130**n, black steatite; **130**o, p, black and white limestone; **130**q, clear green serpentine; **130**r, black and white porphyry. Type B, **130**s, shell carved in basket pattern, with hook at lower end to hold up a veil. Type C, **130**t, u, shell, carved as female figures.

Materials. Shell 16, Black and white limestone 2, Black steatite, 1, Black and white porphyry 1, Clear green serpentine 1, Copper 1.

Position. On forehead, as found in burials, and curved to fit the position.

Collection. Univ. Coll. P. 21.

131. KNOTTED CORD.

Meaning. No statement of the meaning remains in Egypt, but in Europe we find according to Pliny (xxviii, 27) seven knots in the girdle effective for catching hyaenas; in xxviii, 12, a thread knotted with the names of widows is used for inguinal hernia; and knotted hairs of a she-mule for conception (xxx, 49). In modern times we read of untying knots in cord to liberate a sailing wind, in the Isle of Man, Finland and Germany; and three times three knots cast, three on each of three coloured threads in order to check a man's movements. "Among the Hadendoa, knots which have been tied by a holy man, or even by a *fiqi* (teacher), while a text of the Koran is recited, are protective, just as the ordinary *hegab*," or written charm in a leather case (Seligmann). The essential idea seems to be making anything certain, or controlling others.

Period. XIIth to XXVth dynasty.

Figures. **131**a, knot of cord, of hollow gold, Dahshur XIIth dynasty; **131**b, cords with sard pendant, blue-glazed *uzat* open work, papyrus charm pendants, cowry shells and *uzat* eye; **131**c, cords with bronze Nefertum, *uzat* eyes and cowries; **131**d, knotted card with papyrus charm pendants, *uzat* eyes, and Isis seated of blue glaze; **131**e, with cowry shells, *uzat* eyes of blue glaze and bronze open-work, papyrus charm pendant; **131**f, knotted cords with baboon of Tahuti seated, *uzat* eyes open-work, Taurt, tooth of hyaena, cowry shell, papyrus charm pendant; **131**g, cord with cowry shells, *uzat* eyes, Bast, and papyrus charm. All from Kafr Ammar, xxiii—xxv.

Position. On the neck and chest.

Collection. Univ. Coll. P. 7.

132. WOVEN CHARM.

Meaning. Protection.

Period. Coptic.

Figure. **132**, COHCΘE ΔWPE, "May thou be saved, O! Doros," in white on a purple band. Illahun. (An Arab philosopher of this name is mentioned by Suidas.)

Collection. Univ. Coll. P.

133. CHARM CASE.

Meaning. To hold a written charm.

Varieties. A, vertical. B, horizontal. C, square. D, heart-shaped. E, crescent-shaped.

Period. XIIth dynasty to Modern.

Figures. A, **133a**, limestone model inscribed "Bast lady of the city," early; **133**b, gold foil over resin body, XIIth dynasty (?); **133**c, bronze case, in form of obelisk, with doors engraved on one side, inscribed, *Asar men f Seka du as f neb ta:* "For Seka; may Osiris establish him, and may the lord of the land give his tomb," XXVth dynasty; **133d**, iron case, Balyzeh, Coptic; **133**e, durite, with cross lines, imitating binding (see next); **133**f, roll of leather, elaborately bound with thread. For imitation charm cases in the XIIth dynasty see *Dahchour*, xvii, xviii, xix, xxiv; and later rough rolls of papyrus on the cords, **131** above. Imitated also by small cylinders of wood worn against witchcraft in Central Africa (Leicester Museum). See also imitation charm rolls in **131**b, d, f, g.

B. The horizontal charm case is later. **133**g, pottery model, Memphis, Roman; **133**h, black glass rod, gold ends; **133**j (pl. xliii), wood, Tell el Amarna, Roman, group 21; **133**k, dark violet opaque glass; **133**l, green glaze; **133**m, bronze, Wushim, all probably of Roman age; **133** n, bronze, Arab.

C. The square package is of Arab origin. **133**o, cast lead, inscribed, *La illaha illa Allah wa khadamu la sawyd* . . "There is no god but Allah, and his servant shall not be put to shame": probably intended for a Copt to wear, with a colourable imitation of the Muslim formula; **133**p, leather case, containing Arabic charms written on a sheet of paper, 12 × 17 inches, folded in 8 folds each way; it bears 57 lines with one magic square of 6 × 8, and another of 5 × 6, and a pentacle; modern, brought by Martyn Kennard from Nubia, 1854.

D. **133**q (pl. xliv), silver, peacock-blue enamel, loose plug at the top with slip inside to hold a written charm or relic; **133**r, bronze imitation of previous, not opening.

E. **133**s, gold hollow, with imitation Runic inscription; **133**s 2, small copy in lead, Coptic; **133**t, gold, probably a copy of an amulet case. The charm of writing 2468, the number value of the name of Baduh the spirit of carrying, is still written on letters in Egypt.

134. HYPOCEPHALUS.

Meaning. Derived from the papyrus with the figure of a cow, which was placed under the head of the dead according to the 162nd chapter of the Book of the Dead. For an account of some fine examples see *Abydos*, I., p. 50, pl. lxxix.

Period. XXXth dynasty.

Figures. **134**a, the deceased mummy on the back of the cow, with the winged disc and uraeus over it, fragments of formula around; cartonnage coloured red and black; **134**b, reverse of a, the four-ramheaded form of Amen, adored by two baboons, two men and two women; above, the bark of the Sun; below, reversed, the cow, with the winged disc and uraeus over it; fragments of inscription: black on yellow ground. **134**b 2, a larger disc with more figures (like *Abyd.* lxxix), and on reverse the baboons adoring the shining disc, and Isis and Nebhat mourning with the crowned *zed* sign between: being black with fine yellow lines it will not photograph; **134**c, eight crocodile heads around a disc, with eight baboons above, and below Paunhatef offering Maat to the hawk of Ra; yellow and red with black drawing on cartonnage.

135. INSCRIBED STONE CHARMS, GREEK.

Those on the left side of pl. xxi are the inscribed reverses of those on the right side in the same order, each to each.

Figures and Materials. **135**a, black glass, Serapis with Isis and Nephthys; "Isis conquers"; **135**b, hard black limestone, Aphrodite drying her locks, *S. Ps.*; **135**c, brown limestone, Isis nursing Horus, *Athlthaththab*, blundered for *Athlathanalba*: Bes standing, *Tas Berberete* for *Beberete* (see **135**t); **135**d, black steatite, *Mormoron to Kobbli*, possibly "A scaring for rascals," or perhaps connected with mormorion—a transparent black stone from India (Pliny, xxxvii, 63); reverse in an unknown alphabet; **135**e, brown jasper, Anubis standing by a mummy laid on a lion's back, *Abrasax*; **135**f, green chalcedony, lion-headed serpent radiated, three serpents across a staff behind; *O Thmouēr Khnoumis, Z, M, KH*=647; **135**g, black limestone, Set standing holding serpents and *onkh*; *Iō Sēt Iaiō; Iaeō ba phren emoun* (see **135**aa); **135**h, haematite, hawk . . . *atha*, five letters in an unknown alphabet; . . . *ōr;* **135**j, haematite, the sun's disc in an enclosure (see **135**v, pl. xxii) with ears of corn and serpents, Isis and Anubis (?) above it, *Iaō orō riouth; Aphreni, Sambēl, Mekhtu, Pskhr* (? Sokar) *eimi, Ikhankhala, Eoulkheōukh*, apparently the names of genii; **135**k, haematite, body of Harpekroti upon a galloping lion; wreath and leaf, *Eukairian*, "good fortune"; **135**l, black limestone, figure standing with uraeus on head, *Atherne Minō Pisiduos Thibrim, Psausilōi*: four blundered cartouches, among them the two cartouches of Ramessu II, and that of Merneptah. Tell el Yehudiyeh; **135**m, blue glass, Horus radiated in a bark, between Isis and Nephthys winged; *Sabaōth Adōnai*, "Lord of Hosts"; **135**n, blue glass, Horus on the lotus in a bark, above him three khepers (triune Creator), behind him three goats (evil persons), before him probably were three hawks (justified persons), as on **135**y; around, a ram, a lion, Set, Anubis and four signs lost; *Phrē* (the sun) *thbain* . . . *ōōi* . . . and three lines of unknown letters; **135**o, Prussian blue glass, heart of Osiris and heart of Isis facing; *He Kharis*, "favour." This may belong to the followers of Marcus, who taught the partaking of the *Kharis* in the wine (Iren., *adv. Haer.*, I, xiii, 1—3); **135**p, black steatite, lion-headed uraeus of Khnumu, over the sun's disc in an enclosure, traces of inscription around; Bennu bird (soul of Osiris) with triple plant on a stand, (compare the triple plant on stand behind Min), *Iaō*; **135**q. black steatite, the bennu as before, crescent above, two serpents across a staff below; *Eupepti*, "good digestion"; **135**r, black steatite, lion-headed uraeus, in circle, two serpents across staff; bennu bird as on **135**p (see **135**v, w, next plate). Pl. xxii; **135**s, black haematite, sun's disc in an enclosure, lion-headed serpent over it, figure in front, bar behind; **135**t, black steatite, *Tas beberte*; **135**u, black jasper, head of Serapis, *diliullsse* (division uncertain); **135**v, w, as **135**r. On pl. xlvi, **135**x, jasper, dark green blood stone, Harpokrates on the lotus in a papyrus bark, with a crowned hawk on either end, star in front; **135**y, haematite, figures holding a spear, star before, crescent behind; on the back *Mikhaēl*; **135**z, lazuli, crowned seated figure holding *phialē*; on the back *Primou*.

135aa, bronze; for the details of this elaborate amulet it will be best to examine the facsimile on an enlarged scale (pl. xlix), with transcription and translation of the intelligible parts. On the first face is a large central figure of Bes, with two additional human faces, one on either side. The elaborate head-dress of animal heads, the four wings, and the serpent at the feet enclosing various noxious animals, are all seen on a bronze figure of Bes from the Serapeum, and on the Metternich stele (Lanzone, *Diz. Mit.*, lxxx, lxxxi). At the proper right is *Bakhakhukh*; this phrase repeated adding a syllable each time, occurs in the Greek and Demotic magical papyri. The four-headed ram comes next, with the name *Khab*, a god of the north with four rams' heads (Lanz., *Diz. Mit.*, 1190). Next is the name *Rau* for Ra, the four-headed ram (L., *D. M.*, clxxxii). Following is the title *Ph nes khērphi*, probably connected with *kriphi* in the Iaeō formula. This is followed by *Phōkhōs*, a word found in the Leyden magical papyrus, and as *Phōx* in the Demotic magic papyrus. *Phylax*, "the guardian," is the title of the sphinx on the opposite side of the axis. Beyond this is a gryphon, with the words *Rē gom ph.* . . . In the next register is a bandaged mummy, holding scourges on each of which are two uraei; by the side is *Ablanathanalba*, a word often found in magic papyri (Greek in British Museum, Paris, and Leyden, also Demotic), and on gems. It is a reversible phrase, the latter half made by reversing the former part; *ablanath* is the group to be explained. Opposite is Anubis standing, with *Aleximandre-ula*, "bark, guardian of man." Behind him is *Iaō-la-ila-ma*; it is tempting to see in this an early type of the formula of Islam, "la illaha illa Allah"; *ma* might be an Egyptian form of Aramaic *imi*, "with me," Egyptain *my*, "with me," Arabic *mdi*. Thus the formula might be rendered, "I AM, there is none else with me," testifying the Unity. The phrase is common in the Paris and British Museum Greek papyri.

In the third register is a partly defaced figure with two large animal legs, and a crown of seven uraei. Compare with parts of Horus in LANZ., *D. M.*, ccxvii. By this begins the *Akrammakhamarix*, which occurs with the termination *marei* in the British Museum and Paris papyri. It is almost a reversible word, and *akhramakh* is the group to be explained. Possibly the Semitic *kerim*, gracious or noble, may be the source, and the phrase be "thy most gracious one." This would agree with the subject of Horus, trampling on crocodiles, and subduing the noxious animals. The lion in the group has *Saba* by it, the Arabic *sabá*, "a lion," justifying our looking to an Arabic form for the phrase *akhramakh*. Above this is a lion trampling on a skeleton, a group seen in other Gnostic objects—a magical papyrus in Paris, and a gem. Below is *Abrasax*, the mysterious word commonest on Gnostic amulets, which has not been explained. The numerical values of the letters total to 365. Irenaeus (*adv. Haeres*, i, xxiv, 7) says that the Basilidians declare that their chief is *Abrasax* (Greek) or Abraxas (Latin version). It is therefore a divine name.

On the reverse of the amulet are, at the top, the Divine names, *Iaō Iēsous*. Below these are three scarabs, the self-becoming animal, emblems of the Creative Trinity. Below is Horus in the bark, which shows the direction to be facing the three hawks. These birds are the souls of the Just, standing before the Trinity; behind are the evil animals going away, three goats, three serpents, and three crocodiles. Under the hawks is the reversible inscription *Iaeō ba phren emoun othilari on aeu* (reversing) *ea iphirk ira litho nuome nerph ab ōeai*. This sentence is found elsewhere in completely reversible form, with *kriphi* in place of *on* in the first half, in magical papyri of British Museum, Paris, and Berlin. The substitution of *on* for *kriphi* here is of value, as showing how the sentence is to be divided, and that some equivalence may be looked for in these two words. Also the sentence breaks after *emoun*, as shown by **135**g. In the centre is Horus seated in the lotus flower in a boat, with a figure before him. Behind is *Brinteti ēn*, which must be compared with the phrase below, *Brintat ēnōphri*, clearly ēnōphri is *un-nefer*, "the good Being," and ēn may be *un*, "the being." Behind this is a radiated lion-headed god, holding a radiated lion-headed serpent, and the *onkh*. This is a form of Khnumu, as he is called *Khnoubis Kharnous*, which is a late form of Khnumu *kahran*, "the horned."

In the second register is a figure wrapped in wings, holding a standard. In the middle is a four-armed crowned Horus; the inscription is only legible at the end, *Ph noeouonti*, a prolonged form of *pa nuter*, "the god." In front is another Horus with the royal attributes of the scourge and tail (LANZ., *D. M.*, ccxxvii, 1).

In the third register is Thoth seated, with a female figure before him, carrying a standard and other objects. Before these is a hawk with serpent tail, carrying a branch. This is named *Ar po khnouphis*, "Horus the creator," and behind is *Brintat ēnōphri*. This combination is found in Demotic and in the Paris Greek papyrus. Below *khnouphi* may possibly be *Rōsthi Thuth neortou*. Below can be distinguished a lion, with perhaps *Saba* behind it, and a baboon of Thoth with the head of the ibis of Thoth on the back; the other signs and letters can hardly be settled without some better example of such figures.

At first sight the mixture of Egyptian, Semitic and Greek would seem incredible to a scholar of any one of the languages; yet there can be no doubt of each of these elements. The names and figures of the gods show how largely the Egyptian enters into the mixture; the Semitic is shown by *Saba*, the lion, which makes more probable the readings of *Akhrammakh* and *Iao la ila ma*; and the Greek is evident in *Aleximandreula* and *Phylax*. The looseness, of the equivalents is seen in the variants Rē, Rau, Iaeō, Iaō, Khnoubis, Khnouphis, Brintat, Brinteti, so that we cannot take literal accuracy as a criterion. The main value of this amulet is in the figures which help to attach a meaning to the phrases in the magical papyri.

The following references to papyri containing these names I owe to the kindness of Sir Herbert Thompson:—

Bakhakhukh, etc., W. S. V. p. 19, No. 16, l. 50 and 70. B. M. G. P. xlvi, l. 11, 362. G. P. M. D., v 8, vi 25, viii. 10. xxvii, 13 (see note to v 8).

Phōkhōs. L. P. G. in D. A. 1891, pp. 180, 184. G. P. M. D. iv 18.

Ablanath, etc. B. M. xlvi, l. 63, 478 (B. M. G. P., I., 67, 80). P. P. l. 3030, L. P. G., V, 4a 3, 5a 15. G. P. M. D., I., 16, verso xxii 13, xxvii 8. Also often on gems.

Lailama. P. P. 1625, 1804, 1983. D. A., p 5. B. M. xlvi, l. 349. See index of B. M. G. P., I., p. 261.

Abrasax. P. Z. G. P., I, l. 303, II, l. 154. D. A., p 182.

Akhrammakh, etc. B. M. xlvi, l. 63; B. M. G. P., I., index, p. 256. P. P. 982, 3030. Mimaut pap., l. 79 (see Wessely).

Lion treading on skeleton. D. A. p. 53. P. P., l. 2132.

Iesous. P. P. 1233, 3020.

Iaeo ba phren emoun, etc. P. P., l. 398. B. M. xlvi, col. 5 verso. P. Z. G. P., I. Mimaut pap. l. 59.

Arpokhnoupi, etc. P. Z. G. P., I, 237. P.P., 2199. G. P. M. D. xvi 6—7.

The above initials are: B. M. G. P., *British Museum Greek Papyri.* D. A., Dietrich, *Abraxas.* G. P. M. D., Griffith, *Pap. mag. demotic.* L. P. G., Leyden, *Pap. Grk.* P. P., Paris papyrus in Wessely, *Griechische Zauberpapyrus von Paris u. London,* Wiener Denkschr. 1888. P. Z. G. P., Parthey, *Zwei griechische Papyri d. Berliner Mus.* 1866. W. S. V., Wünsch, *Sethianische Verfluchungstafeln.*

136. INSCRIBED STONE CHARMS, NON-GREEK.

Figures and Materials. Pl. xxi, **136**a, black steatite, Horus hand in hand with another figure; two lines of inscription. Pl. xxii, **136**b, five views, basalt; a divinity holding a branch standing on the back of a couchant bull; a tree, with two lines of inscription below; four lines of inscription on the base; a palm tree with two young ones; a mountain, like Mt. Argaeus on the coins of Caesarea, two lines of inscription. From the types and characters it appears to belong to the Cilician region; **136**c, black steatite, Horus on crocodiles of usual type, but with hieroglyphs reduced to a barbaric imitation, as also on the back; **136**d, black steatite, a figure standing with a staff in the hands, lines of characters on the back resembling Mandaite; **136**e, limestone blackened, two bird-headed figures over a worshipper; four lines of degraded Semitic; **136**f, two figures with a serpent coiled on a staff; three lines of degraded Semitic; **136**g, slate, an ass-headed figure with legs ending in serpents; four lines of degraded characters; **136**h, onyx, figure standing with four characters behind; **136**j, grey steatite, unknown signs. Pl. xxiii, **136**k, l, slate tablets with degraded Kufic inscriptions; **136**m, black jasper, the moon and Cancer, the house of the moon; the sun and Leo, the house of the sun; barbaric imitation of inscription; this stone has been broken, and mounted in a silver band, with the suspension ring at the bottom.

137. CROSS.

Name. *Stauros.*

Meaning. Salvation and protection.

Varieties. A, plain cross. B, *Chi-rho* cross.

Period. Coptic.

Figures. A, **137**a, b, c, c 2 to 6 d, bronze; **137**d 2, lead; **137**e, f, g, g 2 smaller, h, bronze; **137**j, mother of pearl; **137**k, bronze; **137**l, lead; **137**m, black steatite, Koptos; **137**n, n 2, with two balls on ends, o, o 2, bronze; **137**o 3, lead; **137**p, bronze; **137**q, wood, and q 2, rougher; **137**r, s, bone; **137**t, t 2, iron; **137**u, wood; **137**v, y, bronze Memphis; **137**w, bronze; **137**x, lead; **137**z, bronze, hollow reliquary case with aquamarine on the centre. B, **137**aa (xliv), dark blue glass, cross white, red spots around, aa 2, similar in light blue glass. On pl. xlvi, A, **137**ab, bone; **137**ac, lead; **137**ad, lead; **137**ae, af, lead, cross in circle.

Materials. Bronze 22, Lead 8, Wood 3, Iron 2, Bone 2, Black steatite 1, Mother of pearl 1.

CHAPTER VII

AMULETS OF HUMAN-HEADED GODS

THEOPHORIC AMULETS, 138—179.

When the dim ideas of similars and of charms—such as the Eskimo now use—had given place to a belief in gods with intelligence and feelings akin to those of men, it was quite natural that the images of such deities should take the place of the stocks and stones which had been venerated. The system of amulets was at once adapted to the theistic beliefs, and figures of the gods became the most popular of all amulets. The very different numbers of amulets of the various gods show clearly which were the most generally worshipped. Horus, Isis and Osiris account for much more than half of the human-headed figures. As the eye of Horus was one of the earliest amulets, we begin with it here, as introducing the Horus group.

138. UZAT EYE OF HORUS.

Name. *Uzat* (MacG. 52).

Meaning. The eye of Horus. The *uzat* eyes are properly a pair, right and left, representing the two eyes of Horus, which are also compared to the sun and moon. The 140th chapter of the Book of the Dead refers to the sun as the eye, and was to be "Said on an eye of pure Lazuli or *mak* stone ornamented with gold; an offering is made before it of all things good and holy; . . . another is made of jasper, which a man will put on any of his limbs that he chooses." The 167th chapter refers to an *uzat* eye brought by Tahuti.

Varieties. The main classes are put under different numbers here, from 138 to 142. In this class, 138, we may discriminate A, the earliest form (Old Kingdom) with very short appendages, imitating the pattern of feathers below the hawk's eye; B, larger appendages, with a flat surface; C, coloured surface; D, incised surface. The order in the plates is that of the age as nearly as can be estimated. The order of numbering and description is that of the classification.

Period. VI to Ptolemaic.

Figures. Type A, **138**a, brown limestone group 8; **138**b, c, d, sard, groups 1, 2, 7; **138**e, green felspar, group

30; **138**f, bone, group 13; **138**g, sard, group 14; **138**g 2, sard, group 7; **138**h, bone, group 5; **138**h 2, sard, group 2; **138**j, j 2, j 3, k, k 2, sard, group 3; **138**j 4, sard, group 7. Type B, **138**l, hard white calcite, back similar; **138**l 2, same, back plain; **138**m, volcanic ash; **138**m 2, 3, diorite; m 4, syenite; m 5, grey porphyry; m 6, pink limestone; m 7, chlorite; m 8, haematite; m 9, grey marble; m 10, dark blue glass; **138**n, porphyry; **138**o, diorite; **138**o 2, jade; **138**p, steatite, XVIII, Tell Amarna; **138**p 2, grey porphyry; **138**q, porphyry. Type C, **138**r, blue glaze, black relief; **138**s, same, Memphis, XXIII; **138**t, same, faded; **138**u, blue, black lines, Karnak, XXV; **138**u 2, similar; **138**u 3, green glaze, Naukratis. Type D, **138**v, jade; **138**v 2, green glaze; **138**w, olive green glaze; **138**x, carnelian; **138**x 2, dark blue, three joined; **138**x 3, blue paste, Naukratis; **138**y, apple-green glaze, Gizeh; **138**y 2—5, blue glaze, Naukratis; **138**z, diorite; **138**aa, yellow green glaze; **138**ab, blue and black glaze; **138**ab 2, green glaze; **138**ac, green glaze, Memphis; **138**ad, light blue-green glaze; **138**ad 2—9, green glaze; **138**ae, faded blue and black glaze; **138**ae 2—19, blue and black glaze, Zuweleyn and Tanis; **138**af (pl. **xliv**), green and black glaze, Dendereh, Ptolemaic; **138**ag (xliv), gold, XVIII. (See **131**b, c, d, e, f, also four early examples in *Deshasheh* and many of XXII to XXV in *Hyksos and Israelite Cities*).

Materials. Sard 29, Green and blue glaze 46, Porphyry 15, Amethyst 5, Green felspar 5, Gold 5, Carnelian 3, Diorite 3, Calcite 2, Grey agate 2, Haematite 3, Lazuli 2, Bone 2, Jade 2, and 1 each of Syenite, Volcanic ash, Serpentine, Chlorite, Steatite, Brown limestone, Grey marble, Pink limestone, Blue glass, Blue paste.

Position. Forehead (3); throat (5); chest (14); stomach (3); arms and hands (3).

Collection. Univ. Coll. P. 39, E. 47. The lack of detail in most catalogues prevents the statement of these different classes.

139. UZAT EYE (UNUSUAL TYPES).

Varieties. A, open work. B, inlaid. C, metal plate. D, engraved on ring. E, in square form. F, in cartouche.

Period. XII to Ptolemaic.

Figures. Type A, open work, **139**a, b, silver; **139**c, electrum ring; **139**d, green glaze; **139**e, amethyst, Koptos, XII (?); **139**f, g, deep blue glaze, curved to fit the wrist, *Uzat* with *nefer*, XVIII; **139**h, olive and black glaze, XXIII; **139**h 2—5, blue glaze; **139**h 6, blue and black glaze, large; **139**j, k, deep blue glaze, modern amulet beads, copied from *uzat*. Type B, inlaid, **139**l, blue and black glaze, inlaid with white glaze eye, and red glaze cheek; **139**m, green and black glaze, traces of red paste, inlay; **139**m 2, blue glaze, Nebesheh; **139**m 3—12, green glaze, Naukratis. Type C, metal plate, **139**n, silver plate, incised; **139**n 2 (xlvii), lead plate, similar but larger, scale 2 : 5; **139**n 3 (xlvii), larger pewter plate cut to outline of eye, scale 2 : 5; **139**n 4 (xlvii), copper plate, eye embossed, scale 2 : 5; **139**o, bronze, eye inlaid with coloured limestone, and coloured glass above and below. Type D, on ring, **139**p, jasper ring, engraved with *uzat*. Type E, square, **139**q, green and black glaze; **139**q 2—7, green, Nebesheh; **139**r, dull green glaze; **139**r 2, green glaze (xlvii); **139**s, green glaze burnt brown; **139**t, green glaze; **139**u, bronze. Type F, **139**v (pl. xliv), yellow glaze.

Materials. Green and blue glaze 34, Silver 3, Bronze 3, Lead 2, Electrum 1, Amethyst 1, Jasper 1, Yellow glaze 1.

Collection. Univ. Coll. P. 24, E. 22.

140. UZAT EYE, MULTIPLE.

Varieties. A, bead cylinder. B, double eye. C, quadruple eye. D, multiple eye.

Period. XXIIIth to XXVth dynasty.

Figures. Type A, **140**a, green glaze gone brown, two eyes alternate with two *onkhs*; **140**b, green and black glaze, three eyes; **140**c, deep blue and black glaze, two eyes. Type B, **140**d, light green, inscribed *Sekhmet* on back, Zuweleyn. Type C, **140**e, yellow paste, with traces of blue paste inlay, reverse below; **140**f, blue glaze, black lines and yellow rosette; **140**g, green and black glaze, two *uaz* plants between the eyes; **140**g 2, 3, similar, Memphis; **140**g 4, 5, flat plate, green, yellow. Type D, **140**h, green glaze and black, rosette on back, 20 eyes; **140**h 2, green gone brown; **140**j, green faded and black, *uzat* on back, 28 eyes. Another in Price Collection had 21 eyes.

Materials. Green and blue glaze 13, Yellow glaze 1.

Collections. Univ. Coll. P. 10, E. 4.

141. UZAT EYE, WITH GODS.

Meaning. The 163rd chapter of the Book of the Dead concerns the mystic eyes, and is to be "Said on a serpent having two legs, and bearing a two-horned disc. Two eyes are before him, having two legs and two wings." This may refer to some such figure as the type A.

Varieties. A, vulture and uraeus. B, wing and arm. C, with cats. D, with bull. E, with apes. F, with lion. G, on hills. H, with Ra. J, with Sekhmet or Bastet.

Period. XXIIIrd dynasty.

Figures. Type A, **141**a, the vulture's legs and wings below the eye, and a uraeus before it. Type B, **141**b, blue glaze, with white glaze eye and obsidian pupil, and red glaze inlay above and below the vulture's wings, and an arm grasping an *onkh*, Ramesseum, XIXth dynasty (?). Type C, **141**c, green-blue glaze, flat back, with 19 cats, and secondary *uzat* above the pupil; **141**d, blue and black glaze, with 13 cats; **141**e, blue and black glaze, with 9 cats. Type D, **141**f, green glaze faded, with bull; **141**g, green glaze, bull on platform, lotus in front, 7 uraei above. Type E, **141**h, green glaze, two baboons adoring the *uzat* eye, with *neb* below, plain back (compare MacG. 74). Type F, **141**j, light blue glaze, couchant lion above, resting on three *uzat* eyes, behind which are 12 uraei; **141**k, apple-green glaze, couchant lion, resting on 9 uraei, behind which are three *uzat* eyes. Type G, **141**l, jade, partly decomposed, the *uzat* engraved on both sides, resting upon the triple hill sign, representing Horus in the horizon. Type H, **141**m (pl. xliv), Ra on back, green glaze. Type J, **141**n, o, p, 9, green glaze, with Sekhmet.

Collection. Univ. Coll. P. 12.

142. UZAT EYE, INSCRIBED.

Meaning and Varieties. The *uzat* is associated with a group of seven goddesses, whose names are found singly on the square eyes, or altogether on one eye.

Period. XXIInd dynasty.

Figures. **142**a, green-glazed square with *uzat* in relief, on back is impressed the name of the goddess Uazet; **142**b, same with Bastet; **142**c, with Aset; **142**d, with Nebhat; **142**e, with Sekhmet; **142**f, with Selket; **142**g, with Neit, all from Zuweleyn; **142**h, blue paste, with names of Uazet, Bastet, Aset, Nebhat, Sekhmet, Selket, and Neit; **142**j, light blue glaze, gone white, *uzat* in relief with name of Aset (?); **142**k, green glaze, reverse of **141**n, name of Uazet.

Materials. In general, the various types of *uzat* not being sufficiently distinguished in catalogues, the materials in other collections of Nos. **138** to **142** are here stated together; the materials in University College collection are stated above in detail. Green glaze 178, Blue glaze 116, Carnelian 34, Lazuli 25, Red jasper 23, Haematite 22, Obsidian 13, Porphyry 8, Serpentine 7, Prase 7, Limestone 6, Steatite 6, Syenite 6, Diorite 4, Granite 4, Green felspar 4, Blue glass 4, Basalt 3, Silver 3, Red glass 3, Gold 2, Calcite 2, Grey agate 1, Brown and green limestone 1, Crystal 1, Slate 1, Brown limestone 1, Beryl 1, Silver gilt 1, Black glass 1, Green glass 1.

Collections. Univ. Coll. P. 100, E. 84, Price 124, St. Petersburg 85, Turin 84, Alnwick 75, Cairo 71, Athens 16, Edinburgh 10.

143. HORUS THE HUNTER.

Name. *Har.*

Meaning. The overcoming of evil beasts.

Period. XXXth dynasty.

Figure. **143.**

Material. Bronze.

Collection. Univ. Coll. P.

144. HORUS ON THE CROCODILES.

The great example of this usual household amulet is the Metternich stele, published by Golenischeff, 1877. Perhaps the earliest are two in limestone, which by the work may be of the XXVth dynasty, one in Cairo, 9,403, and one 14 inches wide, 15 high to broken top, with fifteen lines of inscription on the back, in University College, P., as also a smaller one in limestone 8 inches wide, perhaps XXXth dynasty.

Meaning. Protection from noxious animals.

Period. XXV (?) to Roman.

Figures. **144**a, white marble, ten lines of inscription on back; **144**b, black steatite, reverse six lines, "Beloved of Set, Anhur and Tahuti (?). Hail to thee god son of a god; hail to thee heir son of an heir; hail to thee bull son of a bull, born of the great cow," see Metternich stele, ll. 101—5; **144**b 2, blue glaze, small, very rough; **144**c, black steatite, reverse four lines, "Become Horus, Osiris, Amru and Ptah," etc.; **144**d, cast lead, for reverse, see below it, hawk on standard as net, Isis standing behind, Gurob; **144**e (see pl. xliii), black steatite, reverse (see pl. xli), described under No. **241**; **144f**, light green glaze, Isis and Nebhat standing at the sides, winged Isis on the back (similar at St. Petersburg).

Collections. Cairo 27, Univ. Coll. P. 8, E. 1, Turin 6, Price 4, St. Petersburg 5, Alnwick 3.

145. HORUS THE CHILD.

Name. *Har-pe-kroti.*

Meaning. Horus as an infant.

Varieties. A, seated. B, on goose. C, standing.

Period. VI to Roman.

Figures. **145**a, bone, group 8, VIth dynasty (see *Deshasheh*, xxvi, 32); **145**b, blue-glazed quartz crystal, XIIth dynasty; **145**c, d, bronze; **145**d 2, black steatite; **145**e, black steatite, Horus seated on the ground, XIIth dynasty (?); **145**f, g, silver, group 16; **145**g 2, bronze; **145**h, black steatite; **145**j, silver, group 17; **145**k, silver on ring; **145**l (pl. xlv), quartz crystal; **145**m—m 5 (pl. xlv), carnelian; **145**n, blue glaze, Roman; **145**nn (xlvi), blue glaze, Illahun, XXII; **145**o, bronze; **145**p, p 2, q, r, r 2, bronze; **145**s, on lion throne, blue glaze, Memphis; **145**t, blue glaze. Type B, **145**u, v, blue glaze with yellow points, group 22, Roman; **145**v 2, coarse blue glaze. Type C, **145**w, x, blue glaze with yellow points, group 22, Roman. Similar figures of B and C types, of large size, in rough terra cotta, are very common as household amulets of Roman age; **145**y (xlvii), dark blue glaze, holding club; **145**z, green glaze, phallic, holding baboon and vase (xxvii).

Materials. Blue glaze 13, Bronze 9, Green glaze 7, Silver 4, Carnelian 4, Quartz crystal 1, Black steatite 2, Glazed quartz 2, Lazuli 2, Grey glaze 1, bone 1.

Collections. Univ. Coll. P. 20, E. 5, St. Petersburg 10, Turin 4, Murch 6.

146. HORUS ON LOTUS.

This is not known before Greek times, and so may easily be an Indian idea imported; but Horus in the marshes of Buto is so ancient an idea that the type might well arise in Egypt.

AMULETS OF HUMAN-HEADED GODS

Figure. **146**, gold, with traces of blue glass inlay in the lotus, group 15. From north of Abydos.

Materials. Blue glaze with yellow points 2, Green glaze 1, Gold 1.

Collections. Turin 3, Univ. Coll. P. 1.

147. HEAD OF HORUS.

Period. Roman.

Figures. **147**a, b, blue-green glaze.

Collections. Univ. Coll. P. 2.

148. ISIS AND HORUS.

Name. "The heir and Isis" (see MacG. 60).

Meaning. The protection of Isis.

Varieties and Period. A, seated on ground, VIth dynasty. B, seated on throne. XXVI to Roman.

Figures. Type A, **148**a, b, steatite, glazed, with geometrical patterns below, VIth dynasty. B, **148**c, d, e, f, g, g 2, g 3, g 4, blue glaze; **148**h, j, silver, group 16; **148**k, bronze; **148**l, blue and black glaze; **148**m (pl. xlvi), bronze; **148**m 2, bronze; **148**m 3, 4, 5, 6, 7, green glaze.

Materials. Green glaze 19, Blue glaze 14, Bronze 5, Silver 2, Steatite 2, Lazuli 1, Agate 1, Blue glass 2, Grey glaze 1.

Collections. St. Petersburg 18, Univ. Coll. P. 15, E. 6, Turin 5, Athens 2, Murch 2.

149. ISIS.

Period. XVIII to Roman.

Varieties. A, statuette. B, outline on plaque (Hawara 4, pl. l). C, bust.

Figures. Type A, **149**a, bronze, fringed garment; **149**b, dark blue glass, orange glass crown; **149**c, d, dark blue glass; feet of d, green glass, another figure; **149**e, bright blue glaze, Ramesseum, XXth dynasty (?); **149**f, gold, group 15, Isis or Mut, not Neit by the uraeus, see 164 Mut; **149**g, silver, group 15; **149**h, pewter plate, group 18; **149**j, glaze faded white, Hawara, group 32; **149**k, gold, Memphis, group 27; **149**l, blue glaze with yellow points, Roman, group 22; **149**m, green-black glaze, possibly Neit; **149**m 2, 3, 4, 5, green glaze. Type C, **149**n (pl. xlvi), bronze.

Materials. Green glaze 20, Blue glaze 13, Grey glaze 7, Lazuli 7, Blue glass 4, Gold 3, Silver 1, Bronze 2, Pewter 1, Brown glaze 1.

Position. Throat (1); on chest in row of gods (13); stomach (1).

Collections. Turin 22, St. Petersburg 17, Univ. Coll. P. 13, E. 4, Murch 2, Athens 1.

150. ISIS MOURNING.

Meaning. Protection by Isis.

Varieties. A, kneeling with hand raised. B, standing winged. Both as a pair to Nephthys.

Period. Ptolemaic.

Figures. Type A, **150**a, b, b 2, gilt wax, Dendereh, group 20; **150**c, (d, not in plate), e, green and black glaze, Dendereh, group 21; **150**f, blue and black glaze, Dendereh, 21, with two feathers on head, as **149**g. Type B, **150**g, blue and black glaze, standing, Dendereh, 21; **150**h, green and black glaze, Dendereh, 21.

Materials. Blue or green glaze 5, gilt wax 3.

Position. Shoulders and chest (4).

Collection. Univ. Coll. P. 8.

151. ISIS PHARIA.

Name. Isis Pharia, of the Pharos at Alexandria, entirely of Greek origin.

Meaning. Protection of sailors; the goddess is reclining in a barge and holding a steering oar.

Period. Ptolemaic and Roman.

Figures. **151**a, green glaze faded brown; **151**b, violet-blue glass; **151**c (xlvi), pale blue glass, on back, *Uēl*; **151**d, coin of Gallienus, showing the type clearly.

Material. Green glaze 1, Violet glass 1, Pale blue glass 1.

Collection. Univ. Coll. P. 3.

152. ISIS, NEBHAT, AND HORUS.

Meaning. The goddesses as protectresses.

Period. XXVI to Roman.

Figures. **152**a, b, green glaze, no inscription, loop on back; **152**b, 2, 3, 4, green glaze; **152**c, bronze, the right-hand figure has the hair dressed in two horns as Isis, between the busts is a minute bust of Horus crowned.

Materials. Green glaze 49, Blue glaze 13, Grey glaze 4, Yellow glaze 1, Bronze 1.

Position. On breast (2); along with large *zad*, or line of *zad* amulets, on chest or stomach (4); on thighs.

Collections. Alnwick 21, St. Petersburg 8, Price 4, Univ. Coll. P. 3, E. 3.

153. GROUPS OF GODDESSES.

Period. XXVth to XXVIth dynasties.

Figures. **153**a, green glaze, Isis, Hathor, Mut, Nebhat, Sekhmet; these can be better identified on a blue-glazed pentad found at Hawara (*Labyrinth*, xxxi); **153**a 2, green glaze Isis, Bast and Hathor (Edw.).

Collections. Univ. Coll. P. 1, E. 1, Manchester.

154. NEBHAT.

Meaning. Protection, as Nebhat protected Horus.

Varieties. A, statuette. B, outline on plaque (Hawara, 4, pl. xlix).

Period. XXVI.

Figures. **154**a, green glaze; **154**b, brown glaze (burnt); **154**c, olive glaze; **154**d, e, blue glaze; **154**f, olive glaze; **154**g, g 2, green glaze faded, Hawara; **154**g, 3, 4, green glaze; **154**h (pl. xliii), light green glaze, inscribed on back, "Nebhat give life to Nes . . ."; **154**j (pl. xlv), light green glaze.

Materials. Green glaze 2, Grey glaze 7, Blue glaze 6, Lazuli, 4, Yellow glaze 2, Brown glaze 1, Blue glass 1.

Position. Chest (11); stomach 1.

Collections. Turin 18, St. Petersburg 10, Univ. Coll. P. 8, E. 2, Murch 2, Athens 1.

155. NEBHAT MOURNING.

Meaning. Protection, as Nebhat protected Osiris.

Period. Ptolemaic.

Figures. **155**a, gilt wax, Dendereh, group 20; **155**b, blue glaze, Dendereh, group 21.

Position. With No. **150**, Isis mourning.

Collection. Univ. Coll. P. 2.

156. OSIRIS, ISIS, AND HORUS.

Meaning. Protection by the Triad. Horus always in front, and Isis behind.

Period. Ptolemaic and Roman.

Figures. **156**a, a 2, gilt wax, Dendereh, group 20; **156**b, blue and black glaze, Dendereh, group 21; **156**c, dark blue and black glaze, group 26; **156**d, black steatite, the heart of Osiris, between Isis wearing the two feathers, and Horus crowned, with the club in his hand; the back divided into 8 by 6 squares; traces of Greek cursive writing scratched on the ground between the figures.

Materials. Blue glaze 2, Steatite 1, Gilt wax 1.

Collection. Univ. Coll. P. 4.

157. OSIRIS.

Varieties. A. Standing alone. B. Double figures. C. Osiris-Min. D. Osiris and mummy.

Period. XXVI to Roman.

Figures. **157**a, a 2, 3, 4, b, b 2, c, c 2, c 3, bronze, b from Memphis; **157**d, gilt wax, Dendereh; **157**e, e 2, blue glass; **157**f, green glaze, Dendereh, group 21; **157**g, h (pl. xlv), wax.

Materials. Bronze 20, Blue glaze 5, Green glaze 1, Wax 3.

Position. Stomach (1); feet (1).

Collections. Univ. Coll. P. 8, E. 5, Turin 8 (B and C), Athens 4, St. Petersburg 3.

158. HEART OF OSIRIS.

Meaning. The heart of the god supplied to the deceased; this branched into the idea of the heart scarab.

Varieties. A, plain. B, with shrine and scarab on front. C, with figures of gods.

Period. XVIII to Roman.

Figures. Type B, **158**a, black-green chlorite, XVIIIth dynasty; shrine on front, Osiris and Ra seated at the sides; around the figure six lines of inscription, beginning, "Speech of the Osirian (an official) of Amen, Pa Shedet, and continuing with a random portion of the usual chapter of the heart, xxx B. The person may be that named on a Cairo stele, quoted in Lieblein, *Dict.*, 657. Type A, **158**b, black steatite, with female head, XIXth dynasty; **158**c, alabaster; **158**d, black steatite; *bennu* bird on front; on back *Asar neb zad*, "Osiris lord of Mendes"; **158**e, brown steatite, traces of shrine on front; **158**f, white quartz; **158**g, blue and black glaze, XIXth dynasty; **158**h, bronze, disc on head, Memphis. Type B, **158**j, black steatite, blue paste inlay, scarab on front. Type C, **158**k, bronze, on front, shrine, disc, scarab with wings, two gods at sides; **158**l, bronze, two uraei head dress; shrine with a hawk on each corner and disc above it, disc and uraei below, scarab winged; six figures of gods at sides; **158**m, bronze, shrine, winged scarab, on back lotus; **158**n, green glaze, shrine; **158**o, bronze, on front heart amulet, shrine with two seated figures, scarab, at sides four figures with raised hands adoring, two seated figures below; **158**p, bronze, shrine, disc and uraei, scarab, at sides two figures with raised hands; **158**q, mottled black and white steatite, shrine, winged scarab with disc; on back a hawk displayed with two feather fans; **158**r, brown pottery, scarab (?) on front, Roman; **158**s, brown pottery, winged scarab and disc, shrine below.

Materials. Bronze 7, Steatite 5, Pottery 2, Alabaster 1, White quartz 1, Chalcedony 1, Agate 1, Blue glaze 1, Green glaze 3, Chlorite 1, Limestone 1.

Collections. Univ. Coll. P. 18, Cairo 4, Athens 2, Beck, 1.

159. ORACULAR BUST.

Name. *Hez medu Asar* (repeated with other gods, Kheper, Atum, and Ra) LEPSIUS, *Denk.*, iii, 224 i.

Meaning. "Illumination by speech of Osiris," or of Kheper, Atum, or Ra. This appears to show that the bust was an oracle of the god, and being called the "illumination" or "clearing," it may be connected with the Semitic oracular Urim. It appears on a stele, adored by a woman making offerings (MARIETTE, *Abydos*, ii, 60); as a bust between two jackals on a stele (ROSELLINI, *Mon. Civ.*, cxxxiv, 2); and as a glazed pottery bust at Tell Amarna (*Amarna*, xvii, 277—8). The form of it, a head and chest only, would accord with the idea of the power of speaking.

Period. XVIII to XIX dynasties.

Figures. **159**a, wood, XVII; **159**b, limestone, XVIII (reduced about a tenth); **159**c, d, blue glaze with black paint, XVIIIth dynasty; **159**e, violet glaze, Tell Amarna, XVIII; **159**f, green glaze, faded, XVIII; **159**f 2, blue glaze; **159**g, bronze, with arms on the breast; **159**h, bronze, flat behind head, as if fitted against a surface, with bust full thickness below; **159**j, ivory with electrum loop, prehistoric; may be an early form of the oracular bust.

Materials. Blue glaze 3, Green glaze 2, Bronze 2, Violet glaze 1, Limestone 1, Ivory 1, Wood 1.

Collections. Univ. Coll. P. 9, E. 1, Turin 1 (1231).

AMULETS OF HUMAN-HEADED GODS

160. HORUS AND MIN.

Name. Min is named "Horus, son of Isis of Koptos" (LANZ., *Diz. Mit.*, xvii).
Period. XXVI (?).
Figure. **160**, bronze.
Collection. Univ. Coll. P.

161. MIN.

Period. XXVI to Roman (?).
Figures. **161**a, bronze, Memphis; **161**b, c, c 2, d, bronze; **161**e, f, f 2, g, green glaze; **161**h, green glaze, Dendereh, group 21; **161**j, green glaze, with yellow points, group 23, Roman; **161**k, grey steatite, part of a tablet, Min and heads of Hathor; on back, winged disc and uraei, "Ra," two *uzat* eyes, etc.
Materials. Green glaze 32, Bronze 5, Steatite 1, Wood 1.
Position. Chest (1).
Collections. Cairo 21, Univ. Coll. P. 9, E. 2, St. Petersburg 4, Turin 2.

162. AMEN.

Period. XXVI.
Figures. **162**a, a 2, bronze; **162**b, light blue glaze; **162**c, blue plaque; **162**d, light green head.
Materials. Green glaze 5, Blue glaze 2, Bronze 4, Gold 1, Silver 1, Granite 1.
Collections. Turin 5, Cairo 4, Univ. Coll. P. 4, E. 1.

163. AMEN, MUT AND KHONSU.

Period. XVIII.
Figure. **163**, dark blue glaze.
Materials. Green glaze 1, Blue glaze 1.
Collections. Turin 1, Univ. Coll. P. 1.

164. MUT.

Period. XXVI (?).
Figures. **164**a, blue glaze; **164**b, bronze; **164**b 2, pewter, b 3, 4, 5, blue glaze; **164**c, silver, group 16: **164**d (pl. xlv), violet glaze, Rifeh, XIXth dynasty; **164**e, apple-green glaze (xlvii); **164**f, head on cylinder, blue glaze (xlvii).
Materials. Green glaze 4, Silver 2, Bronze 2, Blue glaze 5, Pewter 1.
Collections. Univ. Coll. P. 4, E. 5, Turin 3, Cairo 2.

165. KHONSU.

Period. XXVI.
Figures. **165**a, bronze; **165**b, green glaze (pl. xxxi).
Collection. Univ. Coll. P. 2.

166. ANHUR.

Period. XXVI (?).
Figure. **166**, bronze.
Materials. Bronze 1, Green glaze 1.
Collections. Cairo 1, Univ. Coll. P. 1.

167. SHU.

Period. XII, XXX.
Figures. **167**a, silver, hollow; **167**b, carnelian, both XIIth dynasty (?); **16**c, d, e, f, light blue glaze; **167**e 2, 3, 4, 5, 6, green glaze.
Materials. Green glaze 65, Blue glaze 7, Grey glaze 6, Bronze 2, Silver 1, Carnelian 1, Yellow glaze 1.
Position. Chest (2); stomach (1).
Collections. Cairo 33, Turin 22, St. Petersburg 14, Univ. Coll. P. 6, E. 5, Murch 1.

168. NEIT.

Varieties. A, standing. B, suckling two crocodiles.
Period. XXVI to XXX.
Figures. A, **168**a, pewter plate. B, **168**b, light blue glaze, Neit suckling two crocodiles (see LANZ., *Diz. Mit.*, clxxv). Seated figure (see MacG. 75); **168**c, lazuli (xlvii).
Materials. Lazuli 7, Green glaze 3, Blue glaze 3, pewter 1.
Position. Chest (5).
Collections. Cairo 3 (2 B), St. Petersburg 3, Univ. Coll. P. 2, E. 1, Turin 1, Murch 1.

169. UNKNOWN DIVINITIES.

Period. Ptolemaic to Roman.
Figures. **169**a, bronze, female in Greek chiton with hands advanced, on the back of the head the face of a bear; possibly Artemis Brauronia; **169**b, blue glaze with yellow points, Roman, squatting female; **169**c, blue glass, female holding breasts, Syrian influence (?); **169**d (pl. xxxi), male figure green glaze with yellow points, Roman; **169**e, squatting female, dark blue glaze (pl. xlvi); **169**f, squatting female, blue glaze with yellow points (pl. xlvi).
Materials. Blue glaze with yellow points 2, Green glaze with yellow points 1, Dark blue glaze 1, Blue glass 1, Bronze 1.
Collection. Univ. Coll. P. 6.

170. HATHOR.

Name. "The habitation of Horus," apparently the mother of one of the forms of Horus, distinct from the Isis tradition. Especially venerated as the Mother Goddess.
Varieties. A, standing. B, seated.
Period. Ist to XXXth dynasty.
Figures. Type A, **170**a, gold, group 15; **170**b, silver, group 16; **170**c, c 2 (pl. xliii), bone, group 5, VIth dynasty; **170**d, gold, Hathor and *zad*, group 4, VIth dynasty. Type B (pl. xxvii), **170**e, e 2, f, f 2, carnelian, e 3, porphyry; **170**g, g 2, carnelian; h, h 2, h 3, carnelian, porphyry, XVIIIth dynasty; rudely cut open work. Hawara. These figures all have long hair, and appear to be female; they have a crescent and disc on the head, probably Hathor; they appear to be engaged in forming the body of the deceased person for future life, in the attitude of the

Khnumu creative figures, as Lanz., *Diz. Mit.*, cccxxxvi, 3. Perhaps, therefore, they are the seven Hathors who create a person. **170**j, bronze (xlvi).

Materials. Carnelian 4, Blue glass 4, Porphyry 2, Gold 2, Silver 1, Bone 2, Bronze 1, Limestone 1.

Collections. Univ. Coll. P. 15, E. 1, Murch 2.

171. HEAD OF HATHOR.

Name. *Her ne pot*, "human faced" (Lacau, 84).

Varieties. The head of Hathor appears worn by King Narmer upon his waist cloth ; also later with a straight wig, and with curling ends to the wig. As an amulet, it appears on the neck of the sacred *Aht* cow (Lanz, *Diz. Mit.*, 1).

Period. I to XXX. Apparently also prehistoric (*Naqada*, lxiv, 94).

Figures. **171**a, b, gold, XVIIIth dynasty; **171**c, grey-green glaze, XXXth dynasty (?); **171**d, blue glaze, XVIIIth dynasty; **171**e, apple-green glaze, piece of large disc, XXVIth dynasty; **171**f, blue glaze; f 2, blue paste, XVIIIth dynasty ; **171**g (pl. xlv), blue glaze, Illahun, XXIInd dynasty.

Materials. Green glaze 8, Blue glaze 3, Yellow glaze 2, Gold 2, Blue paste 1, Black glaze 1, Grey glaze 1, Blue glass 1 (Naqada), Lazuli plaque 1.

Collections. Turin 10, Univ. Coll. P. 7, Murch 2, St. Petersburg 1.

172. MĂOT.

Meaning. Impersonation of Truth, not worshipped as a divinity.

Varieties. A, seated. B, winged.

Figure. **172**, Lazuli.

Materials. Lazuli 10, Green glaze 1, Red glass 1.

Position. Throat (1) ; chest (6).

Collections. Cairo 6, St. Petersburg 2, Univ. Coll. P. 1, Athens 1.

173. HATMEHYT.

Name. *Hatmehyt* the goddess of Mendes, wearing the sacred fish of Mendes. (See No. **255**.)

Period. XXVI.

Figures. **173**a, apple green glaze; **173**b, dull green glaze, blundered inscriptions on the back of each.

Collections. Cairo 5 (glazed), Univ. Coll. P. 2.

174. SELKET.

Period. XXVI to XXX.

Material. Lazuli 14, Schist 1.

Position. Throat (1); chest (3).

Collections. Cairo 11, St. Petersburg 2, Univ. Coll. E. 2.

175. NEFERTUM.

Varieties. A, standing alone. B, standing on a lion.

Period. XXVI.

Figures. Type A, **175**a, violet glaze, no back pillar; **175**a 2, blue glaze; **175**b, green glaze, on back pillar, "Speech of Nefertum, son of Sekhmet, giving life, lady of . . ."; **175**b 2, bronze, b 3, green glaze (xlvi); **175**c, bronze; **175**d, light blue glaze; **175**e, silver, group 17, Memphis. Type B, **175**f, light green glaze. A, **175**g 2, light green glaze, g 3 lazuli, very rude. (See also **131**c.)

Materials. Green glaze 1 B, Blue glaze 8, Bronze 5, Silver 4, Violet glaze 1, Yellow glaze 1, Lazuli 1.

Collections. Cairo 16 and 3 B, Univ. Coll. P. 5 and 1 B, E. 5, Turin 4, St. Petersburg 3 and 1 B.

176. PTAH SEKER.

Name and Meaning. Ptah, god of the dynastic race at Memphis, united with Seker of Saqqareh, the primitive god of the dead, or of "silence"; like Mertseker, "lover of silence," the goddess of the Theban necropolis.

Varieties. A, alone. B, backed by gods on a plaque. C, double.

Period. XVIII to Ptolemaic.

Figures. **176**a, b, black and white porphyry, XVIIIth dynasty; **176**c, blue glaze, XVIII; **176**d, green glaze, XVIII; **176**e, green glaze, side view, XIX; **176**f, blue glaze, with scarab on head, XXII; **176**g, blue glaze, crowned, Illahun, XXII; **176**h, h 2, green glaze, XXVI; **176**j, j 2, burnt green glaze; **176**k, green glaze; **176**l, l, 2, 3, 4, 5, 6, 7, 8, 9, burnt green glaze; **176**m, bronze, solid casting with raised figure; **176**n, blue glaze, eating serpents (xlvi); **176**o, (xlvii), green glaze; **176**p (xlvi), green glaze, Bast with spread wings behind, Illahun, XXIII.

Materials. A, Green glaze 55, Blue glaze 15, Yellow glaze 2, Porphyry 2, Quartz crystal 1, Syenite 1, Carnelian 1, Bronze 1, Ivory 1. B, Green glaze 8. C, Blue glaze 2.

Collections. A, Cairo 21, St. Petersburg 12, Univ. Coll. P. 12, E. 12, Turin 10, Murch 4. B, Turin 5, St. Petersburg 2; backed by Bast, Illahun, Univ. Coll. E. C, St. Petersburg; triple, Cairo.

177. PTAH.

Period. XXVI to XXX.

Figures. **177**a, bronze; **177**b, b 2, green glaze; **177**c, bright green glaze, Memphis; **177**d, schist, Illahun (xlvii).

Materials. Green glaze 15, Blue glaze 5, White glaze 1, Gold 1, Bronze 2.

Collections. Cairo 14, Turin, 4, St. Petersburg 4, Univ. Coll. P. 3, E. 2.

178. DWARF.

Meaning. Compare the *gobbo* in Italy.

Period. Roman.

Figures. **178**a, lazuli, fine work; **179**b, yellow glass.
Collection. Univ. Coll. P. 2.

179. SAINTS.

Meaning. Protection by saints.
Period. Third century A.D. to Coptic.
Figures. **179**a, bronze; **179**b, bronze; **179**c, lead, figure with nimbus in middle, on each side a figure adoring; **179**d (pl. xlv), lead, horseman with nimbus, and spear in hand striking a kneeling figure below, crescent above; reverse, traces of six lines of inscription; **179**e, lead, figure holding long cross, another with arms raised; reverse *Eis theōs ho boethōn*, "In God is help"; **179f** (pl. xlvi), amber-yellow glass, Jonah asleep under the gourd, ship in the background; this class of yellow glass pendant is dated to about 250 A.D. by heads of Philip and Otacilia. Univ. Coll. P. 6.

CHAPTER VIII

AMULETS OF ANIMAL-HEADED GODS

THEOPHORIC AMULETS, 180—203.

THE primitive animal worships of the Egyptian nomes may well have had a totemistic basis—though that is questioned. There is no doubt that they largely modified the ideal of anthropomorphic gods which probably came in with the Libyan race at the beginning of the prehistoric civilisation. The two different ideals were reconciled, like the different races, by fusion. The human figures acquired the animal heads; and in no point is the artistic skill of the Egyptian shown better than in the facile union of such incongruous subjects as the ibis or snake with the man. Each stock of the mixed race clung to its own beliefs, and down to Roman times the animal-headed gods were as much venerated as any others.

180. HORUS.

It is difficult to separate between the figures of the gods Horus and Ra, who were so intimately blended. The only practical course, where no inscription exists, is to class plain hawk-headed figures as Horus, and those with the disc of the sun upon the head as Ra.

Varieties. A, striking with a spear, *Hor-merti* (see inscrip. Cairo, 38618). B, hawk-headed, wearing double crown. C, seated, no head-dress. D, lion-headed, *Hor-akhti* (LANZ., *Diz. Mit.*, 625). E, on crocodiles.
Period. XVIII to Roman.
Figures. Type A, **180**a, bronze. B, **180**b, ebony; **180**c, bronze; **180**d, e, green glaze, and f, Hawara (pl. xlv); **180**d, 2, 3, light blue glaze; **180**g, pewter plate, group 18; **180**h, green glaze; **180**j, blue glaze, Dendereh, group 21; **180**k, green glaze, classed as Hor-behudti in Cairo catalogue; **180**l, blue glass; **180**m, blue glaze, mummiform, perhaps Kebhsenuf, son of Horus (see **182**); **180**n, lazuli, perhaps Kebhsenuf (pl. xlv), group 28; **180**o, o 2, blue glaze, probably Kebhsenuf (**182**); and **180**o 3, steatite, but no fellow figures are known of the other genii. Type D, **180**p (pl. xxiii), blue glaze, yellow points, Roman; Horus of the eastern and of the western horizons hand in hand. Type E, **180**q, green glaze.

Materials. Green glaze 54, Blue glaze 9, Yellow glaze 6, Grey glaze 4, Red glaze 1, Lazuli 5, Blue glass 2, Bronze 2, Pewter 1, Ebony 1. Type C, Green felspar or prase 10. Type D, blue glaze with yellow points 7 (4 at St. Petersburg).
Position. In main row of gods on chest (10); stomach (1).
Collections. Cairo 40, Turin 24, St. Petersburg 18, Univ. Coll. P. 13, E. 2.

181. RA.

Varieties. A, standing, or B, seated; always hawk-headed with disc.
Period. XXVI to XXX.
Figures. **181**a, bronze; **181**a 2, green glaze, small, a 3, alabaster, small; **181**b, bronze, having a crescent below the disc it appears to be Ra-Khonsu; with the crescent the god is named as Khonsu, never as Ra; but this is Ra-Khonsu, as Khonsu strictly is human-headed with the youthful lock of hair; **181**c, c 2, olive-green glaze; **181**c 3—7, blue glaze; **181**d (pl. xlv), green glaze faded, Hawara; **181**e (pl. xlv), shell, Illahun, XXIInd dynasty; **181**f, apple-green glaze plaque, holding the *uas* sceptre, and called Hor-mer-tef (LANZ., *Diz. Mit.*, xvii); **181**g, white glass; **181**h, blue glaze, Ra in his boat adored by the baboons, XVIIIth dynasty.
Materials. Green glaze 28, Blue glaze 12, Yellow glaze 2, Grey glaze 5, Lazuli 1, Bronze 2, White glass 1.
Position. In the row of gods on the chest (6); throat (1).
Collections. Turin 16, Cairo 14, Univ. Coll. P. 7, E. 9, St. Petersburg 7, Athens 1, Murch 1.

182. FOUR SONS OF RA.

Names. *Amset*, human head; *Hapy*, baboon head; *Duat mutef*, jackal head; *Kebhsenuf*, hawk head.
Meanings. Amset or Mestha, probably the "statue" or image. Hapy, perhaps Hapy the bull god of Memphis, who presided over the great cemetery of Memphis. Duat mutef, "the underworld is his mother." Kebhsenuf, "Coolness is his brother." Each son protected one part of the body; Amset the stomach and large intestines, Hapy the small

intestines, Duat mutef the lungs and heart, Kebhsenuf the liver and gall. The four are often shown standing together on a lotus flower before Osiris.

Varieties. Executed in all kinds of material, metals, wax, pottery, vegetable paste, bead-work, etc.

Period. XXIII to Roman. (On tops of jars from XIIth dynasty, but all human-headed.)

Figures. **182a**, gold; **182b**, pewter, group 18; **182c**, gilt wax; **182d**, red pottery; **182e**, e 2, blue glaze with red paint, with winged scarab; **182f**, green glaze, with applied blue; **182g**, wax; **182h**, white and red glass; **182j**, red glass; **182k**, blue glaze; **182l**, dark blue glaze, with black heads, also with scarab and girdle tie; **182 l2**, Duat mutef, blue glazed schist; **182m**, blue glaze; **182n**, black wax; **182o**, black clay, with blue paint on heads; **182p**, green glaze; **182q**, blue glaze, with black paint, Dendereh, Ptolemaic, group 21; **182r** (pl. xxxiii), blue glaze on one plaque, Dendereh, group 21 and see **93f**, g (pl. xi.)

Materials. Blue glaze 40, Green glaze 11, Wax 9, Clay 8, Pewter 6, Green glass 6, Red glass 5, Blue glass 4, Pottery 4, Gold 2, White glass 1, Wood 1.

Position. Usually in two pairs facing, on the chest (9) or stomach (2), below the winged scarab.

Collections. Univ. Coll. P. 49 (others in funerary section), Turin 27, St. Petersburg 7, Murch 4.

183. SET.

Period. XXVI (?). Extremely rare as an amulet, as well as in larger figures.

Figure. **183**, bronze, wearing double crown, the upright ears shown on either side.

Materials. Bronze 1, Blue glaze 1, Red wood 1.

Collections. Cairo 1, Univ. Coll. P. 1, Turin 1.

184. SPHINX, MALE.

Period. VI, XVIII, XXVI.

Figures. **184a**, brown limestone, fine work, XVIIIth dynasty; **184b**, green glaze, of Graeco-Assyrian style; also **184a** 2, lazuli, of Ramessu II; **184a** 3, blue paste, of Sety II.

Materials. Green felspar 4, Amethyst 2, Lazuli 2, Carnelian 1, Limestone 1, Green glaze 1, Blue paste 1.

Collections. Murch 8, Univ. Coll. P. 4, Athens 1.

185. SPHINX, FEMALE.

Varieties. A, bird body. B, cat body.

Period. VI to Ptolemaic.

Figures. A, **185a**—d, bone, possibly intended for a human-headed vulture of the goddess Mut, group 13. Type B, **185e**, f, f 2, green felspar, apparently a cat body, group 30; **185g**, h, carnelian, group 14; **185j**, green glaze faded, Memphis, XXIIIth dynasty by the form of hair; **185k**, k 2, l, green glaze, black hair, XXVI; **185m**, green and black glaze, Dendereh, Ptolemaic; **185m** 2, yellow glass, small.

Materials. Green felspar 23, Amethyst 4, Carnelian 2, Bone 4, Green glaze 5, Lazuli 1, Yellow glass 1.

Collections. Murch 25, Univ. Coll. P. 13, E. 2, St. Petersburg 1.

186. HATHOR COW-HEADED.

Period. XVIII to XXVI.

Figures. **186a**, dark blue glaze, XVIII; **186b**, light green glaze, XXVI; **186c**, d (pl. xlv), green glass, burnt.

Materials. Green glaze 2, Blue glaze 2, Green glass 2.

Position. Throat (1); chest (1).

Collections. Cairo 2, Univ. Coll. P. 4. (See also 210.)

187. KHNUMU.

Meaning. The Creator, popular in late times as Khnouphis.

Varieties. A, statuette. B, outline on plaque (Hawara 4, pl. I).

Period. XXVI.

Figures. Type A, **187a**, bronze; **187b**, dark green glaze; **187c**, coarse green glaze; **187d**, red glaze (? burnt green); **187e**, f, f 2, Hawara, group 32, f 3, g, all green glaze.

Materials. Green glaze 46, Blue glaze 8, Yellow glaze 3, Grey glaze 3, Red-grey glaze 7, Red glaze 1, Carnelian 1, Bronze 1, Blue paste 1.

Position. In row of gods on chest (4); stomach (1).

Collections. Cairo 30, Turin 20, St. Petersburg 11, Univ. Coll. P. 8, E. 1, Murch 1.

188. BES OR BESA.

Name. *Besa*, the native name of *Cynaelurus guttatus*.

Meaning. The god of children, of dance and games.

Varieties. Dealt with under **189**, **190**.

Period. XVIII to Roman.

Figures. Pl. xxxiv, **188a**, b, gold, XVIII; **188c**, red paste, Tell Amarna, XVIII. Pl. xxxiii, **188d**, schist, dark green glaze, XVIII; **188e**, dark blue glaze, XVIII; **188e** 2, blue glaze; **188f**, steatite, XIX (?); **188g**, silver, XIX (?), head-dress very high; **188h**, white schist; **188h** 2, blue glaze, larger; **188j**, j 2, green glaze; **188k**, dark blue glaze with yellow points, Roman; **188l**, light blue, similar; **188m**, green, n, o, p, blue, with yellow points, Roman; **188q**, bronze; **188r**, bright blue, XX (?); **188s**, dark green, thin, XVIII; **188t**, light blue glaze, Memphis; **188u**, light green glaze; **188v**, grey glaze; **188w**, w 2, green gone brown, blue and yellow applied, Roman; **188x**, dark violet glass, seated; **188y**, light green, seated; **188z**, green gone grey, with yellow points, Roman, Bes under archway with two columns; **188aa**, ab, blue glass impressed; **188ac**, violet glaze, XVIII.

Materials. Green glaze 52, Blue glaze 46, Blue or green with yellow points 7, Red glaze 2, Grey glaze 4, Blue glass 3, Green glass 1, Gold 4, Silver 1, Bronze 4, Carnelian 2, Steatite 2, Schist 1, Violet glaze 1.

Collections. Cairo 59, Univ. Coll. P. 27, E. 9, Turin 13, Alnwick 18, Murch 3.

189. BES, UNUSUAL FORMS.

Varieties. A, profile holding *sa*, for protection. B, dancing in profile with tambourine. C, front face between two in profile dancing. D, with lyre. E, armed. F, with cylinder on head. G, winged, holding *uzats*. H, with two uraei. J, masculine and feminine. K, feminine, Beset. L, quadruple. M, as sphinx. N, between two Taurts.

Period. XVIII to Roman.

Figures. Type A, **189**a, blue glaze, holding *sa* before him, the other hand holding the tail of the skin, XVIII. Type B, **189**b, blue glaze. Type C, **189**c, violet glaze, XVIII. Type D (see Cairo). Type E, **189**d, faded blue glaze, yellow points, Roman; **189**e, blue glaze, Roman (type common in household pottery amulets). Type F (see Turin). Type G, **189**f, violet glaze, XVIII. Type H, **189**g, blue glaze, Roman. Type J, **189**h, blue glaze, yellow points, Roman. Type K (only in household pottery amulets). Type L, **189**j, light blue glaze, a double figure with four heads. Type M, **189**k, glaze faded white, figure on top, and central figure missing, XXVI.

Materials. Green glaze 14, Blue glaze 15, Blue with yellow points 2, Yellow glaze 3.

Position. Necklaces, especially of children.

Collections. A, Univ. Coll. P. 1. B, Univ. Coll. P. 1, St. Petersburg 1. C, Univ. Coll. P. 1. D, Cairo 3. E, Univ. Coll. P. 2, Cairo 1. F, Turin 1. G, Univ. Coll. P. 1. H, Univ. Coll. P. 1. J, Turin 1, Cairo 1, Univ. Coll. P. 1. K, Turin 4. L, Cairo 1, Univ. Coll. P. 1, Turin 1. M, Univ. Coll. P. 1. N, Turin 6, St. Petersburg 1.

190. BES HEAD.

Varieties. A, alone. B, on plaque. C, on *uzat*. D, on disc.

Period. XXIII (?) to Roman.

Figures. Type A, **190**a, light green, probably part of a figure; **190**b, light green glaze; **190**b 2, violet glaze, large; **190**c, d, d 2, blue glaze, XXIII; **190**e, yellow and brown glaze; **190**f, green glaze, part of a figure; **190**g, blue glaze, faded; **190**h, violet glass, Roman; **190**j, clear white glass, Roman; **190**k, green glaze; **190**k, 2, 3, green glaze, small, Naukratis; **190**l, blue glaze, Memphis; **190**m, blue glaze, Roman. Type B, **190**n, plaque of schist, both sides shown. Type C, **190**o, blue glaze, lotus on back; **190**p, green glaze. Type D, 190q, glaze burnt black, reverse shown below; **190**q 2, blue glaze; **190**q 3, green glaze, pierced; **190**r, light green glaze, reverse *uzat* eye; **190**s, pottery mould, Memphis. A, **190**t (pl. xlvi) green glaze; **190**u, blue paste with four-winged Bes straddling on the base.

Materials. Green glaze 11, Blue glaze 9, Yellow glaze 3, Limestone 1, Violet glass 1, Clear glass 1, Blue paste 1, Violet glaze 1.

Collections. Univ. Coll. P. 20, E. 6, Turin 4, Murch 2, St. Petersburg 1.

191. TAHUTI OF PANEBES.

Name. "Tahuti of Panebes in Nubia" (Lanz., *Diz. Mit.*, cccciv), probably known as the deity of the malachite mines there (B. D. G. 335).

Period. XXVII (?).

Figure. **191**, light blue glaze, good sharp work.

Collection. Univ. Coll. P. 1.

192. MAHES.

Name. *Măa-hes*, "the striking lion."

Period. XXVI to Ptolemaic.

Figures. **192**a, bronze, with *ătef* crown on head; **192**b, b 2, 3, 4, c, light green glaze; **192**d, violet glass; **192**e (pl. xxxix), light blue glaze, Mahes (?) holding two lions (?).

Materials. Green glaze 23, Blue glaze 3, Bronze 3, Blue glass 2.

Collections. Cairo 15, St. Petersburg 6, Univ. Coll. P. 5, E. 3, Turin 2, Athens 2.

193. ANHUR AND TEFNUT.

These deities are associated on a group in the Louvre, (Lanz., *Diz. Mit.*, 77).

Period. XVIII.

Figures. **193**a, b, blue glaze.

Collection. Univ. Coll. P. 2.

194. SEKHMET OR BASTET.

Many figures cannot be separated between these two lion- or cat-headed goddesses, so they are here classed together.

Period. XVIII to XXX.

Figures. **194**a, blue glaze, faded, the dress suggests a male god, but the head is exactly like those of the goddesses (see Cairo 38,587); **194**b, bronze, holding sistrum, basket, and aegis, certainly Bastet; **194**c, blue paste, on back "Speech of Bast . . ."; **194**d, green glaze; **194**e, silver, group 16 (see pl. xxxvi); **194**f, g, blue glaze, XIX (?), Sekhmet, by disc on head; **194**h, blue glaze, Illahun, XXII; **194**h 2, green glaze; **194**j, k, l, light green glaze; **194**ll (pl. xlvi); ll 2, 3, 4, 5, 6, 7, blue glaze; **194**m, light blue glaze; **194**n, schist, figure of Sekhmet, probably part of a *menat*; reverse, Nehebka and other figures, see below; **194**o, alabaster, tapering body and legs, Saft; **194**p, dark blue glaze, female kneeling, offering to Bastet, name twice on back, see below; **194**q, blue glaze, Ramesseum. On pl. xlv, **194**r, blue faded, Sekhmet, Memphis; **194**s, bronze, with double crown; **194**t, wood, XXII, Illahun. On xlvi, **194**u, green glazed, seated; **194**v, head on a pillar, blue glaze (xlvii).

Materials. Green glaze 48, Blue glaze 36, Grey glaze 3, Silver 1, Bronze 2, Electrum 1, Schist 1, Blue paste 1, Gypsum 1, Alabaster 2, Wood 1.

Collections. Cairo 36, Univ. Coll. P. 16, E. 8, Turin 20, St. Petersburg 17, Murch 1.

195. AEGIS OF BASTET (AND MUT ?).

This is in form of a deep collar of beadwork, usually surmounted by a lion's head; it has a *menat* attached to it at right angles behind (see the socket of **195**a), and it is carried by the *menat* in the left hand of Bastet. The name and meaning of it are unknown.

Period. XXII to XXVI.

Figures. **195**a, bronze, front and back of both aegis and *menat*; **195**b, b 2, blue glaze, faded white; **195**c, blue glaze, side view of head, with Nehebka, uraeus and *uzat*; reverse, collar; **195**d, green glaze with yellow lines, Roman; **195**e (pl. xlv), silver gilt; **195**f, silver; **195**g, g 2, blue glaze, head of Mut (?), Illahun, XXII; **195**h, bronze, female head; **195**j, blue glaze, head of Mut (?); **195**k, l, bronze, female head with disc and horns, Isis (?); **195**m, n, bronze, lion head.

Materials, as above, Univ. Coll. P. 13, E. 2, St. Petersburg 1, green glaze.

196. SHU AND TEFNUT.

The heads of these twin deities are often figured at the top of a *menat* of bronze.

Period. XXVI.

Figures. **196**a, bronze, inscribed "To Shu and Tefnut. Thapa, son of Duaha, born of Kare-za"; the name Thapa, after the hippopotamus goddess Apit, belongs to the XIXth dynasty (Lieb., *Dict.*, 760); Duaha, called after the moon god, suggests the XXVIth dynasty; and Kareza, "son of the Karian," points also to the Early Greek age (L., *Dict.*, 2396); **196**b, bronze; **196**b 2, bronze. At St. Petersburg, 1 of bronze with lion head.

197. ANPU.

Meaning. Anpu, Anubis, was the protector of the dead, the god of the cemetery frequented by the jackals.

Period. XXVI to Roman.

Figures. **197**a, b, c, d, bronze; **197**a 2, 3, 4, green glaze, smaller: **197**e, f, violet glass; **197**f 2, 3, 4, 5, 6, 7, 8, green glaze; **197**g, blue glaze; **197**h, steatite; **197**j, blue glaze, Dendereh, Ptolemaic, group 21; **197**k, blue glaze with yellow points, Roman; **197**l, bronze, kneeling, pouring water (see Cairo, 38,569; see **35**m); **197**m (pl. xlv), bone, Illahun, seated; **197**n (pl. xlv), ebony, seated.

Materials. Green glaze 60, Blue glaze 19, Grey glaze 5, Black and yellow glaze 2, Red glaze 1, Blue glass 3, Grey glass 2, Yellow glass 2, Bronze 8, Wood 7, Bone 1, Porphyry 1, Quartz crystal 1, Carnelian 1, Agate 1.

Position. Chest (2).

Collections. Cairo 44, Turin 17, St. Petersburg 14, Univ. Coll. P. 13, E. 10, Murch 7, Athens 3.

198. UPUATU.

Names. "The opener of the ways."

Meaning. Guidance to the soul, as the jackal's tracks show the best way in the desert.

Period. Ptolemaic (?).

Figure. **198**, black steatite, kneeling figure with a hawk's body behind, and with two jackal heads, the god being double, of the north and of the south.

Collection. Univ. Coll. P. 1.

199. JACKAL-HEADED ARCHER.

This god is not identified.

Period. XXII (?).

Figure. **199**, wood. (See Cairo Catalogue, 38,857.)

Collections. Cairo 1, Univ. Coll. P. 1.

200. SHREWMOUSE-HEADED FIGURE.

This appears to be a male figure; as the shrew mouse was sacred to Horus, it may be a form of that god.

Figures. **200**, bronze. (See Cairo Catalogue, 38,859.)

Collections. Cairo 1, Univ. Coll. P. 1.

201. SEBEK.

Period. XVIII.

Figure. **201**, light blue opaque glass (see Lanz., *Diz. Mit.*, ccclv).

Material. Above; and gold, Cairo.

Position. Chest (1).

Collections. Univ. Coll. P. 1, Cairo 1.

202. TEHUTI.

Principally honoured as the god of writing and knowledge.

Period. XXVI to XXX.

Figures. **202**a, green glaze, Tehuti holding an *uzat* eye in each hand; on back "Speech of Tehuti, lord of Shmun great god, lady (*sic*) of heaven . . ."; **202**b, green glaze faded, Hawara; **202**b, 2, 3, 4, 5, 6, green glaze; **202**c, blue glaze, with violet beak; **202**c 2, 3, lazuli; **202**d, green glaze; **202**e, e 2, pewter plate, group 18; **202**f, bronze; **202**g, green-blue glaze; **202**h, steatite charm tablet, with figure of Tehuti; rosette and line of Demotic on reverse; **202**j, j 2, 3, blue glaze; **202**k, bronze; **202**l, green glaze (pl. xlvi).

Materials. Green glaze 83, Blue glaze 23, Grey glaze 6, White glaze 1, Red glaze 1, Lazuli 7, Blue glass 2, Bronze 3, Pewter 1.

Position. In the main row of gods on the chest (9); stomach (1).

Collections. Cairo 51, Turin 36, St. Petersburg 15, Univ. Coll. P. 13, E. 8, Athens 2.

203. SERPENT-HEADED GOD.

Name. *Khet-ba-mutef* is represented crowned with a disc, perhaps the same as **203**b, which has disc and crescent (Lanz., *Diz. Mit.*, 993).

Figures. **203**a, blue-green glaze, two serpent heads, on back a blundered inscription, beginning *Ra nofer ar* . . .; **203**b, bronze, Khet-ba-mutef (?); **203**c, bronze; **203**d, lead, possibly a serpent head.

CHAPTER IX

AMULETS OF ANIMAL GODS

Theophoric Amulets, 204—261.

Miscellaneous, 262—275.

The worship of sacred animals survived in Egypt for thousands of years alongside of higher beliefs. Beginning probably before the earliest civilisation of which we have remains, it is found to be prominent in all the great centres, and most of the nomes. The bulls of Memphis and Heliopolis, the ram of Thebes, the hawk of Edfu, are the remains of older faiths, long before Ptah and Amen and Horus had eclipsed them in those cities. The popularity of the animal worship did not wane till Roman times; the abundance of amulets of sacred animals shows how much was thought of them. Though some animal figures here are not known to be connected with a god, that is to be expected, as it was not always that a junction with later theology could be performed. The old independent animal worships would not have any priesthoods or inscriptions by which we can recognise them; and it is only the making and wearing of these figures which shows what animals were venerated.

204. APE STANDING (*Cercopithecus*).

Period. XXVI to Ptolemaic (?).

Figures. **204**a, a 2, faded green glaze; **204**b, b 2, violet glass; **204**c, faded green glaze, Memphis; **204**d, green glaze, burnt brown, ape standing over kneeling woman; **204**e (xlvii), green glaze.

Materials. Green glaze 20, Blue glaze 11, Lazuli 1, Blue glass 2, Basalt 1, Bronze 1.

Collections. Cairo 17, St. Petersburg 5, Turin 4, Univ. Coll. P. 4, E. 3, Murch 35 (amethyst 27, carnelian 4, lazuli 3, green felspar, attitude not stated).

205. APE SEATED.

Period. VI to XXX.

Figures. **205**a, bone, VIth dynasty, group 4; **205**b, green glaze, burnt red; **205**c, blue glaze faded white, Memphis; **205**d, green glaze, faded.

Materials. Green glaze 4, Yellow frit 2, Blue glaze 1, Bone 1.

Collections. Univ. Coll. P. 4, Cairo 3, St. Petersburg 1, Murch.

206. BABOON (*Papio*).

Period. VI to Ptolemaic.

Figures. **206**a, bone, group 6; **206**b, bone, group 8; **206**c, green-blue glaze, group 9; **206**d, blue glaze, group 12; **206**e, green glaze, XIX (?); **206**f, two baboons, crowned with disc and crescent, electrum, XVIII; **206**g, blue glaze, XVIII; **206**h, white schist, on back "Tehuti lord of Shmun"; **206**j, bronze; **206**k, green glaze, holding *uzat;* **206**l, blue glaze, Dendereh, Ptolemaic, group 21; **206**m, (pl. xlv), green glaze, Illahun, XXIInd dynasty. (See also **131**f.)

Materials. Green glaze 15, Blue glaze 9, Yellow glaze 3, Red jasper 1, Carnelian 1, Agate 1, Red glaze 1, Blue glass 2, Lazuli 1, Bronze 2, Bone 2, Onyx 1, Schist 1, Electrum 1.

Collections. Turin 19, Univ. Coll. P. 12, St. Petersburg 9, Cairo 5, Murch 4, Athens 1.

207. APIS.

Name. *Hap.* There is no connection yet known between this and *Hap*, the Nile, or *Hapy*, one of the four sons of Horus.

Meaning. The sacred bull Hap was the primitive worship of Memphis, like the sacred bulls with other names in other cities.

Varieties. A, bronze figures. B, square tablets or pectorals.

Period. XXVI to Roman.

Figures. Type A, **207**a, bronze, on a sled, disc and uraeus between the horns; **207**b, c, bronze, with disc and uraeus; **207**b 2, blue glaze. Type B, **207**d, green glaze; **207**e, silver embossed plate, bull regardant, with garland hung over it; **207**f, cast lead plate, bull fed by a kneeling priest, garland above; **207**g, blue glaze, with black and yellow applied, bull regardant; **207**h (pl. xlv), blue glass impressed.

Materials. Bronze, 14, Yellow glaze 9, Blue glaze 10, Green glaze 3, Yellow glass 2, Blue glass 3, Silver 1, Lead 1, Schist 2.

Collections. Cairo 12, St. Petersburg 10, Univ. Coll. P. 9, E. 1, Turin 9, Athens 3, Alnwick 2, Murch 1 B.

208. HATHOR COW.

Name. *Erpet ăht* (MacG. 53); the Aht cow belonged to Hathor, by the amulet or badge worn on the neck (LANZ., *Diz. Mit.*, I).

Varieties. A, couchant. B, standing.

Period. XVIII to Roman.

Figures. **208a**, fine blue glaze, mid XVIII; **208b**, light green glaze, XXVI; **208c**, blue glaze, moulded, flat back, XIX; **208d**, bronze, cut out of a sheet; **208e**, moulded wax, gilt, group 20; **208f**, apple green glaze, Dendereh, Ptolemaic, group 21; **208g**, blue glaze, couchant (xlvi).

Materials. Blue glaze 3, Green glaze 3, Carnelian 2, "Black and white stone," Cairo 2, Bronze 3, Red glass 2, Red and yellow glass 1, Yellow glass 1, Red glaze 1, Jasper 1, Wax 1.

Position. Chest (1); stomach (2).

Collections. Univ. Coll. P. 6, Cairo 5, Athens 4, St. Petersburg 2, Turin 2, Alnwick 1.

209. HATHOR COW ON SQUARE.

Varieties. A regular naos, on a plain square plaque.

Period. XXVI to Ptolemaic (?).

Figures. **209a**, light blue glaze, with dark green-blue inlay; **209b**, blue-green glaze, impressed cow, with relief of *uzat* above; **209c**, green glaze, faded brown, disc between the horns; **209d**, light blue glaze, disc between the horns; **209e**, cast lead plate, disc between the horns, feeding stand in front, star and crescent above. The last is distinctly a cow, the previous four might be intended for a bull, but the similarity of *c*, *d*, and *e* points to the same meaning.

Materials. Bronze 11, Blue glaze 6, Green glaze 6, Steatite 3, Green frit 2, Lead 1.

Collections. Cairo 23, Univ. Coll. P. 5, St. Petersburg 1, Athens 1.

210. HATHOR COW HEAD.

Period. XVIII (?).

Figures. **210a**, white opaque quartz, covered with green glaze, inscribed on back "Hathor lady of N . . .," broken from a figure; note the two plumes above the disc; **210b**, bronze, human face on back, short stem below; **210c**, bronze, cow head (back up); **210d**, apple green glaze; **210e**, violet glaze, human wig at sides.

Materials. Bronze 2, Quartz glazed 1, Apple green glaze 1, Violet glaze 1.

Collection. Univ. Coll. P. 5.

211. RAM.

Name. *Sera.*

Meaning. Creator, as Khnumu, Amon and Ra.

Varieties. A, couchant. B, standing. C, four-headed emblem of Ra, at Mendes, the souls of Ra, Osiris, Shu, and Khepera.

Period. Prehistoric to Ptolemaic.

Figures. **211a**, noble serpentine; **211b**, dark green steatite, both prehistoric; **211c**, lazuli, with the characteristic long fleece; **211d**, d 2, light green glaze; **211e**, silver; **211f**, green glaze burnt brown, Memphis; **211g**, dark blue glaze; **211h**, light green glaze; **211j**, deep blue glaze with yellow points, group 22, Roman; **211k**, apple-green glaze, Dendereh, Ptolemaic, group 21; **211l**, schist, ram couchant under tree, uraeus in front; reverse, title and name of Shabaka, XXVth dynasty; **211m** (pl. xl), bronze, with two heads. C, **211n** (pl. xlvi), lazuli.

Materials. Blue glaze 26, Green glaze 15, Lazuli 5 (4 of C), Steatite 2, Silver 1, Bronze 2, Schist 2, Carnelian 1, Serpentine 1, Red glaze 1.

Collections. Cairo 16 (2 of C), Turin 10, Univ. Coll. P. 10, E. 1, St. Petersburg 6, Alnwick 5, Athens 2, Murch 4.

212. RAM'S HEAD.

Varieties. A, flat prehistoric, with round neck. B, late relief, without neck. C, on column.

Period. Prehistoric to Ptolemaic.

Figures. Type A, **212a**, black steatite; **212b**, noble serpentine; **212c**, carnelian; **212d**, noble serpentine, pale oil-green; **212d 2**, green serpentine, Tarkhan; **212e**, e 2, ivory, stained green; **212f**, durite; **212g**, g 2, alabaster; **212h**, brown serpentine, veined; **212j**, carnelian; **212k**, dark green serpentine; **212l**, alabaster; **212m**, black serpentine, ostrich eggshell eye. Type B, **212n**, silver; **212o**, bronze; **212p**, green glaze faded brown; **212q**, blue glaze, Dendereh, Ptolemaic; **212r**, hollow bronze case, with blue glass eyes, ring for hanging beneath mouth; **212s**, schist scarab with ram's head, name of Shabaka on reverse, XXVth dynasty. Type C, **212t** (two views), green glaze, serpent on one side, winged serpent on other, on front disc with uraei, *si ra Amen mery*, and blundered signs.

Materials. Prehistoric, Alabaster 3, Carnelian 3, Noble serpentine 2, Ivory 2, Green serpentine 1, Black serpentine 1, Black steatite 1, Brown serpentine 1, Durite 1. Historic, Grey glaze 3, Green glaze 2, Green felspar 1, Blue glaze 1, Blue paste 1, Gold 1, Silver 1, Bronze 2, Schist 1, Brown limestone 1.

Collections. Univ. Coll. P. 21, Turin 4, Murch 4, Athens 1.

213. HARE.

Name and Meaning. *Sekhat.* Used probably as the hieroglyph for *un*, being, and hence probably used for *Un-nefer*, the good being, or Osiris.

Period. XXVI to XXX.

Figures. **213a**, light green glaze; **213b**, glaze faded white; **213b 2**, green glaze; **213c**, light blue glaze.

Materials. Green glaze 22, Blue glaze 17, Yellow glaze 1, Carnelian 1.

Collections. Cairo 22, St. Petersburg 8, Turin 5, Univ. Coll. P. 3, E. 1, Athens 1, Murch 1.

214. IBEX (*Capra nubiana*).

Meaning. "Ba the divine, above the gods" (Lanz, *Diz. Mit.*, 190).

Figure. **214**, green glaze, *onkh* on base.

Collections. Univ. Coll. P. 1, E. 1, Murch 1.

215. BARBARY SHEEP (*Ovis lervia*).

Figure. **215**, serpentine, green partly gone brown, no horns, but a heavy long head.

Collection. Univ. Coll. P. 1.

216. KLIPSPRINGER (*Oreotragus*) (?).

Period. XVIIIth dynasty.

Figure. **216**, green glaze on schist, two scrolls on base. The small head, long neck, and marking of coarse hair seem to define this identification. Short curved horns have lain over to the shoulder, but are broken away.

Collection. Univ. Coll. P. 1.

217. CAMEL.

Meaning. Hairs from tail used for quartan fever (Pliny, xxviii, 25).

Period. Roman (?).

Figure. **217**, bronze, flat plate.

Collection. Univ. Coll. P. 1.

218. HAWK-HEADED SPHINX.

Period. Prehistoric.

Figure. **218**, hard white limestone with gold bands, no tail.

Collection. Univ. Coll. P. 1. (See **244**, as Mentu.)

219. LION.

Name. *Seno* (couchant).

Meaning. To guard or defend.

Varieties. A, couchant. B, walking. C, seated. D, with crouching man.

Period. Prehistoric to Ptolemaic.

Figures. Type A, **219a**, hard white limestone; **219b**, black and white porphyry, both prehistoric; **219c**, amethyst, XII; **219d**, d 2, d 3, bone, VI, group 5; **219e**, gold, VI; **219f**, light blue glaze; **219g**, light blue glaze, faded; **219h 2**, light green glaze, XXVIIth dynasty; **219j**, blue and black glaze, Dendereh, Ptolemaic; **219k**, k 2, blue glaze, VI, group, 11, XII, Kafr Ammar; **219l** (pl. xlvi), carnelian, early (see *Naqada*, lviii; *Deshasheh*, xxvi, 15); **219m** (xlvi), green glaze, with flower of Nefertum on head; **219n**, with squatting man before, head turned back, blue glaze with yellow points, Roman (xlvi).

Materials. Green glaze, 16 (2 of B, 2 of C), Blue glaze 16, Grey glaze 1, Gold 1, Bronze 1, Amethyst 1, Carnelian 1, Milky agate 1, Porphyry 1, Lazuli 1, Hard white limestone 1, Bone 3.

Position. Chest (6); Stomach (1).

Collections. Cairo 16, Univ. Coll. P. 14, E. 2, Turin 9, St. Petersburg 7, Murch 2.

220. TWO LIONS.

Name. *Khens* (MacG. 56); two fore-parts joined.

Meaning. The Mahes (see **192**) of north and south (Lanz., *Diz. Mit.*, 269). See vignette of Chapter 17, Book of the Dead.

Varieties. A, two fore-parts joined. B, two lions rampant.

Period. A, VIth to XXVIIth dynasty. B, Prehistoric, Coptic.

Figures. Type A, **220a**, a 2, sard, VIth dynasty, group 7; **220b**, bone, VIth dynasty (?); **220c**, light green glaze, XXVII; **220c** 2, blue glaze; **220d**, ivory, Old Kingdom (?) (see *Deshasheh*, xxvi, 26). Type B, **220e**, iron disc incised, Coptic, Illahun, indistinct signs between and above (see two rampant lions on ivory ring, prehistoric, in *Naqada*, lxiv, 78).

Materials. Green glaze 8, Blue glaze 2, Brown glaze 1, Grey glaze 1, Sard 1, Cloudy agate 1, Ivory 2, Iron B, 1.

Position. Chest (1).

Collections. Univ. Coll. P. 6, E. 1, Turin 3, St. Petersburg 2, Cairo 2, Price 1.

221. LION'S HEAD.

Period. XXXth dynasty.

Figure. **221a**, light green glaze, flat back (similar Alnwick, 604); **221b**, c (pl. xlv), green glaze, Illahun, XXIInd dynasty; **221d**, coarse blue glaze Roman (see **269**).

Collections. Univ. Coll. P. 4, Alnwick 1.

222. LION AND BULL, FORE-PARTS.

Period. XXVII.

Figure. See Cairo catalogue.

Materials. Green glaze 8.

Collections. Alnwick 5, St. Petersburg (695), 2, Cairo 1.

223. TWO BULLS, FORE-PARTS.

Period. This is a very ancient combination, appearing on one of the predynastic slate palettes (Capart, *Primitive Art*, fig. 170). The amulets are of the XXVIth dynasty.

Figures. **223a**, pale green glaze, Hawara; **223b**, green glaze gone brown, Hawara, group 32; **223c**, olive green glaze.

Position. Chest (1).

Collections. Univ. Coll. P. 3, St. Petersburg 1, Price 1.

AMULETS OF ANIMAL GODS

224. CAT.

Name. *Mau.*

Meaning. Emblem of the goddess Bastet.

Varieties. A, seated. B, couchant. C, walking.

Period. XVIII to Roman. Very common on necklaces of XXIInd and XXIIIrd dynasty.

Figures. Type A, **224**a, silver, group 16; **224**b, c, light green glaze; **224**d, green glaze burnt brown; **224**d 2, blue and black glaze; **224**d 3, olive glaze; **224**e, light blue glaze; **224**e 2, bronze; **224**f, blue and black glaze, Dendereh, Ptolemaic, group 21; **224**g, blue glaze, with yellow points, Roman. Type B, **224**h, lion or cat; **224**j, cat, green glaze, XIth dynasty, Kafr Ammar; **224**k, blue glazed schist, *Ymenf* on base, XVIII; **224**k 2, blue-glazed pottery; **224**l, dark blue paste, *Amen-ra* in cartouche on base, dubious. Type C, **224**m, blue glaze, Dendereh, Ptolemaic, group 21.

Materials. Green glaze 22, Blue glaze 13, Bronze 9, Grey glaze 3, Carnelian 1, Yellow glaze 1, Black glaze 1, Purple glaze 1, Black limestone 1, Silver 1, Blue paste 1.

Position. Feet (1).

Collections. Turin 13, Univ. Coll. P. 12, E. 4, Cairo 11, St. Petersburg 10, Edinburgh 3, Murch 3.

225. CAT IN SHRINE.

Period. XXVI.

Figure. **225**, green glaze, papyrus stem and head on each of the three sides, Memphis. Also a rough solid imitation, green glaze (Edw.)

Collection. Univ. Coll. P. 1, E. 1.

226. TWO CATS ON COLUMN.

Varieties. Three in Cairo have only one cat on the column.

Period. XXIII.

Figures. **226**a, b, green glaze, octagonal column, blundered inscription on front, "Speech of Bastet lady of Pa Bastet"; **226**c (pl. xliii), column with feet of cat, inscribed "Speech of Bastet . . ."

Materials. Green glaze 6.

Collections. Cairo 4, Univ. Coll. P. 2.

227. CAT AND KITTENS.

Varieties. A, seated. B, couchant.

Period. XXII to XXVI.

Figures. **227**a, bronze, two kittens; **227**b, light green glaze, five kittens, three in front, one each side; **227**c, green glaze, one kitten.

Materials. Green glaze 7, Green-glazed stone 2, Purple glaze 1, Carnelian 1, Bronze 1.

Collections. Cairo A, 3 (3, 6 and 9 kittens), B, 6, Univ. Coll. P. 3.

228. SET ANIMAL.

Period. XIX (?).

Figures. **228**a, light blue glaze, impressed plaque; **228**b, dark blue glaze, perhaps Mentu as a hawk-headed lion (see also **183** for set, and engraved stone **135** g).

Collection. Univ. Coll. P. 2.

229. JACKAL STANDING.

Name. *Upuatu.*

Meaning. "Opener of ways" for the soul (see **198**).

Figures. **229**a, light blue glaze; **229**b, c, bronze; **229**d, bronze, and d 2, green glaze, with the two serpents in front (compare the two serpents that led the way for Alexander to the Oasis); **229**e, bronze, the four Upuats (of the four quarters) who open the way for the sun in the underworld (LANZ., *Diz. Mit.*, cclvi).

Materials. Bronze 5, Green glaze 1, Blue glaze 1.

Collections. Univ. Coll. P. 5, St. Petersburg 2, Cairo 1.

230. TWO JACKAL HEADS.

Name. *Upuatu* of the south and north.

Figure. **230**, hard brown limestone, pierced under the tip of the ears, flat base.

Collection. Univ. Coll. P. 1.

231. JACKAL COUCHANT.

Name. *Anpu*, Anubis.

Meaning, The guardian of the cemetery, and of the dead in the judgment.

Varieties. A, on ground. B, on shrine.

Period. XXVI to Roman.

Figures. Type A, **231**a, blue glaze, XIX; **231**b, blue glass Ptolemaic; **231**c, blue and black glaze, Dendereh, Ptolemaic, group 21. Type B, **231**d, e, pewter plates with *za* serpent above, group 18; **231**f, g, h, blue and black glaze, Dendereh, Ptolemaic, group 21; **231**j, green glazed schist (pl. xxxviii).

Materials. Blue glaze 8, Black glass 3, Blue glass 1, Pewter 2, Haematite 1, Blue paste 1, Green glaze 1, Grey glaze 1, Bronze 1, Wood 3.

Position. Chest (3); stomach (3).

Collections. Turin 9, Univ. Coll. P. 8, Athens 4, St. Petersburg 2, Murch 2.

232. SHREW MOUSE.

Meaning. Sacred to Horus and Uazet. Passed round boils as a charm (PLINY, xxx, 34).

Varieties. A, standing. B, on box.

Figures. Type A, **232**a, b, c, d, e, bronze. Type B, **232f**, bronze, as also two at St. Petersburg.

Collections. Univ. Coll. P. 5, St. Petersburg 2.

233. DOG.

Meaning. As these dogs are all short-legged, they probably refer to watching and guarding the person, and not to hunting.

Period. Roman and Coptic.

Figures. **233**a, b, bronze; **233**c, red coral, dog seated; **233**d, dark blue glaze with yellow points, Roman, group 22; **233**e, mother of pearl, Coptic; **233**f, f 2, light blue glaze, dog lying down.

Materials. Green glaze 3, Blue glaze 2, Bronze 2, "Black and white stone" (Cairo) 2, Syenite 1, Red coral 1, Shell 1.

Collections. Univ. Coll. P. 6, Cairo 4 (2 seated, 1 lying paws crossed, 1 curled up), Murch 1.

234. PIG.

Names. *Apeh, Rera, Sāau.*

Meaning. Sacrificed to Osiris annually. Pig standard of the sixth and seventh months, Mekhir and Phamenoth (LANZ., *Diz. Mit.*, vii).

Period. XXVI.

Figures. **234**a, b, light blue glaze; **234**c, c 2, light green glaze. All sows.

Materials. Green glaze 20, Blue glaze 11, Black glaze 2, Yellow glaze 1.

Collections. Cairo 18, St. Petersburg 7, Turin 3, Univ. Coll. P. 3, E. 2, Athens 2.

235. HIPPOPOTAMUS.

Name. *Apt.*

Meaning. Sacred as Taurt (see **236**).

Period. Prehistoric. Copper plate, XVIII (?).

Figures. **235**a, noble serpentine, hippopotamus feeding, under the base a wavy line in relief, perhaps a serpent; **235**b, c, brown steatite; **235**d, pink limestone, a frequent ornament for attachment to legs of water skins; **235**d 2, small, round, dolomite, Tarkhan, 1292; **235**e, copper plate.

Materials. Brown steatite 2, Pink limestone 1, Noble serpentine 1, Copper 1, [Green glaze 1, "White stone" 1, Blue glass 1, Cairo.]

Collections. Univ. Coll. P. 5, Cairo 3.

236. TAURT.

Name. *Taurt.*

Meaning. "The great one," the goddess of pregnancy.

Varieties. A, flat. B, round. C, double.

Period. A, VI to XVIII. B, XVIII to Ptolemaic.

Figures. Type A, **236**a, blue glaze, VIth dynasty, Zaraby; **236**b, c, bone, VIth dynasty, group 8. B, **236**d, greenish limestone with gold crown, XXVI, group 15. A, **236**e, f, indigo blue glaze, XVIIIth dynasty; **236**g, indigo blue glaze, Tell Amarna, XVIIIth dynasty; **236**g 2, schist, blue-glazed, XIIth dynasty, Kahun; **236**h, mottled glass, black, white, blue and red, XVIII; **236**j, violet glass, XVIII; **236**j 2, blue glazed schist; **236**k, black steatite, XIX; **236**l, green-glazed schist; **236**m, green glaze; **236**n, violet glass, XVIII; **236**n 2 to 17, necklace of blue glaze, XVIII; **236**o, lazuli, group 28 (pl. xlv); **236**o 2, o 3 (pl. xlv), blue glaze, XIIth dynasty, Kahun. B, **236**p, green glaze, black hair and back; **236**q, bronze; **236**q 2, green glaze; **236**r, white glaze with yellow feathers, fine work, XVIII (?); **236**s, t, green glaze, XXVI; **236**u, red jasper for inlay; **236**v, w, w 2, 3, 4, 5, 6, green glaze; **236**x, bronze; **236**y 2, 3, 4, green glaze; **236**z, glass, burnt; **236**aa, blue glaze, Dendereh, Ptolemaic, group 21. C, **236**ab, double Taurt, violet glaze XVIIIth dynasty. A, **236**ac, black and white serpentine (pl. xlvi).

Materials. Blue glaze 54, Green glaze 51, Yellow glaze 2, Grey glaze 2, Lazuli 2, Violet glass 2, Bronze 2, Haematite 3, Bone 2, Porphyry 1, Red glaze 1, White glaze 1, Violet glaze 1, Red-grey glaze 1, Blue glass 1, Mottled glass 1, Schist green-glazed 1, Schist blue-glazed 2, Jasper 1, Black steatite 1, Limestone 1, Breccia 1, Serpentine 1.

Positions. Diaphragm (2); stomach (1); feet (1).

Collections. Cairo 45, Univ. Coll. P. 41, E. 10, Turin 34, St. Petersburg 25, Murch 5.

237. HIPPOPOTAMUS HEAD.

Period. VIth to XIIth dynasties.

Figures. **237**a, green glaze on schist, button seal with head of Hathor and serpents; **237**b, sard, head and fore-paws broken from a figure; **237**c, carnelian, group 3; **237**d, e, f, carnelian, group 14; **237**g, deep red sard; **237**h, j, k, l, amethyst; **237**m, carnelian; **237**n, black-green jasper; **237**o, p, black-green serpentine; **237**q, green glaze, XIth dynasty, Diospolis.

Materials. Green felspar 18, Amethyst 13, Carnelian 9, Black serpentine 3, Sard 2, Black jasper 1, Glazed schist 1, Green glaze 1.

Collections. Murch 32, Univ. Coll. P. 16.

238. HEDGEHOG.

Period. XX to XXVI (?).

Figure. **238**, on base a fish and a crocodile. (All have incised bases.)

Materials. Green glaze 7, Blue glaze 8, Agate 1, "White stone" 1, Brown agate 1, Black glaze 1, Schist 1 (above), Steatite white glaze 1, Steatite green glaze 1.

Collections. Athens 7, Cairo 6, Alnwick 2, Univ. Coll. P. 1, Murch 1.

239. TURTLE (*Trionyx Triunguis*).

Name. *Opesh.*

Meaning. The animal of death and darkness. The Book of the Dead in Chapter 36 reads: "Chapter whereby the Opshait is kept back. Away from me, thou with parted lips! I am Khnumu the lord of Shennu, who am bringing the words of the gods to Ra, and I announce the news to Nebes." In late papyri it is turned into a blackbeetle; but the name shows it to be the turtle.

Period. Prehistoric to XIIth dynasty (?).

Figures. **239**a, brown agate; **239**b, carnelian; **239**b 2, 3, black serpentine.

Materials. Amethyst **2**, Carnelian 2, Black serpentine 2, Porphyry 1, Brown agate 1, Limestone 1; and coiled gold wire (see *Desc. Eg.*, V, 59, 26—7).

Collections. Univ. Coll. P. 4, Murch 5.

240. CROCODILE.

Name. A, *Hor am utu* (Lanz., *Diz. Mit.*, ccxvii). B, *Emsehu.*

Meaning. Emblem of Sebek the crocodile god.

Varieties. A, hawk-headed and winged, as identified with Horus. B, normal. C, capturing a boy. D, double. E, seven together. F, with feathers, disc and horns.

Period. XIIth to Roman.

Figures. Type A, **240**a, bronze, the Sebek-Ra crocodile, with hawk head, and wings raised, on the head a crown of uraei, two horns and the papyrus crown; upon a corniced stand, without inscription. Type B, **240**b, sard; **240**c, haematite; **240**d, grey steatite, Roman; **240**e, dark blue glaze, XVIII; **240**e, **2**, **3**, rough blue glaze, XIth dynasty, Kafr Ammar; **240f**, black steatite, Roman; **240**g, light green glaze, Memphis; **240**h, blue glaze with yellow points, Roman; **240**j, shell, Coptic (pl. xlii). Type C, **240**k, bronze, crocodile with boy in his mouth, the lower jaw on the front of the boy, and the suspension ring under the throat, Memphis. Type D, **240**l, two crocodiles, grey steatite. Type B, **240**m (xlvi), green glaze, and m 2, 3, **4**, 5, Nebesheh. Type F, **240**n (xlvii), bronze.

Materials. Green glaze 29, Blue glaze 15, Steatite 4, Yellow glaze 1, Grey glaze 1, Bronze 3, Sard 1, Haematite 1, Porphyry.

Collections. Cairo 26, Univ. Coll. P. 12, E. 6, St. Petersburg **4**, Turin 4, Murch 1.

241. WARAN (*Varanus niloticus*).

The short puffy body and narrow tail distinguish this from the crocodile figures.

Period. Prehistoric.

Figure. **241**, ivory, suspension hole under chest.

Collection. Univ. Coll. P. 1.

242. LIZARD.

Period. XXVI.

Figure. **242**, light green glaze, suspension ring at each end, Memphis.

Collection. Univ. Coll. P. 1.

243. MENTU STANDARD.

Meaning. Protection of the god of war. No. **243f**, and perhaps others, seem to be "the harpoon of Horus of Edfu" (Mar., *Dend.*, iii, 63 c).

Varieties. A, with the lance or harpoon point. B, with the aegis of Mentu.

Period. XIXth to XXVth dynasty.

Figures and Materials. A, **243**a, bronze, lance head above the head of Mentu; **243**b, bronze, with the lance head and a hawk over the head of Mentu, forked base to the staff; **243**c, ebony, the Mentu head at the base of a harpoon; **243**d, grey steatite, the lance head above the Mentu head, forked below; B, **243**e, dark blue glaze, aegis of Mentu on head of staff, XXI (?); **243f**, bronze, head of Mentu with disc; **243**g, bronze, aegis of Mentu on staff, double feathers on head, uraeus at each side. (See three large examples from Koptos at Berlin. *Koptos*, xxi. 4, 5, 6.)

Collection. Univ. Coll. P. 7; Berlin 3.

244. HAWK-HEADED SPHINX.

Meaning. The king as Mentu.

Period. XIX.

Figure. **244**, red jasper, with cartouche of Rameses II. on base.

Collection. Univ. Coll. P. 1 (see **218**, as sphinx).

245. HAWK, FALCON.

This royal bird is more correctly called a falcon.

Name. *Bak* (MacG. 55); *Săt* (MacG. 24, B. D. G. 982) = the bandaged hawk (Lacau, 95).

Meanings. The bird of Horus of Edfu. The king's soul. Hawk of Sopd or Seker.

Varieties. A, alone. B, with uraei. C, in shrine. D, of east and west. E, mummified.

Period. Prehistoric to Ptolemaic.

Figures. Type A, **245**a, yellow and black serpentine; **245**b, c, bone; **245**d, greenish limestone; **245**e, bone; **245**e 2, sard, Tarkhan, 1626; **245f**, noble serpentine; **245**g, ivory; **245**h (pl. xlii), grey steatite, all prehistoric; **245**j, j 2, j 3, j 4, bone, VIth dynasty, group 4; **245**k, bone, group 8, VIth dynasty; **245**l, green felspar; **245**l 2, blue glaze, Hu, XIth dynasty; **245**m, n, o, amethyst; **245**p, q, carnelian, group 14: h—q, VIth to XIIth dynasty; **245**r, dark indigo glaze, XVIII (?); **245**s, green glaze, VIth dynasty (?); **245**s 2, sard, Riqqeh, XII; **245**t, green schist; **245**u (xlii), blue glaze, Dendereh, Ptolemaic, group 21; **245**v (xlii), green glaze, on shoulders of Isis; **245**w, black jasper; **245**x, jade, fine work; **245**y, y 2, y 3, y 4, green glaze; **245z**, light blue glaze; **245**aa, hard green limestone; **245**ab, green glaze; **245**ab 2, blue paste, Naukratis; **245**ac, green glass burnt; **245**ac 2, steatite, Nebesheh; **245**ad—ad 4, gold, XVIIIth dynasty, ad 2, larger, silver (see pl. xlv); **245**ae, bronze; **245**af, af 2, af 3, green glaze; **245**ag, blue and black glaze, head turned sideways, Dendereh, Ptolemaic, group 21: **245**ah, blue and black glaze, group 21; **245**aj, light blue glaze, group 21; **245**ak (pl. xlv), red glass, for inlay; **245**al (pl. xlv), silver on resin body, XIIth dynasty. Type B, **245**am, black steatite, Horus with the serpents of south and north, as described in the battles of Horus and Set at Edfu, reverse Horus in triumph (pl. xliii); **245**an, lead plate, the crowned hawk with the serpent before him, and Isis behind him. Type C, **245**ao, blue paste shrine, containing bust of hawk; above it a cornice of seven uraei; on each side the hawk-headed Horus-Ra seated, crowned with disc and crescent; on back a scarab; **245**ap, blue paste shrine, head of the hawk from it here put at the side of it; over the door the disc and serpents, above that the disc and wings; on the side the Horus-Ra seated, on the lotus, and behind that the winged hawk on the *neb*; on the back the disc and scarab; **245**aq, light blue glaze, shrine with hawk and Isis seated before it, Dendereh, Ptolemaic, group 21, as also next two. Type D, **245**ar, hawk crowned with disc, *abt* hieroglyph of the east behind it; **245**as, hawk crowned with feathers, *ament*, west, behind it, both light blue glaze. Type E, gold, Horuza, Cairo. Type A, **245**at (pl. xlvi), quartz crystal.

Materials. Green felspar 42, Amethyst 31, Green glaze 24, Blue glaze 20, Lazuli 26, Bone 8, Gold 6, Bronze 3, Steatite 4, Serpentine 3, Haematite 2, Carnelian 7, Green limestone 3, Blue paste 3, 1 each of Silver, Lead, Quartz crystal, Black jasper, Jade, Green schist, Green glass, Red glass, Yellow glaze, Violet glaze, Grey glaze.

Position. Chest (11); stomach (3).

Collections. Murch 89, Univ. Coll. P. 51, E. 8, Cairo 22, Alnwick 16, St. Petersburg 10, Turin 9, Athens 5.

246. OSTRICH.

Period. Prehistoric.

Figure. **246**, brown serpentine, ostrich seated.

Collection. Univ. Coll. P. 1.

247. IBIS.

Name. *Hàbu*, whence Greek *ibis*.

Meaning. The emblem of Tehuti, the god of wisdom.

Period. XVIII to Roman.

Figures. **247**a, gold, a 2, without feather; **247**b, c, d, bronze; **247**e, blue glaze with black head and tail, inscribed on base "Lord of Khemnu (give life to) Hor-aä-pa-khred"; **247**f, green glaze, Kafr Ammar, XIth dynasty, group 25; **247**g, blue glaze; **247**g 2, green glaze, standing; **247**h, h 2, 3, light blue-green glaze; **247**j, blue glaze, dark blue tail; **247**k, green glaze, Dendereh, Ptolemaic, group 21; **247**l, blue glaze with yellow points, Roman.

Materials. Green glaze 11, Blue glaze 10, Bronze 5, Gold 2, Steatite 1, Lazuli 1.

Collections. Univ. Coll. P. 12, St. Petersburg 8, Turin 5, Alnwick 3, Murch 2.

248. VULTURE.

Name. *Naur.*

Meaning. Devotion to the goddess Mut.

Figures. **248a**, bronze; **248**b, grey limestone (see No. **94**). The latter may perhaps be an eagle.

249. VULTURE FLYING.

Period. XXVI (?).

Figures. **249**a, green-glazed pottery; **249**b, blue-glazed.

Collection. Univ. Coll. P. 2.

250. GOAT SUCKER (*Caprimulgus*).

Period. Prehistoric.

Figures. **253**a, ivory; **250**b, carnelian.

Collection. Univ. Coll. P. 2.

251. BIRD HEADS.

Period. Prehistoric.

Figures. **251**a, b, c, slate; **251**d, slate, 1781 Naqadeh; **251**e, slate, 146 Naqadeh; **251**f, slate, 1865 Naqadeh.

Collection. Univ. Coll. P. 6.

252. COPTIC BIRD AMULETS.

Period. Coptic.

Figures. **252**a, b, b 2, c, c 2, d, shell, perhaps intended for the hoopoe.

Collection. Univ. Coll. P. 5.

253. BIRD'S FOOT.

Period. Coptic.

Figure. **253**, wood, natural branching twigs, the left one broken, Illahun.

Collection. Univ. Coll. P. 1.

254. SERPENT WITH ARMS.

Name. *Nehebka*, one of the 42 judges of the dead.

Meaning. In the Xth domain of the underworld, Nehebkau points out the way to the dead (Book of the Dead, Chapter 149), and the dead says that he "moves eternally like Nehebkau" (Chapter 17). As an amulet, therefore, it is a guide to the soul.

Varieties. A, serpent body. B, human body.

Period. About XXth dynasty.

Figures. **254**a, dull green glaze; **254**b, deep blue glaze; **254**b 2, 3, green glaze; **254**c, green glaze, group 19. B, seated, **254d** (xlvi), d 2, blue glaze, and Cairo.

Collections. Univ. Coll. P. 5, Cairo 1.

255. QARMUT (*Clarias anguillaris*).

Name. *Nar* (in name of early King Narmer).

Meaning. Sacred fish of Mendes, worn on head of Hamehyt, goddess of Mendes.

Figures and Materials. **255**a, b, Silver, XIIth dynasty (?); **255**c, Bone, prehistoric (?) (see **173**).

Collection. Univ. Coll. P. 3.

A fish carved in bone is an amulet against the evil eye in Italy (BELL., xii, 23), and an emblem of fecundity (BELL., *Fet.*, 42).

256. OXYRHYNKHOS (*Mormyrus*).

Name. *Mazed;* as shown by the city Oxyrhynkhos being called Pa-mazed, and *Mizz* or *Mizdeh* being the modern local name of this fish in that district.

Period. XXVI (?).

Figure. **256**, bronze, with horned disc and uraeus on the head.

Collection. Univ. Coll. P. 1.

257. BULTI (*Tilapia nilotica*).

Period. XII to Roman.

Figures. **257**a, bronze; **257**a 2, green glaze, XIIth dynasty, Kahun; **257**b, glazed schist, inscribed below in cartouche . . . *men-neb*; **257**c, grey steatite, Koptos; **257**d, violet glaze, XVIII; **257**e—e 6, carnelian, XVIII; **257**f, gold with green-grey wax inlay, from Nubia (pl. xlvi).

Collection. Univ. Coll. P. **11**.

258. ELECTRIC FISH (*Malopterurus electricus*).

Period. XVIII.

Figure. **258**a—a 7, (pl. xlv) green (6) and violet (1) glaze.

Collection. Univ. Coll. P. 7.

259. LEPIDOTOS (*Barbus bynni*).

Name. *Penpennu* (?), modern *Binny*.

Meaning. Sacred fish at Thebes.

Figures. See Cairo Catalogue.

Materials. Green glazed stone 5, Blue glazed 4, Green glass 1, Amethyst 1 (all Cairo), Sard 1 (Athens).

Collections. Cairo 11, Athens 1.

260. SCORPION.

Name. *Selk.*

Meaning. Emblem of the goddess Selket, one of the four divinities guarding the tomb.

Period. Prehistoric to XXVI.

Figures. **260**a, noble serpentine; **260**b, sard, tail broken off; **260**b 2, sard, Tarkhan; **260**c, bronze, with head of goddess crowned with disc and horns, rising from the scorpion.

Collections. Univ. Coll. P. 4, Edinburgh 1, blue glaze.

261. GREEN BEETLE.

Period. Prehistoric to XII.

Figures. **261a**, noble serpentine (see *Naqada*, lviii); **261a** 2, quartz crystal, Tarkhan; **261**b—b 5, green glaze, Kahun, XIIth dynasty.

Materials. Green glaze 6, Serpentine 1, Carnelian 1, blackened limestone 1.

Collections. Univ. Coll. P. 6, Murch 3.

262. SHUTTLE, OR WINDING FRAME.

Meaning. Emblem of the goddess Neit, one of the four divinities guarding the tomb.

Period. XXVI.

Figures. **262**a, agate; **262**b, carnelian, probably an early form of this sign.

Materials. Carnelian 3, Veined quartz 2, Agate 2, Onyx 1, Alabaster 1, Limestone 1.

Collections. Cairo 7, Univ. Coll. P. 2, St. Petersburg 2, Price 1, Alnwick 1.

263. WOMAN WITH OFFERINGS.

Period. XXVI.

Figure. **263**, light green glaze, woman wearing long flap garment down the back, fringed at the sides, the right hand holding the horns of a gazelle, the left carrying a long jar by a top handle.

Collection. Univ. Coll. P. 1.

264. FIGURE IN TALL HEAD-DRESS.

Period. Prehistoric (?).

Figure. **264**, ivory, tall pointed head-dress, ears projecting as in figures of Ist dynasty, arms raised over chest.

Collection. Univ. Coll. P. 1.

265. FIGURE IN LONG ROBE.

Period. Prehistoric (?), XXII (?).

Figures. **265**a, alabaster, with large collar, and round robe to feet; **265**b (pl. xlv), ebony.

Collection. Univ. Coll. P. 2.

266. FIGURE IN POINTED CAP.

Period. VIth dynasty.

Figures. **266**a, b, sard, group 14.

Collection. Univ. Coll. P. 2.

267. FLOWER.

Period. XXVI to XXX.

Figures. **267**a, blue glaze, Memphis; **267**b, glaze faded white, Memphis, a button; **267**c, green glaze, lotus, XXth dynasty (?) (pl. xlv).

Collection. Univ. Coll. P. 3.

268. PALM COLUMN.

Period. Ptolemaic.

Figure. **268**, blue glass burnt.

Collection. Univ. Coll. P. 1.

269. BUNCH OF GRAPES.

Period. Roman.

Figure. **269**, blue glaze, frothy and bad.

Collection. Univ. Coll. P. 1, with **221**d, similar work.

MISCELLANEOUS AMULETS

270. FLOWERING REED (*Calamus*).

Period. Ptolemaic.
Figure. **270**, blue and black glaze, Dendereh, group 21.
Position. Chest.
Collection. Univ. Coll. P. 1.

271. SEED VESSEL.

Period. XVIII to XIX.
Figure. **271**, blue glaze. Common on necklaces in carnelian and in glaze.
Collection. Univ. Coll. P. many.

272. UNKNOWN OBJECT.

Period. VI.
Figure. **272** a, b, sard.
Collection. Univ. Coll. P. 2.

273. TWO FINGERS.

Name. *Zebo ne dens rud* (MacG. 58).
Meaning. "Finger of heavy stone, at the girdle."
Varieties. Two fingers of right or left hand.
Period. XXVI.
Figures. **273**a, brown limestone, gilt; **273**b, opaque obsidian; **273**c, opaque obsidian, right hand; **273**d, dark purple glass, left; **273**d 2, black glass; **273**e, black glass, left; **273**f, black basalt, right: **273**f 2, brown limestone; **273**g, black basalt; **273**g 2, brown basalt (?); **273**h, light blue glaze, right, Dendereh, Ptolemaic, group 21.
Materials (omitting those in Cairo as uncertain). Black basalt 8, Obsidian 6, Black glass 3, Brown steatite 2, Blue glaze 2, Haematite 1, Purple glass 2, Brown glass 1, Black glass 1, Slate 1, Brown limestone 2, Blackened limestone 1, Brown basalt 1.
Position. Usually left side of pelvis, sometimes base of stomach, or middle of stomach, never higher.
Collections. Cairo 30 R, 2 L, British Museum 10 R, 2 L, Univ. Coll. P. 8, E. 3 (6 R, 2 L), St. Petersburg 4, Murch 3, Price 2, Alnwick 2, Turin 1.

274. UNCERTAIN PENDANTS.

Period. Roman.
Figures. **274**a, black steatite; **274**b, brown haematite.
Collection. Univ. Coll. P. 2.

275. STAR.

Period. XIIth dynasty, Ptolemaic.
Figures. **275**a, blue glaze, XIIth dynasty, Kahun; **275**b, light blue glaze, Dendereh, group 21.
Position. Throat (1); Stomach (1).
Collection. Univ. Coll. P. 2.

CHAPTER X

THE POSITIONS OF AMULETS

In the preceding catalogue the positions of amulets have been stated; and as very few plans of sets of amulets have yet been published, it seems well to set out now the plans which I have long had recorded. These plans were gathered at Hawara, 8 of the XXVIth dynasty; at Abydos, 2 of the XXXth dynasty; at Nebesheh, 4 about the same age; and at Dendereh, 10 of the Ptolemaic age. The last of these groups was recorded by Mr. N. de G. Davies, the Abydos groups by my wife, and the other three groups by myself.

The twenty-four plans of amulet groups are drawn in position on pls. l to liii. Each plan has the site at the top left, and the reference number at the top right hand. Down the side of each plan are letters, T, C, P, etc., indicating the position of the lines of amulets upon the mummies, the meaning of these letters being stated at the beginning of pl. liv. This same plate serves to find all the instances of any amulet, having first the number of the amulet in the catalogue, then the name of the amulet, the numbers of the plans in which it occurs, and the letters of the rows in the plans. These last letters serve also to show at once, without reference to the plans, at what parts of the mummies any amulet is found. The actual drawings here are rather spread out for clearness, so that the lower lines of amulets come lower than their exact places on the mummies: one of the closest is No. 6, on which all the rows from T to the scarabs and eyes in U, were all within 12 inches of height, or from the clavicle to the umbilicus. The materials are listed below No. 1, and the initial letters of the material are placed by the amulets where the material is recorded. All of the Dendereh amulets, 15 — 24, are of blue glaze with black painting.

As on such a scale the distinctions of the minute statuettes of gods would not be clear, the names of the gods are stated instead of a figure. Some of the figures—such as the scarabs—are only conventional, in order to make them as clear as might be. There are obviously certain changing fashions in the kinds and positions of amulets. In the XXVIth dynasty we see a row of *zad* signs across the stomach, above or below them a triad of Isis, Nebhat, and Horus. Rather later were added the counterpoise at the nape of the neck, and the serpent head at the throat. The mummy on the bier, the mourners, and the lion, are Ptolemaic. Many other distinctions between these different ages may be noticed in the arrangements.

THE POSITIONS OF AMULETS

One of the few records of the positions of amulets is from one of the priests of Amen (*Ann. Serv.*, VIII, 35). As this bore dates on the linen of Pisebkhanu son of Pinezem 1006—952 B.C., and the 8th year of Siamen 1014 B.C., it is probably a few years before 1000 B.C. All the groups here given are much later, so this set is important. On the neck was a string of amulets, an *uzat*, uraeus, and vulture, of gold, scarab and engraved *uzat* of lazuli. On clavicle, a hawk of gilt bronze. Pectoral, greenstone scarab. Umbilical, big blue scarab between hands. Over incision in left flank, a plate of copper. Between the legs, a papyrus, the usual position in this age. Under the left hand, a wax figure of Hapi. On left ulna, a long bead of blue paste (the name badge 77), a scarab and an *uzat*. On a string at the side, probably intended to lay across the chest, a uraeus, *uzat*, scarab, heart, *zad*, and two papyrus sceptres. The mummies of the XVIIIth to XXth dynasties have very few amulets. In the Old Kingdom amulets are commoner, usually on necklaces and wrists (see *Deshasheh*, xxvi).

PROPERTIES OF STONES.

Besides the meanings attached to various forms of amulets, the material is also looked on as having important influence. Often the form is disregarded, so long as the special material can be obtained; a mere lump of the required stone, or a plain bead or pendant of it, is sufficient. These properties attributed to the materials are only recorded in general for Italy, by Pliny anciently, and by Bellucci in modern times. These authors are referred to by P. or B.

Adamas, diamond. For poison or delirium, P. xxxvii, 15.

Lead. For suppuration in swine, B. viii, 16, 24.

Pyrites, crystal. To preserve the eyes, B. viii, 23.

Haematite, blood red. Reveals treachery; for success in petitions, P. xxxvii, 60; stops bleeding, B. viii, 17.

Siderites, black haematite, or meteorite. Causes discord in law suits, P. xxxvii, 67; for witchery and evil eye, B. viii, 17.

Apsyctos (haematite?). Against cold, P. xxxvii, 54.

Limonite (hydrous iron oxide) concretion. For pregnancy, P. viii, Am. 19, Fet. 94—5.

Sapphire. For headache: promotes contentment, B. v. 26.

Paeanitis, like ice, quartz crystal. For parturition, P. xxxvii, 66; evil eye, B. x, Am. 64.

Amethyst. For intoxication, P. xxxvii, 15; against spells, hail and locusts, and for access to kings, P. xxxvii, 40.

Chalcedony, white, "milk stone." For increase of milk, B. vi.

Chalcedony, red, "blood stone." For bleeding, especially of nose, B, vi.

Opal. To strengthen the sight. Jackson, "Minerals and their uses."

Agate, concentric, "eye stone." Evil eye, B. vi, Fet. 52.

Agate, Egyptian. Against scorpions, P. xxxvii, 54.

Jaspis, jasper. For public speaking, P. xxxvii, 37.

Heliotropium, blood jasper. For invisibility, P. xxxvii, 60; to stop bleeding, B. v, Am. 18, Fet. 88, 89.

Black jasper, *baetuli* and *keranniae*. Potent in taking cities and fleets, P. xxxvii, 51; against lightning and evil, B. i—iii.

Staurolite. Against witchery, B. v. 27.

Lyncurion, jacinth or yellow quartz. Against jaundice, P. xxxvii, 13.

Smaragdus, emerald. As amethyst, P. xxxvii, 40; for parturition, Jackson.

Jadeite, nephrite. For kidney disease, B. iv.

Amianthus. Against spells, P. xxxvi, 31.

Garnet. For widows, comfort in misfortune, B. v. 10.

Serpentine. Against headache and serpent bites, P. xxxvi, 11; xxxvii, 54; disc, against reptile bites, B. iv, Am. 17; cylinder, phallic, against evil eye, B. iv.

Soapstone, white, mixed in water. For increase of milk, P. xxxvii, 59.

Malachite, "peacock stone." Preserves infants, P. xxxvii, 36; for evil eye, B. x.

Alabaster. For increase of milk, B. vi.

Limestone disc. To get dirt from eye, B. viii, 18; with dendrite, against venom, B. viii, 19.

Selenite. For increase of milk, B. vi; against evil eye, B. x.

Amber. For throat affections, P. xxxvii, 11; on neck for fevers, P. xxxvii, 12; against witchery, B. v.

Coral, white, "milk stone." For increase of milk, B. ix.

Coral, red. Evil eye and menstruation, B. ix, Am. 28, Fet. 46.

Ammonite. Gives prophetic dreams, sacred in Ethiopia, P. xxxvii, 60.

Madrepore. Evil eye and witchery, B. vii, Am. 33; worms in children.

Holed stone. Against witchery, B. viii.

LIST OF GROUPS OF AMULETS

Various strings of beads and amulets have been bought which obviously belong together, by their uniformity of style and material; and although the localities from which they come are not known, it is desirable to keep the record of their grouping. Such are noted by the number of the group when described in the Catalogue, and the list of references to each group is given here. Groups 1 to 13 belong probably to about the VIth dynasty.

Group 1. Types **2**a; **12**a 1—3; **12**b, 2, 3; **12**c 2—4; **15**e 4; **22**f 2; **111**d; **138**b.

Group 2. **2**b; **15**a 2; **15**e 5, 6; **111**f, g, h; **113**d; **138**c; **138**h 2.

Group 3. **2**c; **12**a, b, b 4, c 5; **22**b; **47**a; **111**j; **113**c, c 2; **138**j, j 2, 3, k, k 2; **237**c.

Group 4. **170**d; **205**a; **245**j 1—4.

Group 5. **2**d, e; **27**a, b; **94**a; **113**b; **138**h; **170**c, c 2; **219**d, d 2, 3.

Group 6. **12**a 4; **29**b; **94**b; **206**a.

Group 7. **2**f 2; **12**a 5; **15**c 3; **22**c 2, e 2; **29**a; **94**a 2; **138**d; **138**g 2, j 4; **220**a.

Group 8. **12**a 6; **22**a; **94**c; **138**a; **145**a; **206**b; **236**b, c; **245**k.

Group 9. **2**b 2; **206**c.

Group 10. **22**d 2; **27**b 2.

Group 11. **11**a; **219**k, k 2.

Group 12. **2**f; **206**d.

Group 13. **12**c; **22**c; **77**d; **123**a; **138**f; **185**a—d.

Group 14. VIth to XIIth dynasty. **15**f; **111**c; **129**a, b, b 2; **138**g; **185**g, h; **237**d, e, f; **245**h—q; **266**a, b.

Group 15. From a few miles north of Abydos. **146**; **149**f; **170**a; **236**d.

Group 16. XXVIth dynasty (?). **33**e; **145**f, g; **148**h; **149**g; **164**c; **170**b; **194**e; **224**a.

Group 17. Memphis, XXVI, necklace. **145**j; **175**e.

Group 18. Sheet pewter, figures stamped. **95**c; **149**h; **180**g; **182**b; **202**e, e 2; **231**d, e.

Group 20. Wax impressed, Dendereh, Ptolemaic. **8**a; **30**e; **68**d; **71**c; **88**l; **150**a, b, b 2; **155**a; **156**a, a 2; **157**d; **208**e.

Group 21. From various Ptolemaic tombs, Dendereh. **7**p; **8**b; **28**d; **30**a; **34**e; **36**g; **37**f; **40**b; **58**t, u; **59**d; **71**a, b; **79**c; **84**b: **87**c; **93**e, f; **150**c—h; **155**b; **156**b; **157**f; **180**j; **182**q, r; **197**j; **206**l; **208**f; **211**k; **219**j; **224**f, m; **231**c, f, g, h; **236**aa; **245**u, ag, ah, aj, aq, ar, as; **247**k; **270**; **273**h; **275**b.

Group 22. **13**b; **145**w, x; **149**l; **233**d.

Group 23. **16**b, b 2; **161**j.

Group 24. Tell Amarna, Roman. **74**a, b; **133**j.

Group 25. Kafr Ammar, XIth dynasty. **247**f.

Group 26. Dendereh, Ptolemaic. **7**n; **40**c, d; **88**p; **92**j; **156**c.

Group 27. Memphis, jewellery. **16**c, d; **85**d, e, f; **149**k.

Group 28. **49**d; **88**d, e.

Group 30. VIth dynasty. **22**g 2; **113**e; **138**e; **185**e, f, f 2.

Group 31. Illahun, XXVth dynasty. **34**d 2; **90**aa.

Note.—On pl. xl an unnumbered figure, which entered the collection after cataloguing, has not been described. It is a bronze figure of a hawk with ram's head and human arms. See Lanz., *Diz. Mit.*, cliii p. 558.

INDEX

INDEX

INDEX

INDEX

SIMILARS: PARTS OF HUMAN BODY.

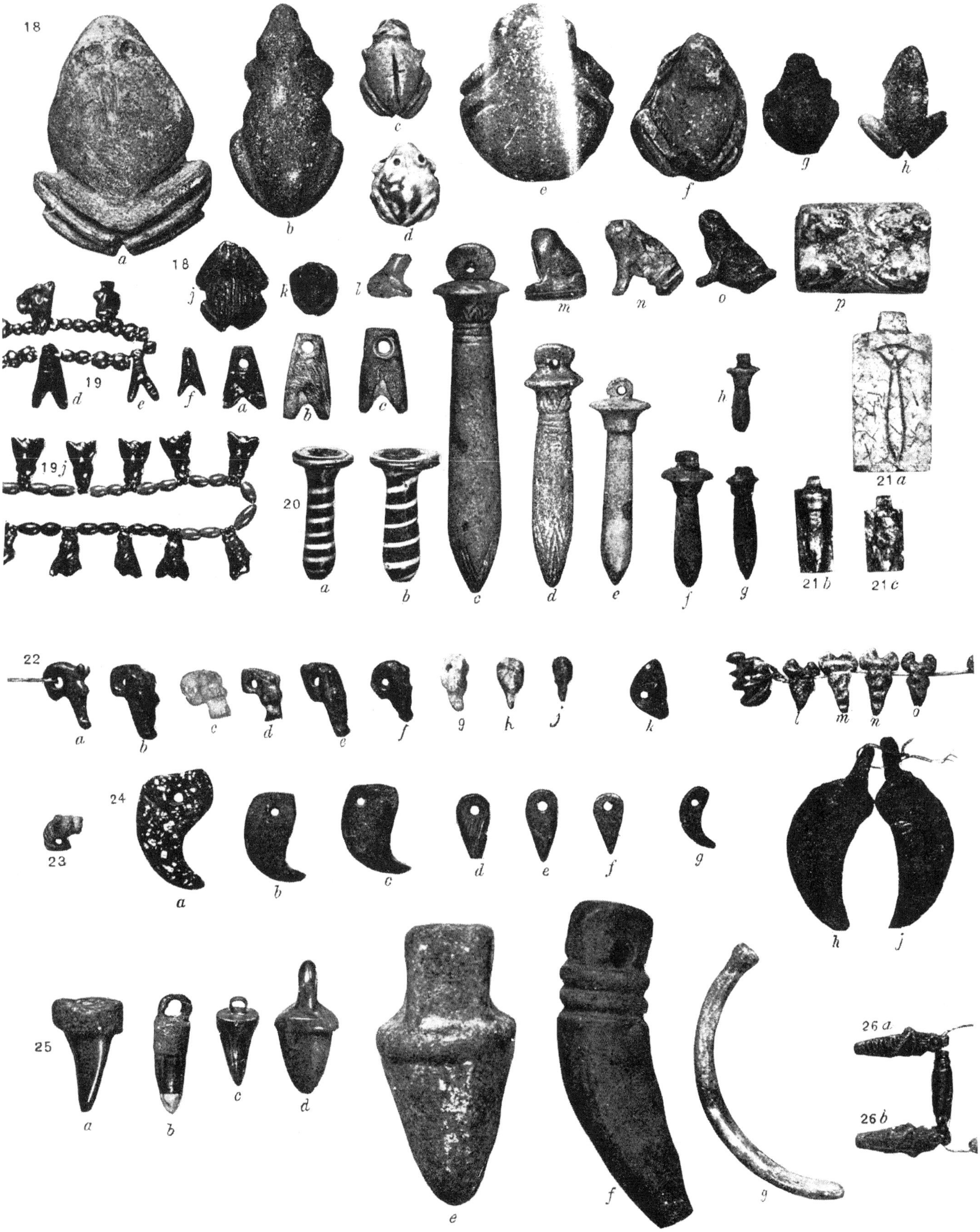

SIMILARS: ANIMAL AND VEGETABLE.

POWERS: SYMBOLIC HIEROGLYPHS.

POWERS: SYMBOLS OF ABILITY AND AUTHORITY.

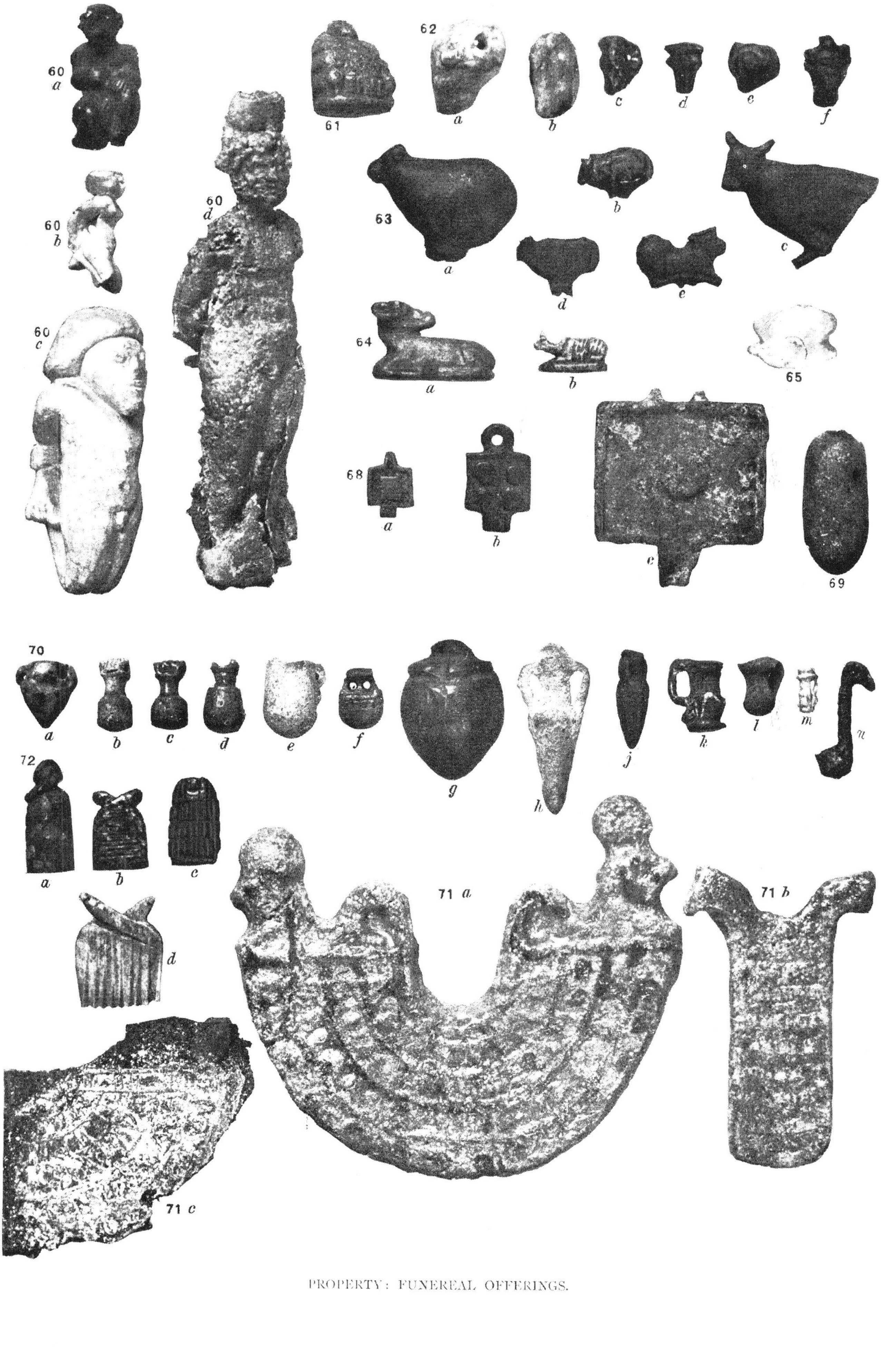

PROPERTY: FUNEREAL OFFERINGS.

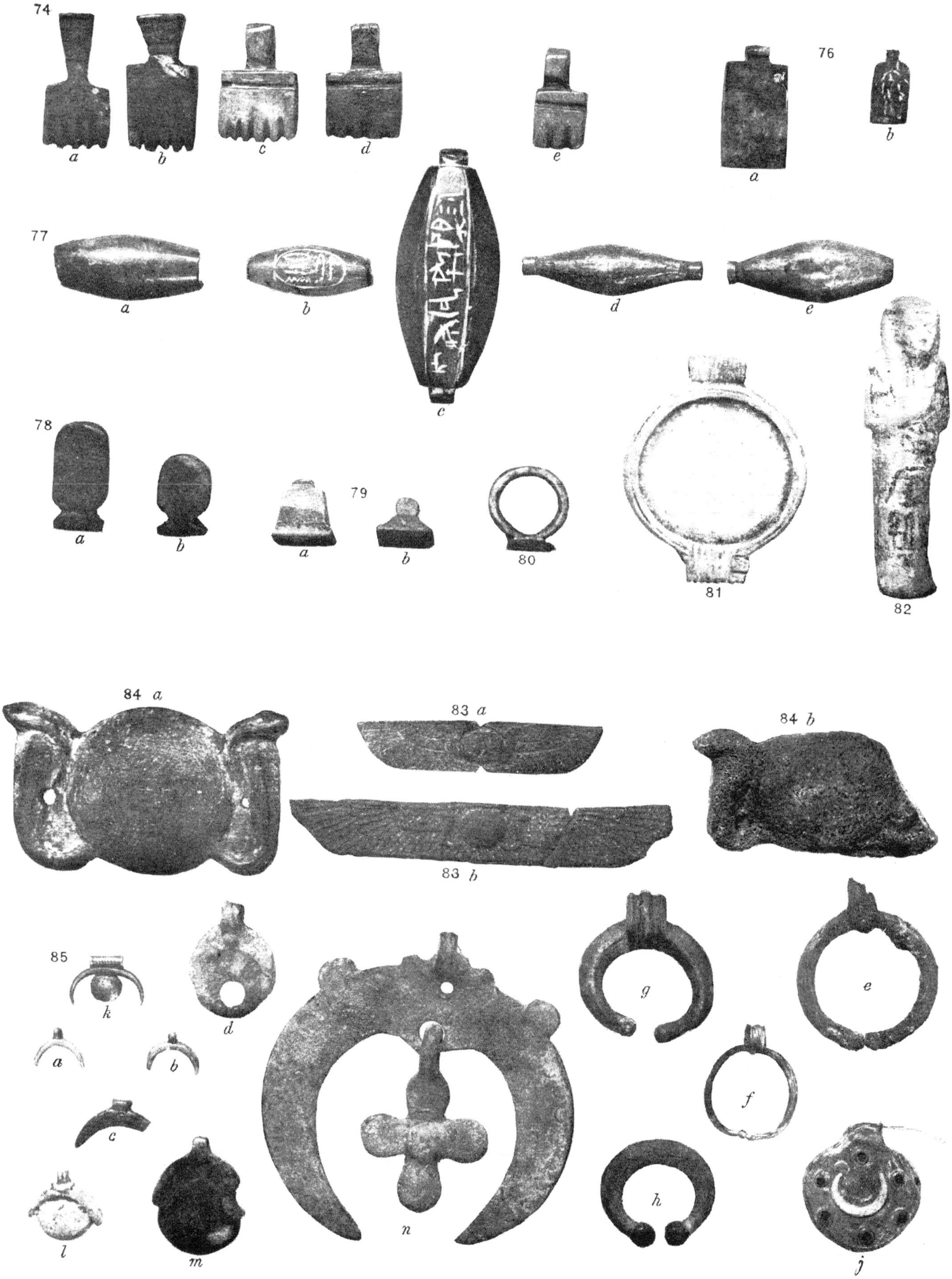

PROPERTY: { POSSESSIONS.
{ PROTECTION CELESTIAL.

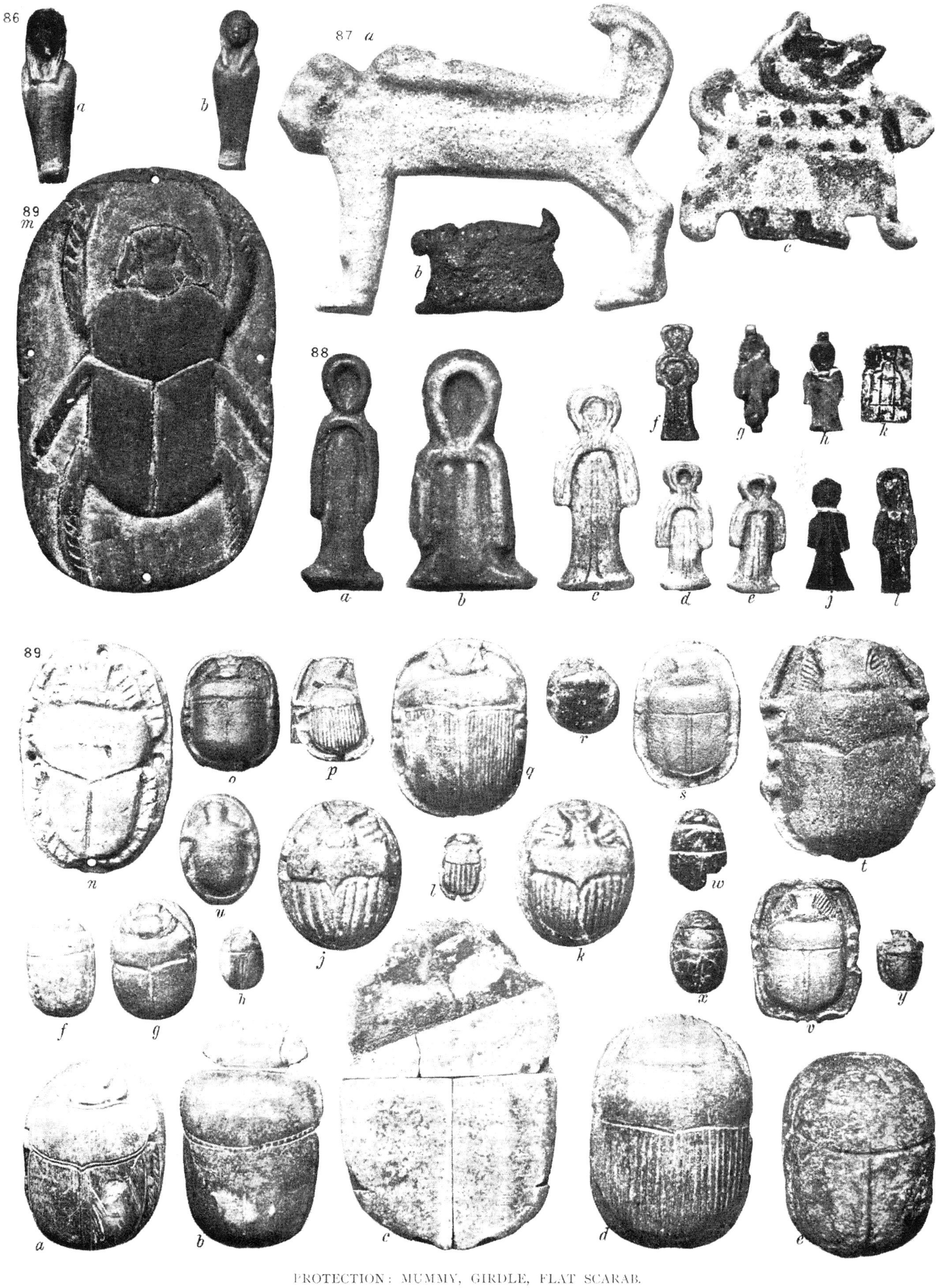

PROTECTION: MUMMY, GIRDLE, FLAT SCARAB.

PROTECTION: INSCRIBED SCARAB, BACKS.

90

PROTECTION: INSCRIBED SCARAB, FRONTS.

91

e

c

g

d

b

a

f

a

PROTECTION: PECTORALS.

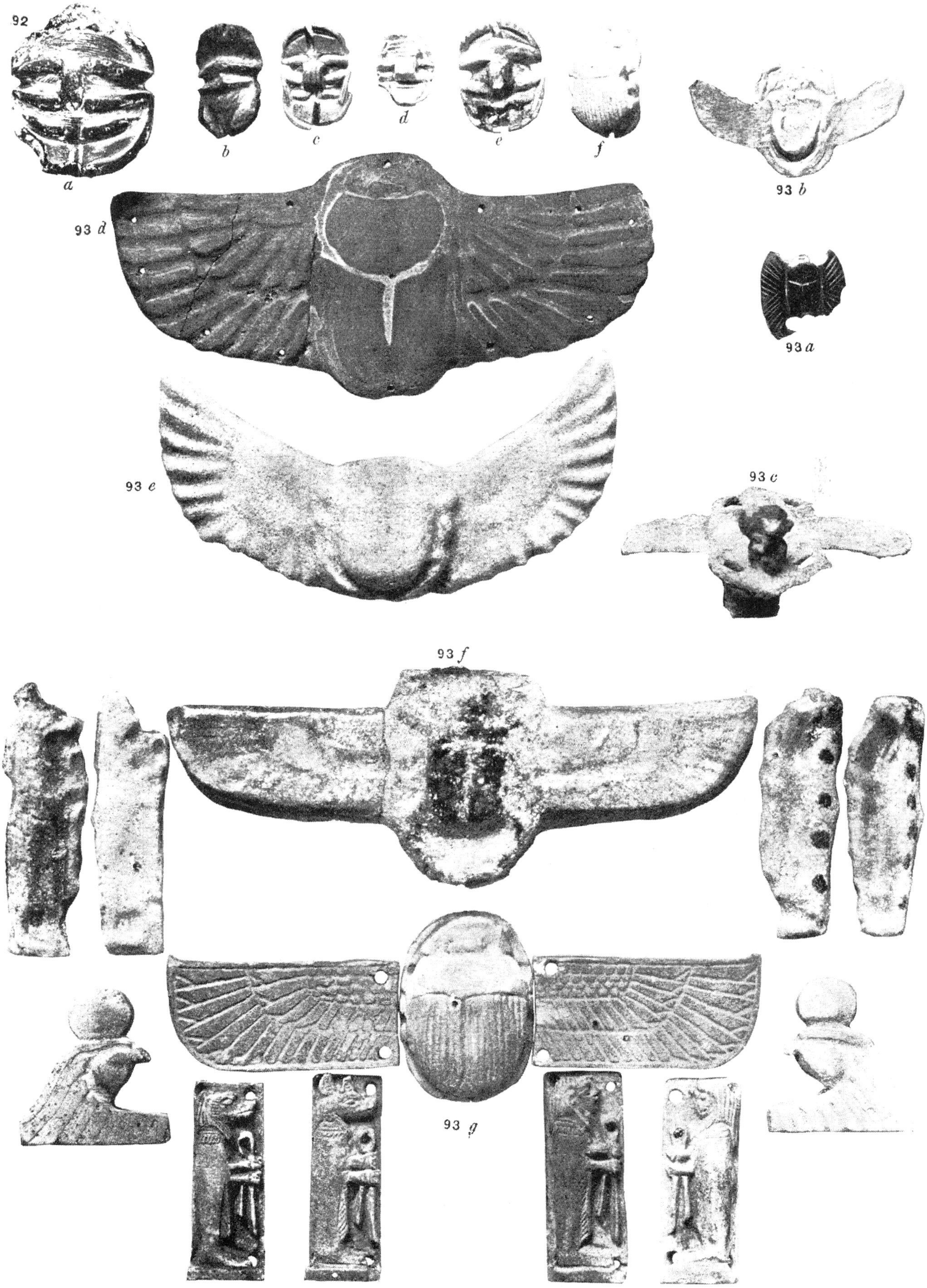

PROTECTION: SCARAB WITH LEGS AND WINGS.

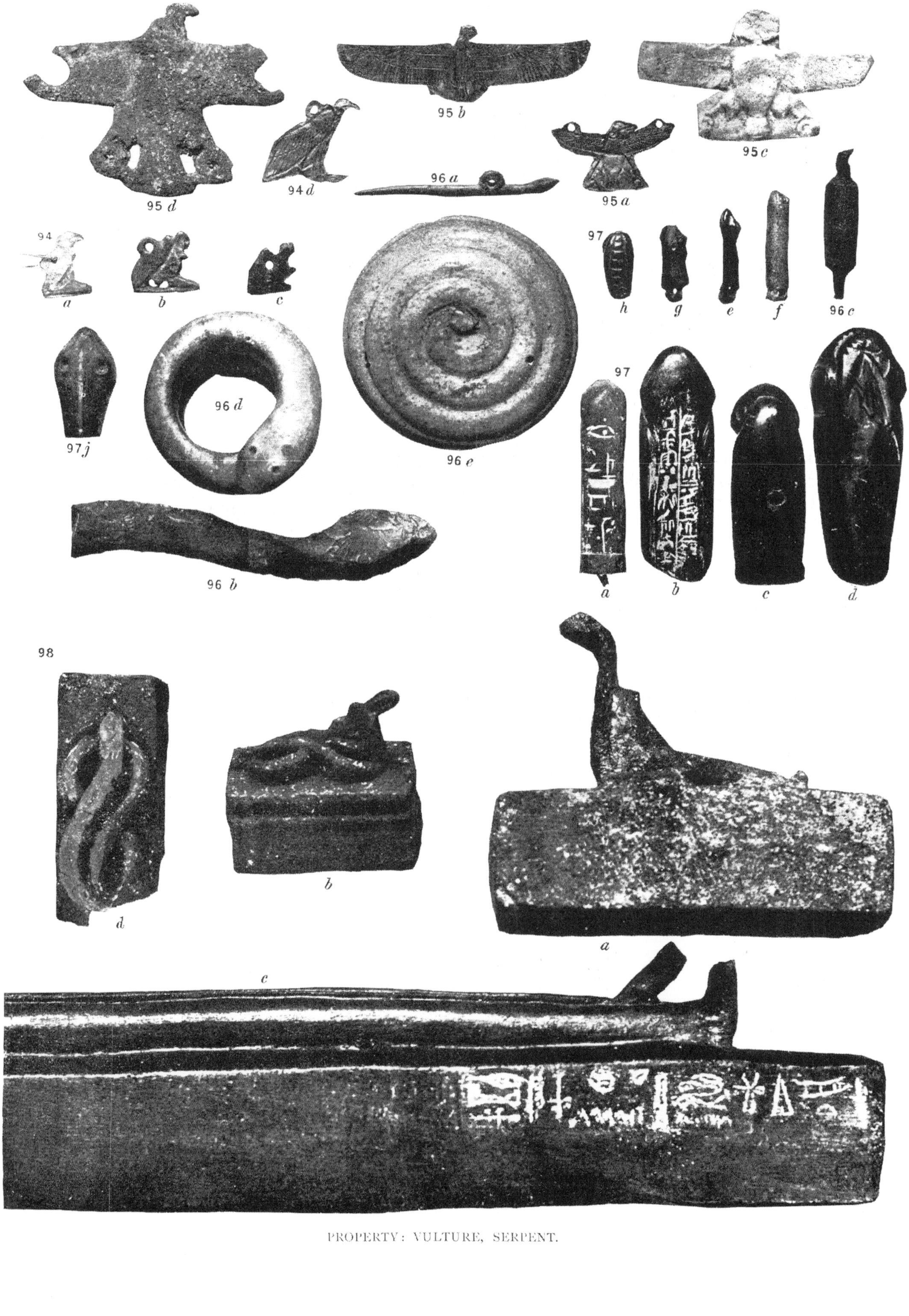

PROPERTY: VULTURE, SERPENT.

PROTECTION: CASES FOR REPTILES.

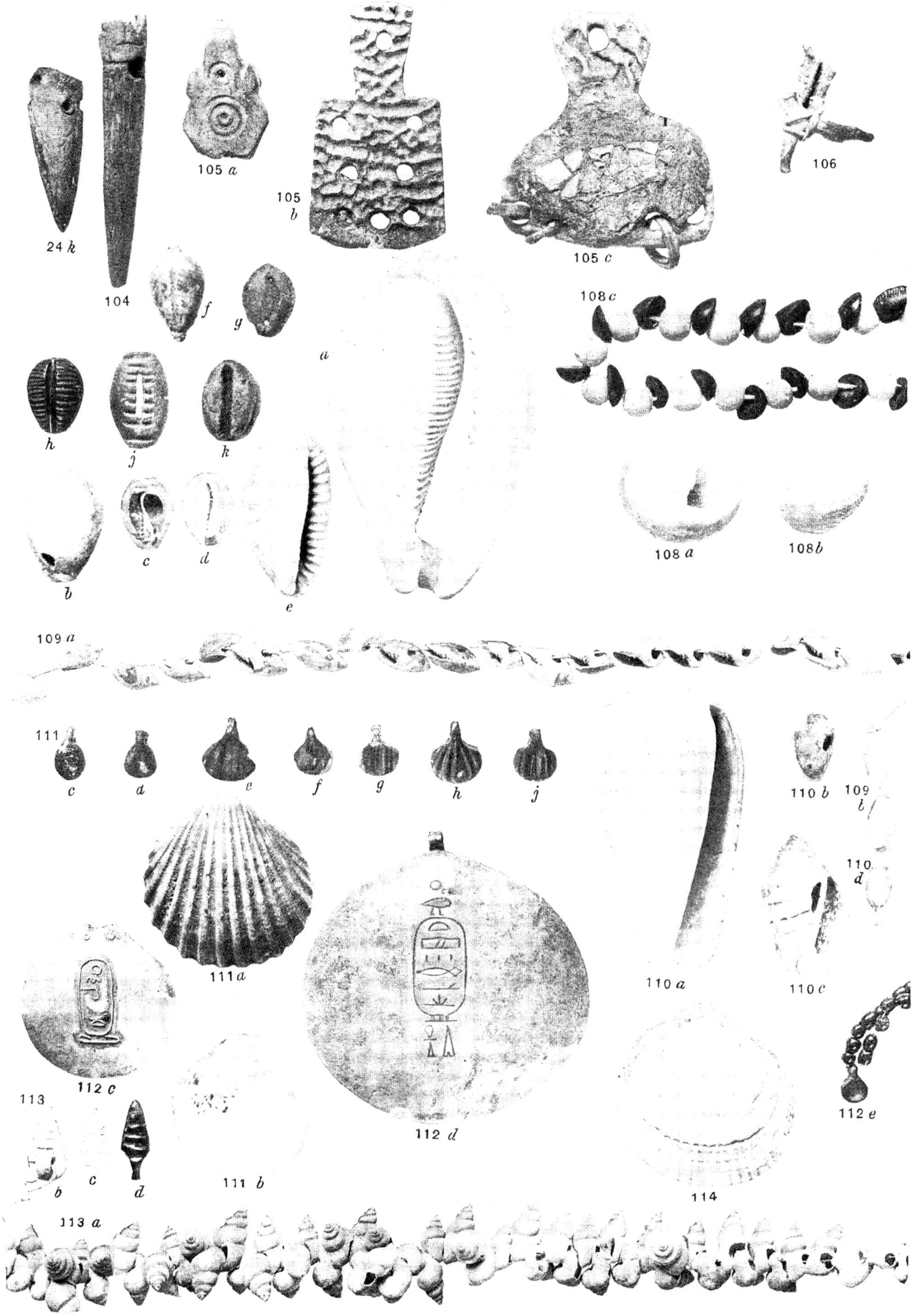

PROTECTION: HORN AND SHELLS.

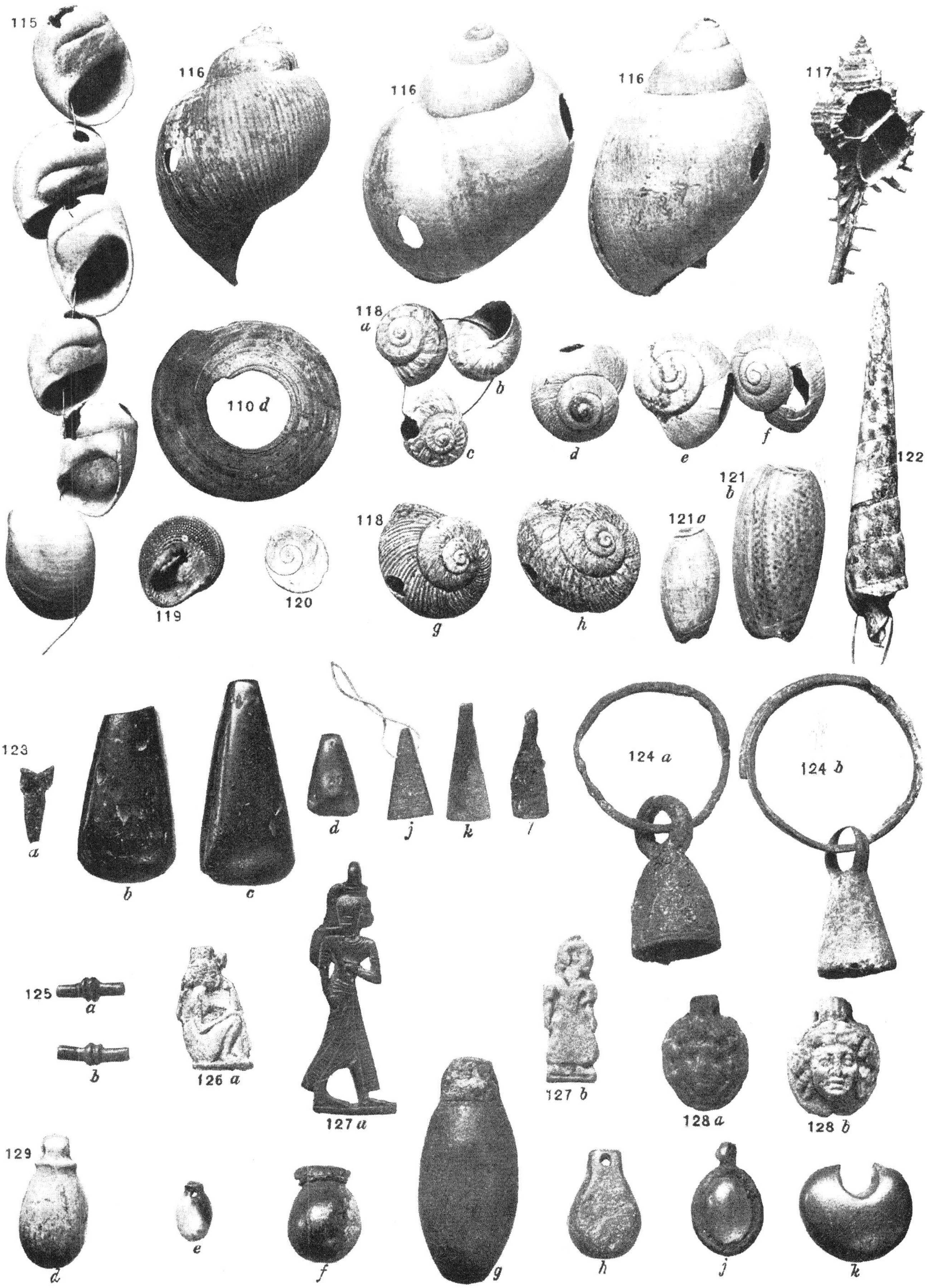

PROTECTION: SHELLS, IMPLEMENTS, FIGURES, BULLAE.

PROTECTION: FOREHEAD PENDANTS.

131

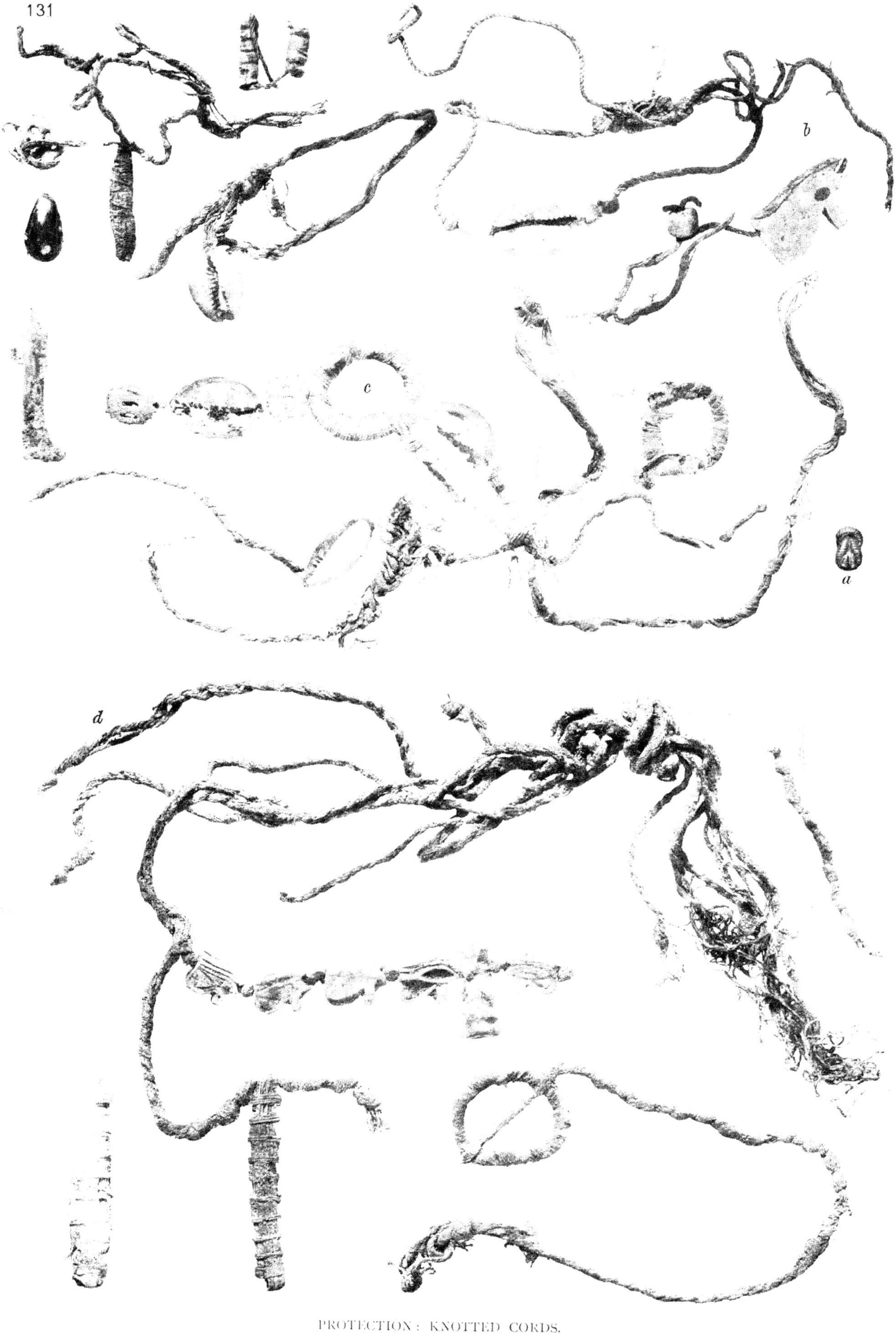

PROTECTION: KNOTTED CORDS.

131. *e.*

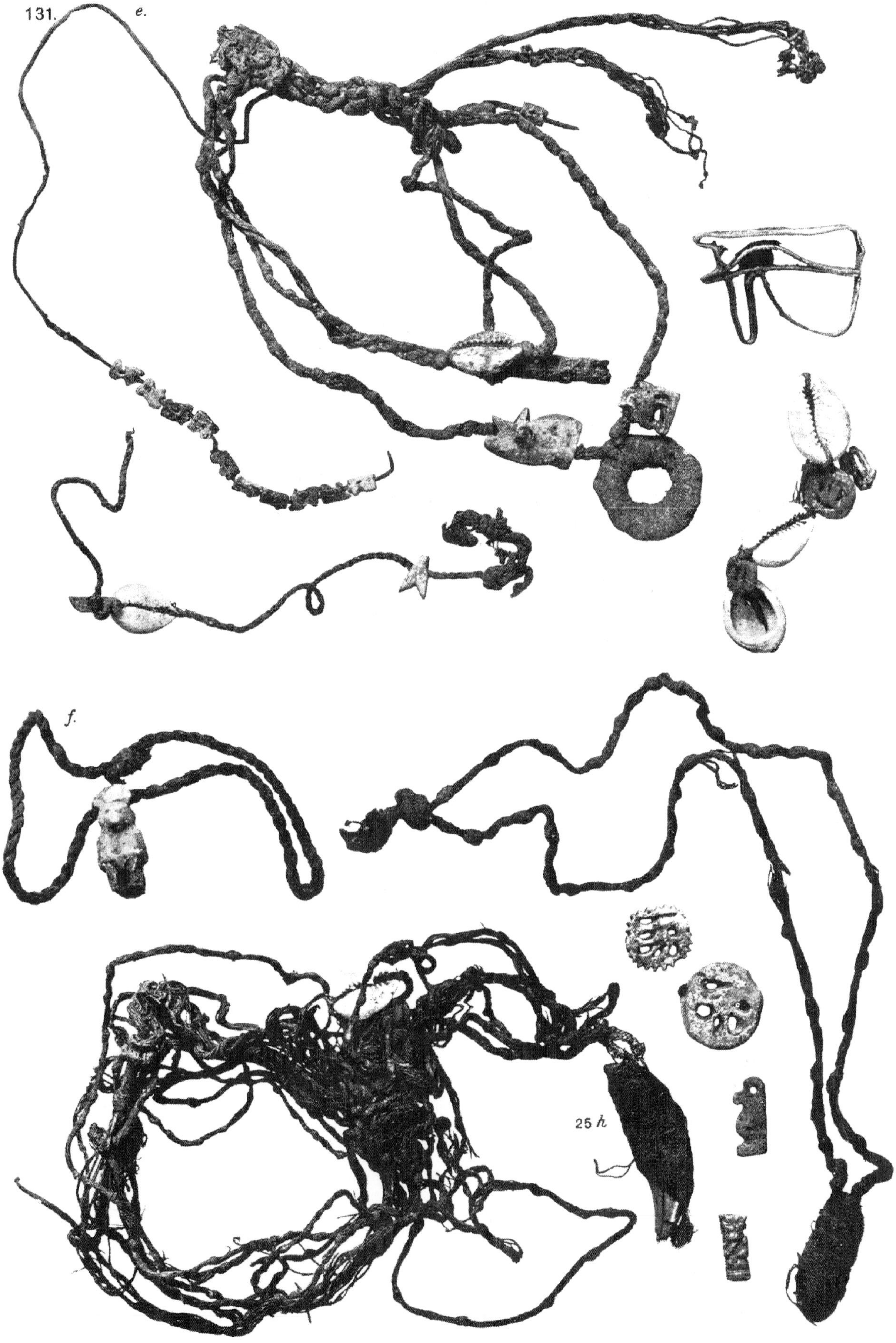

PROTECTION: KNOTTED CORDS.

131 *g*

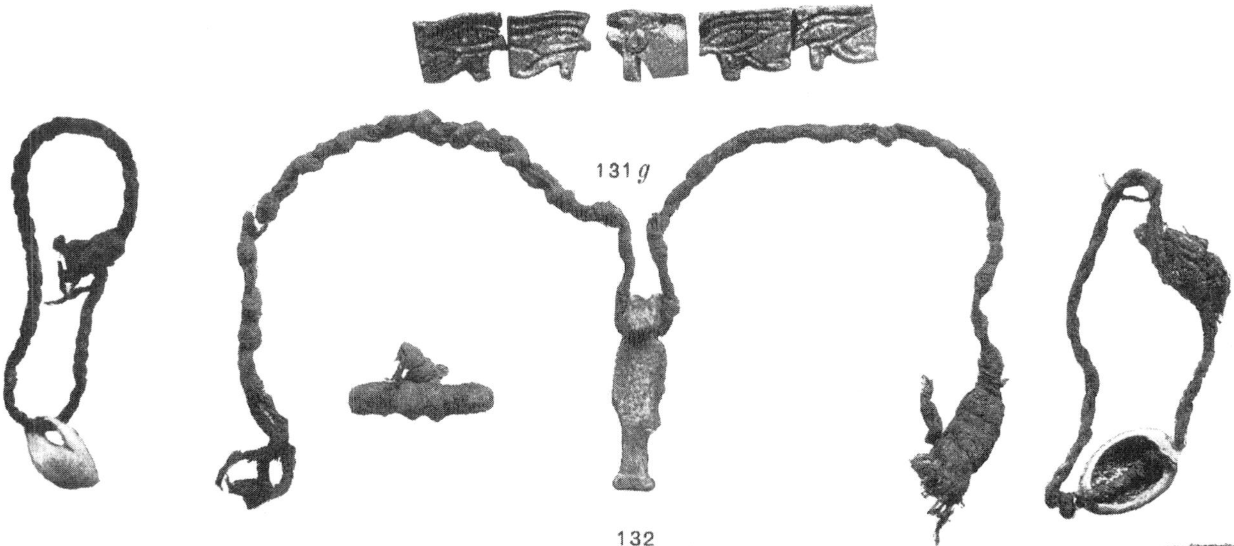

132

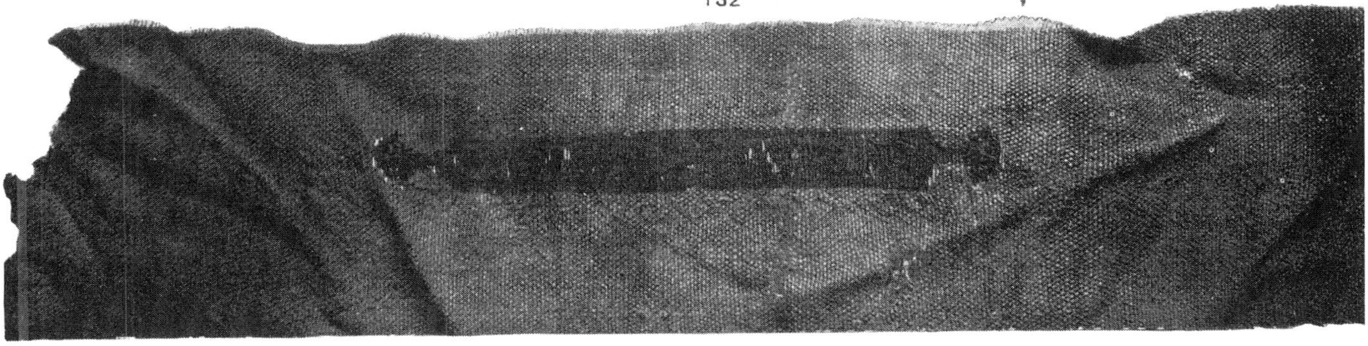

133

PROTECTION: CORDS, WEAVING, CHARM CASES.

134

a

b

c

PROTECTION: HYPOCEPHALI.

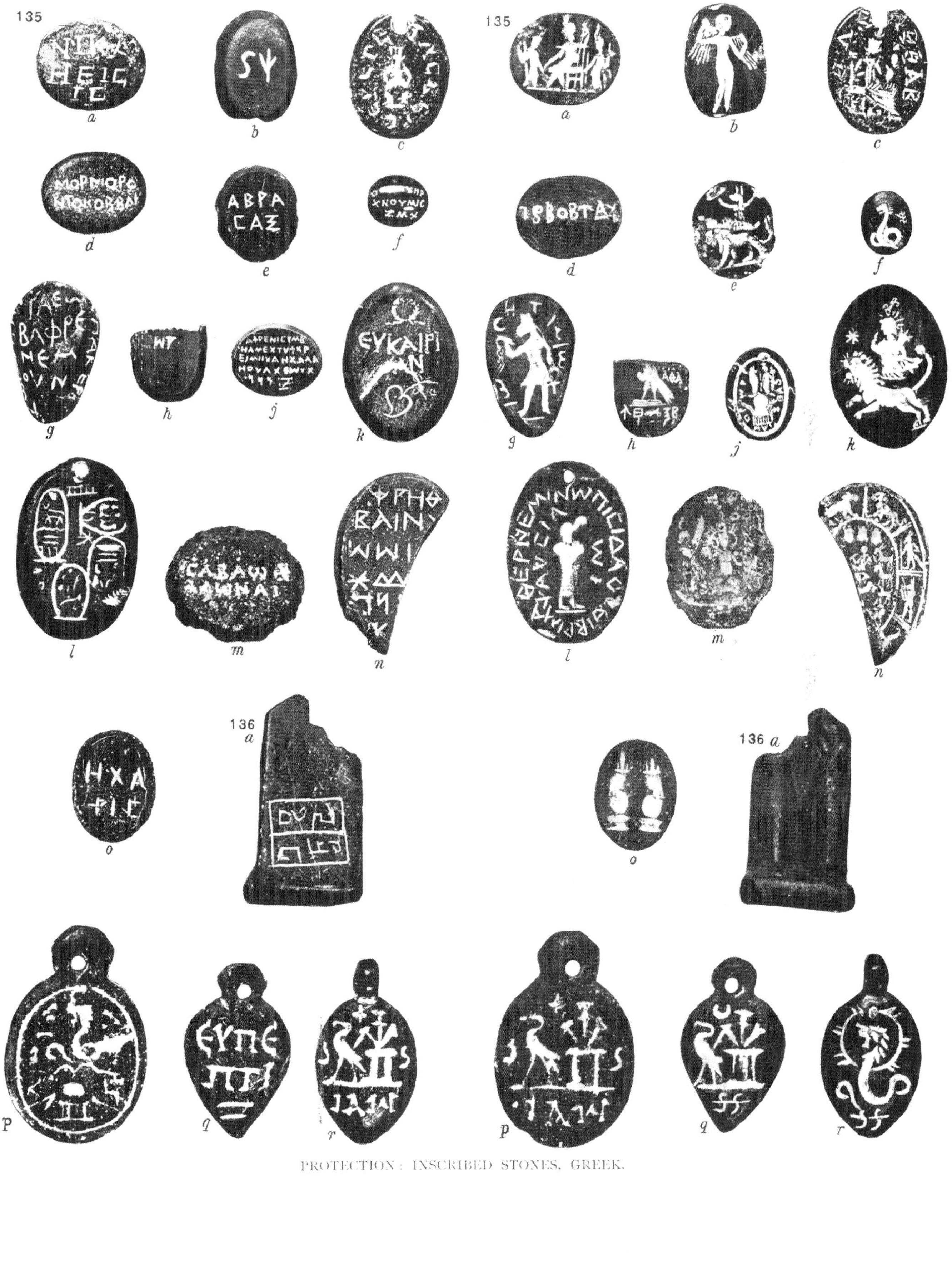

PROTECTION: INSCRIBED STONES, GREEK.

PROTECTION: INSCRIBED STONES, NON-GREEK.

136

137

PROTECTION: INSCRIBED, SEMITIC, CROSS.

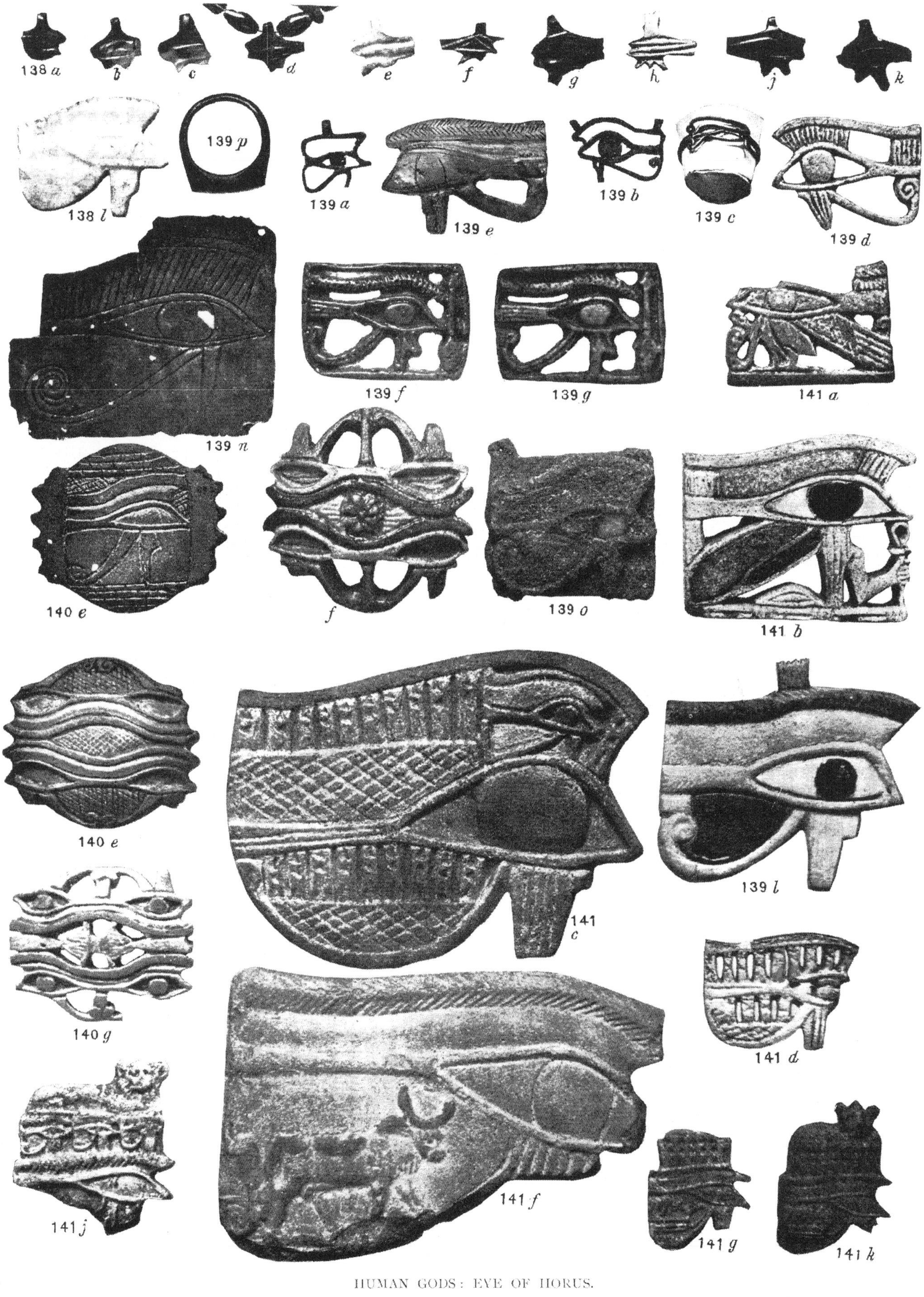

HUMAN GODS: EYE OF HORUS.

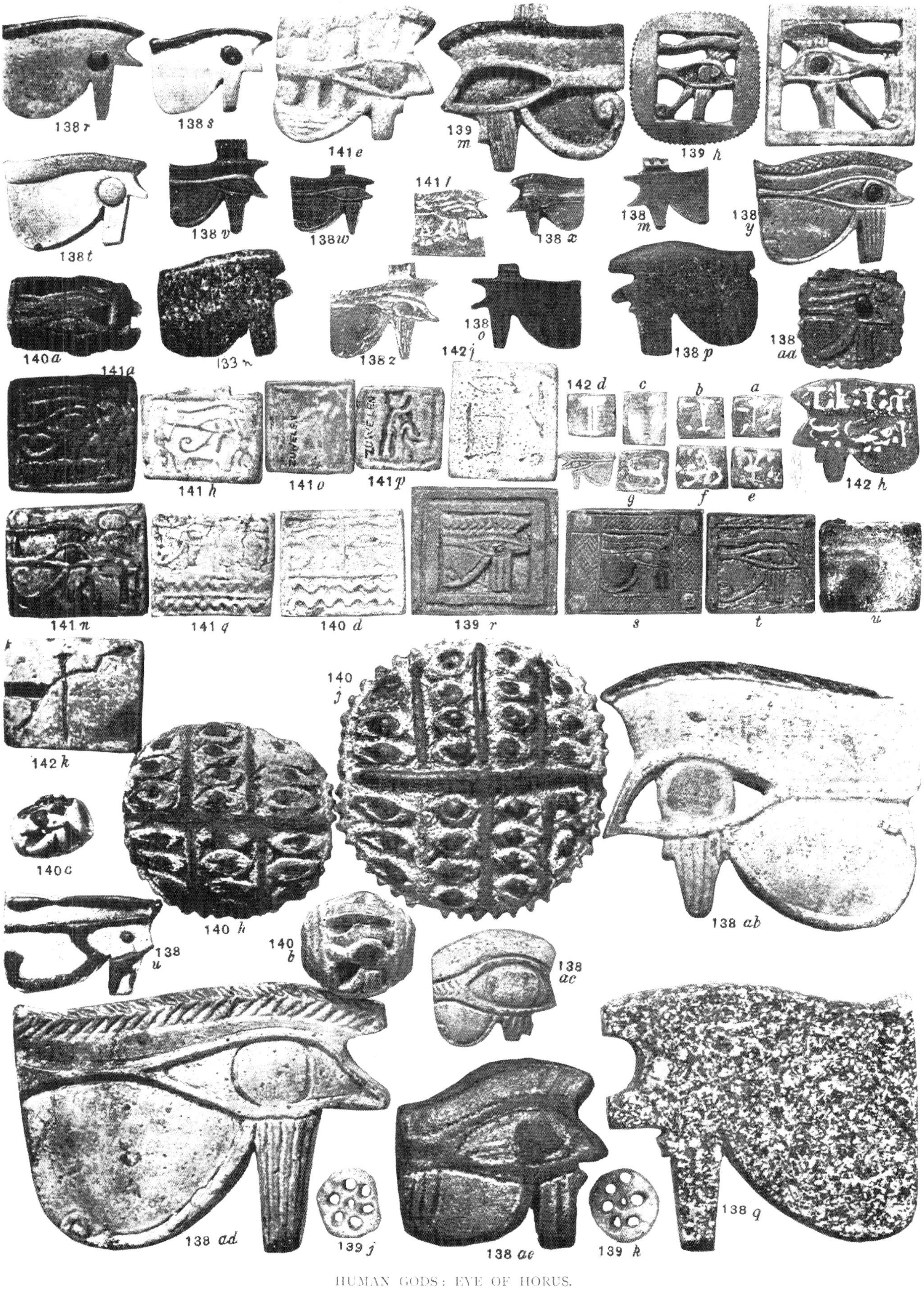

HUMAN GODS: EYE OF HORUS.

HUMAN GODS: HORUS, ISIS.

HUMAN GODS: HORUS, ISIS, OSIRIS, NEBHAT.

HUMAN GODS: OSIRIS, HEART OF OSIRIS.

HUMAN GODS: ORACULAR BUSTS.

HUMAN GODS: MIN TO NEFERTUM.

{HUMAN GODS: DWARFS, SAINTS.
{ANIMAL-HEADED GODS: HORUS-RA.

ANIMAL-HEADED GODS: FOUR SONS OF RA.

ANIMAL-HEADED GODS: SET, SPHINX, HATHOR, KHNUMU, BES.

ANIMAL-HEADED GODS: BES, TAHUTI, MAHES.

ANIMAL-HEADED GODS: ANHUR WITH TEFNUT, SEKHMET, BASTET.

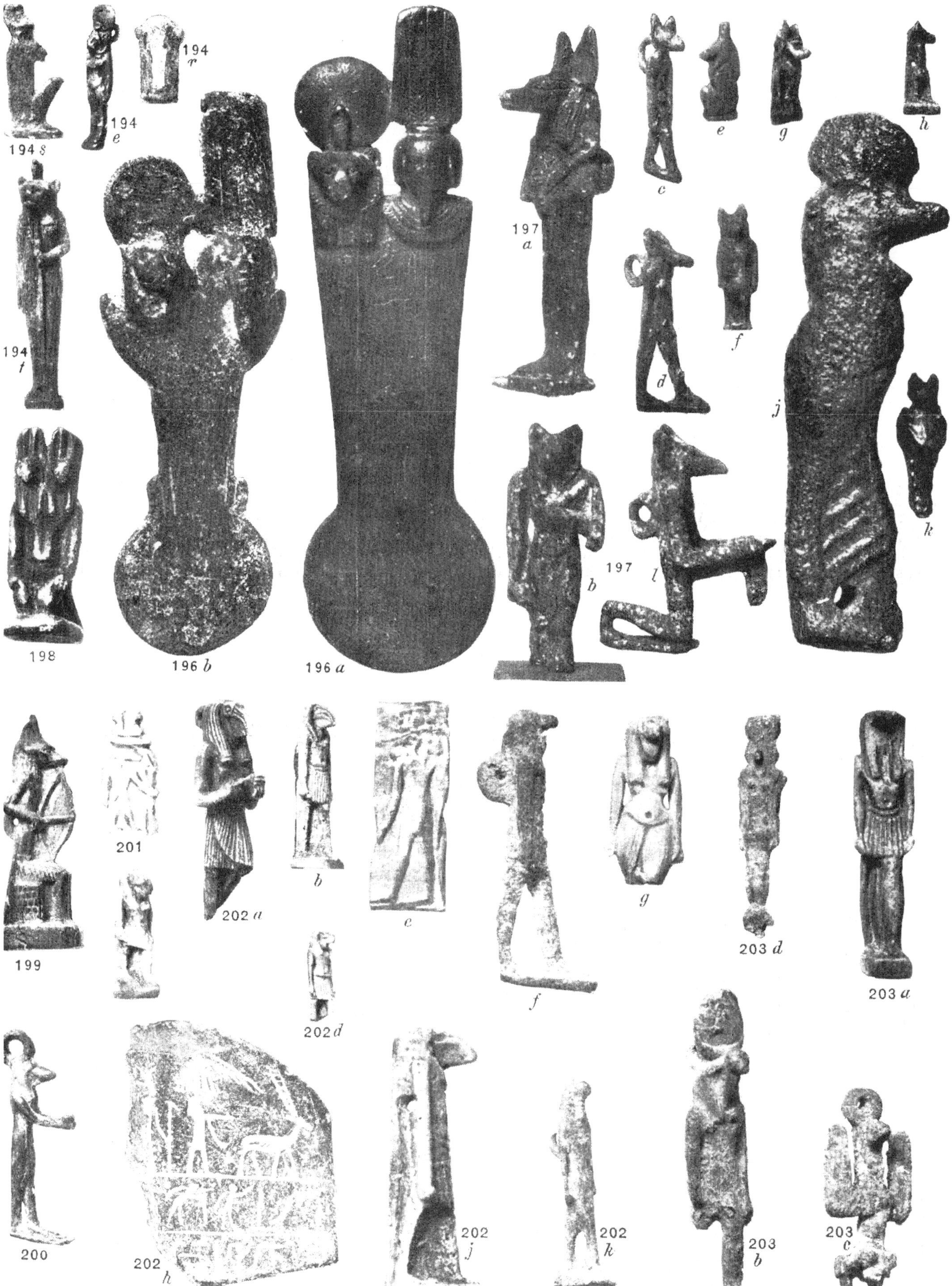

ANIMAL-HEADED GODS: SHU WITH TEFNUT, JACKAL, SEBEK, TAHUTI.

ANIMAL GODS: APE, BULL, COW.

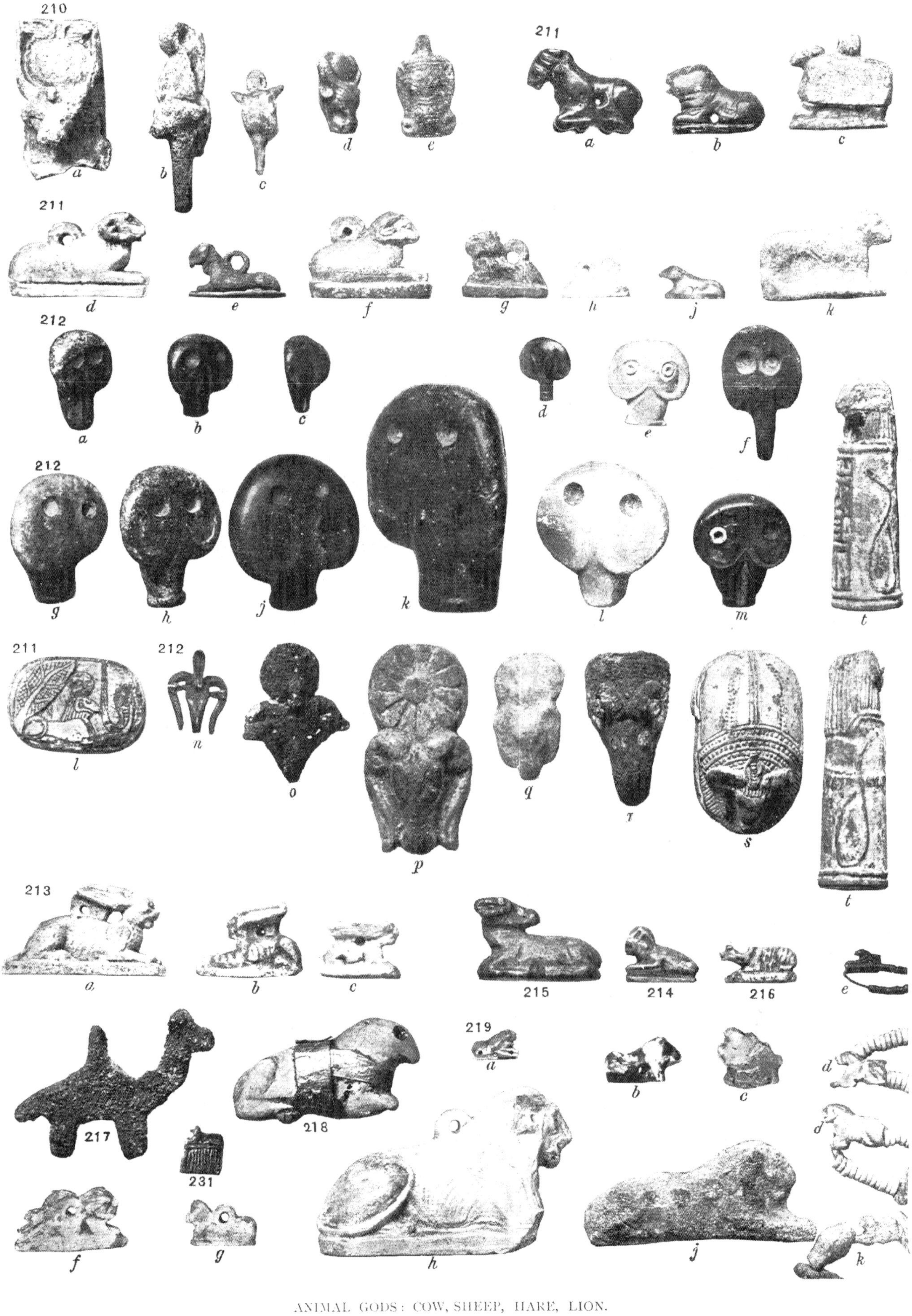

ANIMAL GODS: COW, SHEEP, HARE, LION.

ANIMAL GODS: LION, CAT, JACKAL.

ANIMAL GODS: SHREWMOUSE, DOG, PIG, HIPPOPOTAMUS

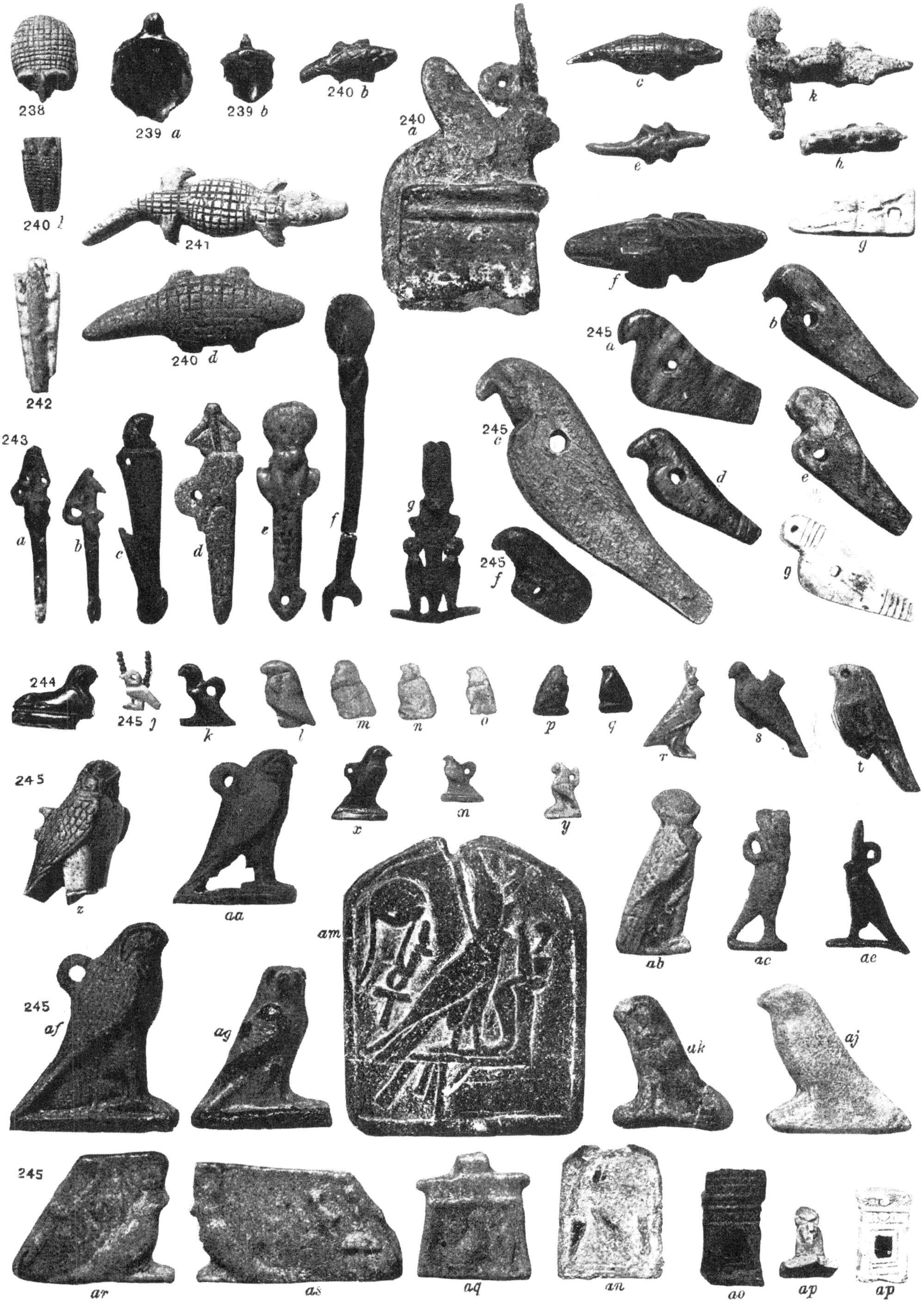

ANIMAL GODS: REPTILES, BIRDS.

ANIMAL GODS: BIRDS.

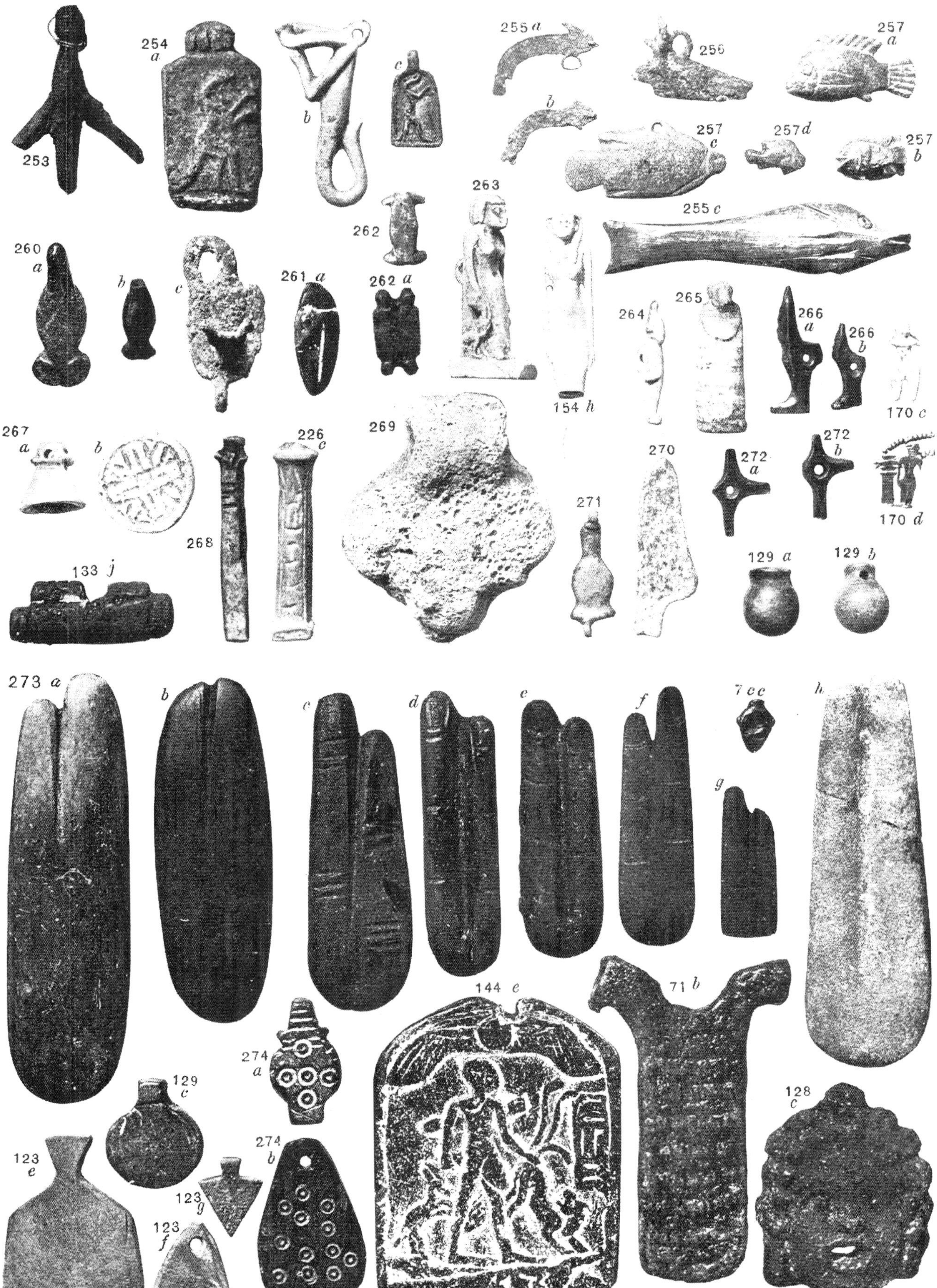

ANIMAL GODS, AND VARIOUS OBJECTS.

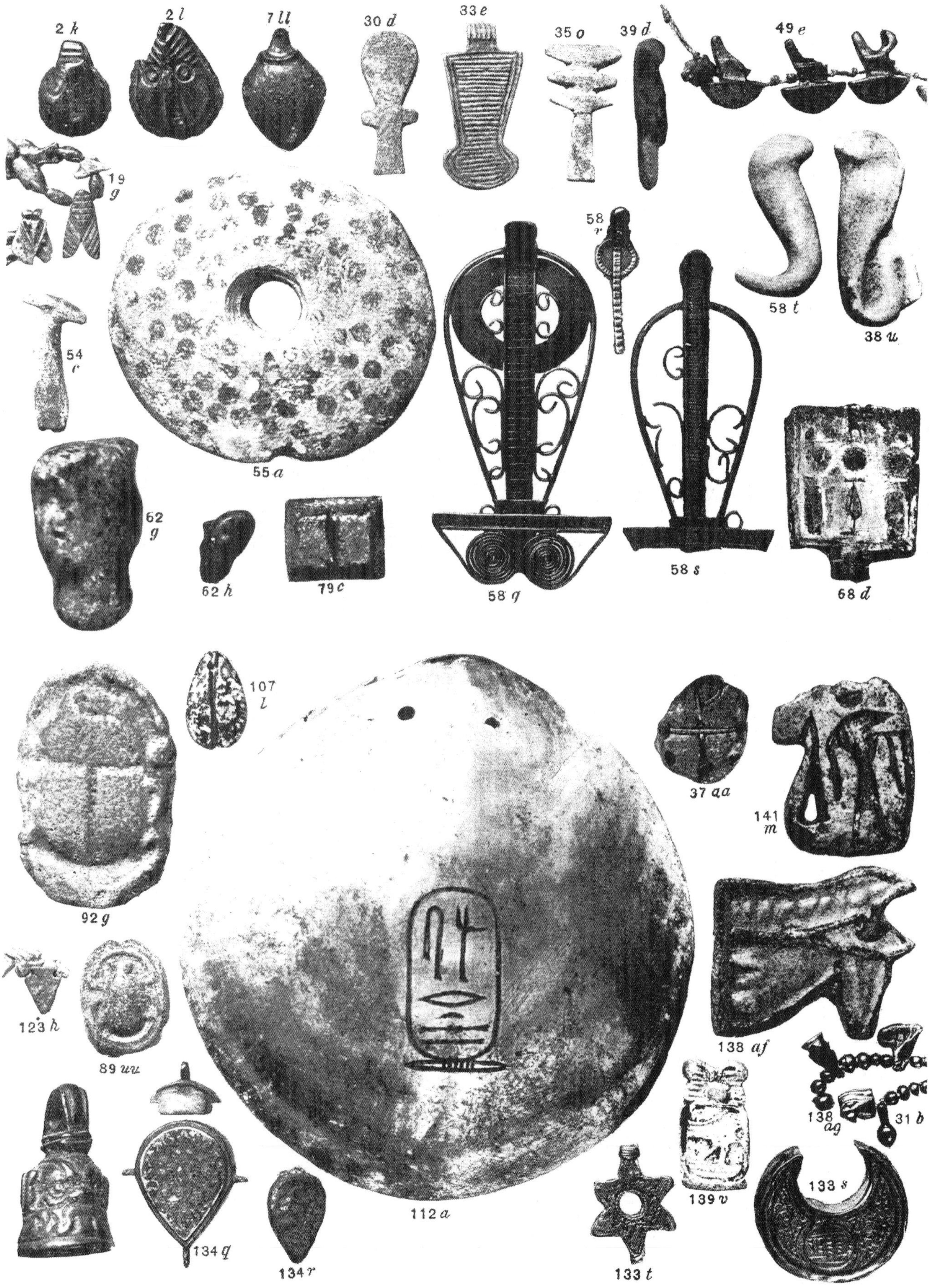
2 k
2 l
7 ll
30 d
33 e
35 o
39 d
49 e
19 g
58 r
58 t
38 u
54 c
55 a
62 g
62 h
79 c
58 q
58 s
68 d
107 l
37 aa
141 m
92 g
138 af
123 h
89 uu
138 ag
31 b
112 a
133 s
139 v
134 q
134 r
133 t

ADDENDA.

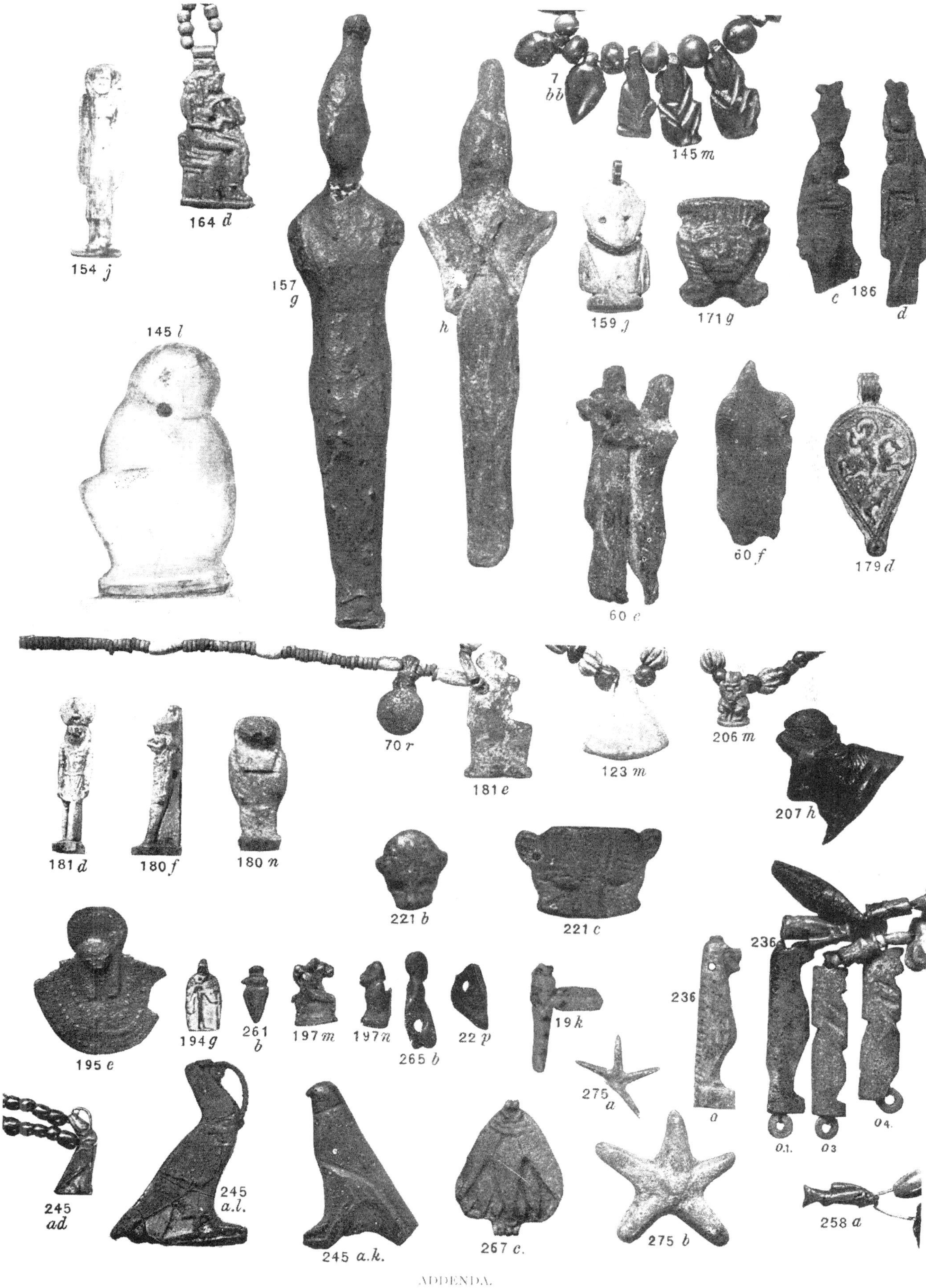
154 j
164 d
157 g
h
7 bb
145 m
159 j
171 g
c 186 d
145 l
60 f
179 d
60 e
70 r
181 e
123 m
206 m
207 h
181 d
180 f
180 n
221 b
221 c
236
236
195 e
194 g
261 b
197 m
197 n
265 b
22 p
19 k
275 a
a
0.1.
03
04.
245 ad
245 a.l.
245 a.k.
267 c.
275 b
258 a

12 e
30 h
70 o
137 ab
137 ac
137 ad
135 x
135 y
135 z
151 c
19 h
68 e
59 e
149 n
148 m
39 c
39 f
137 af
137 ae
129 l
169 e
169 f
202 l
179 f
211 n
190 u
92 h
34 g
245 av
219 l
190 t
236 ac
34 f
90 w
257 f
107 m
124 d
208 g
240 m
219 m
219 n
164 f
175 b3
170 j
176 p
176 n
194 n
194 ll
188 ac

ADDENDA.

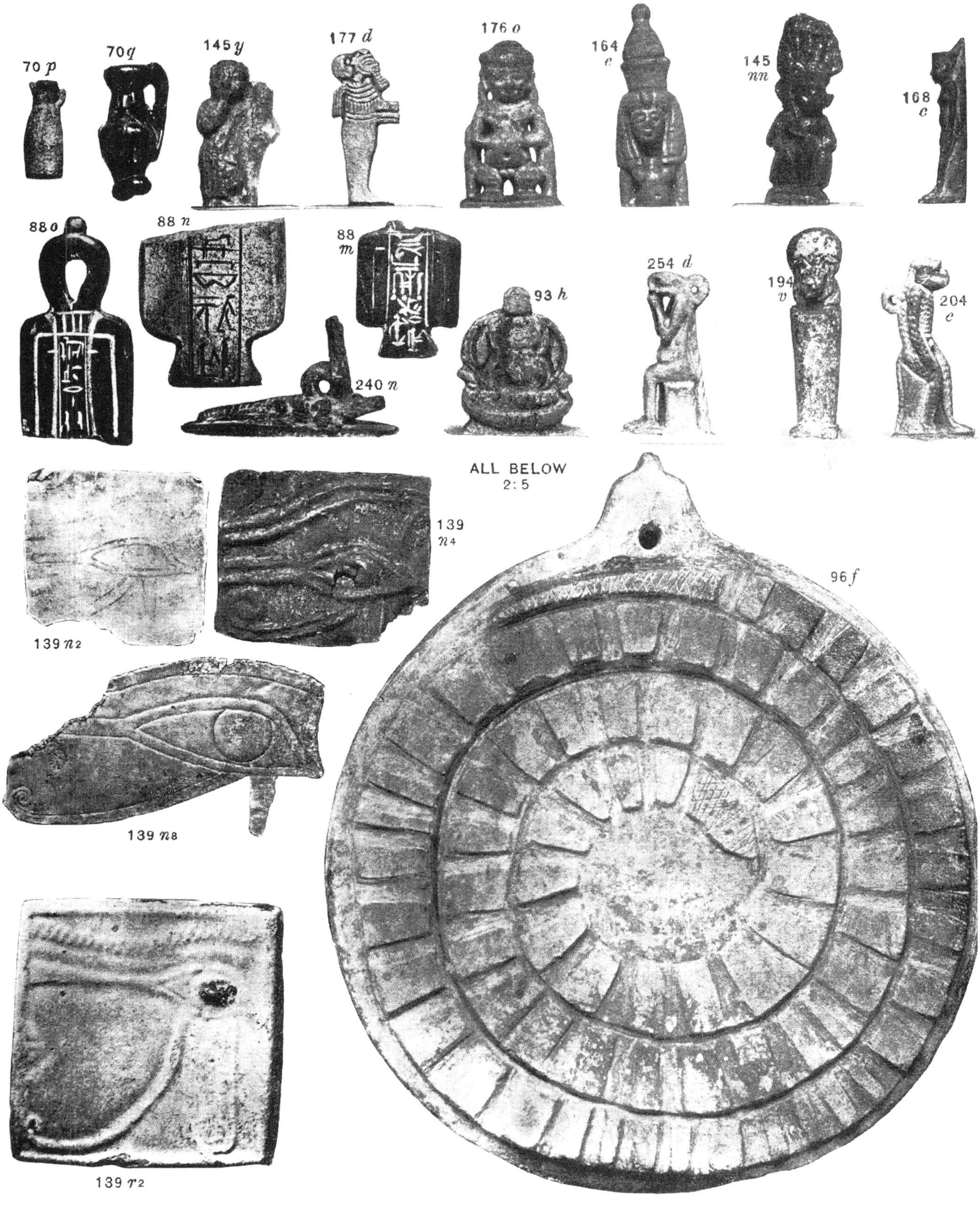
70 p
70 q
145 y
177 d
176 o
164 e
145 nn
168 c
88 o
88 n
88 m
93 h
240 n
254 d
194 v
204 e
ALL BELOW 2:5
139 n2
139 n4
96 f
139 n8
139 r2

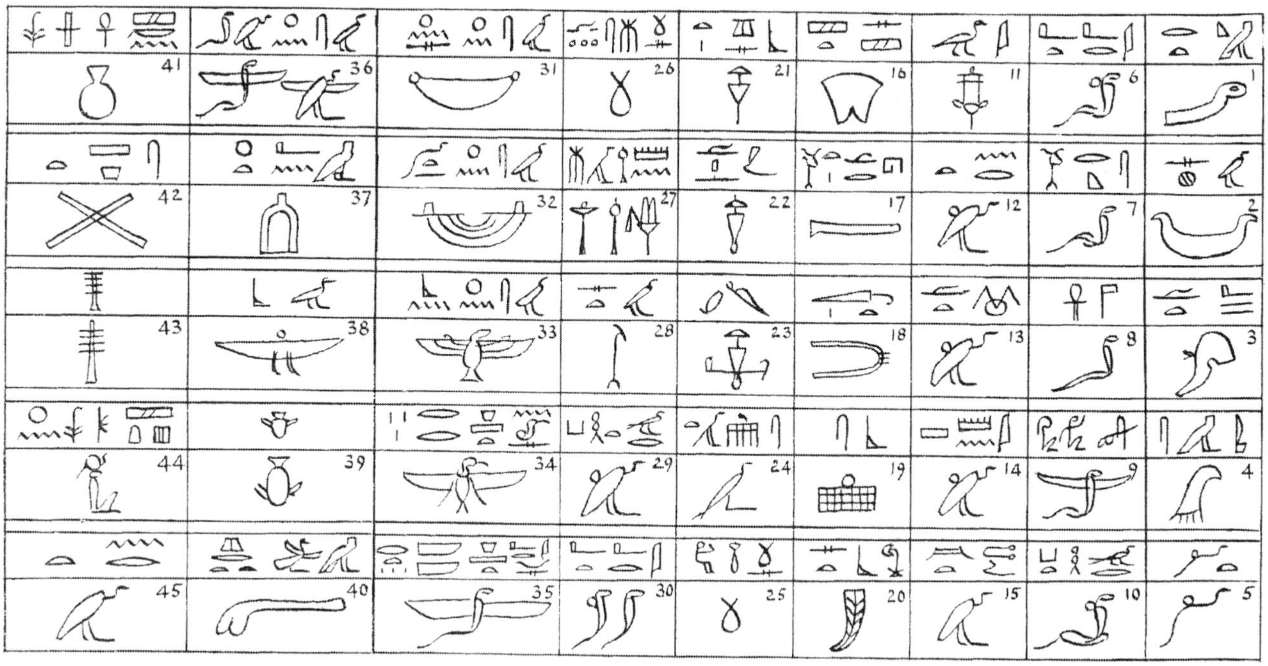

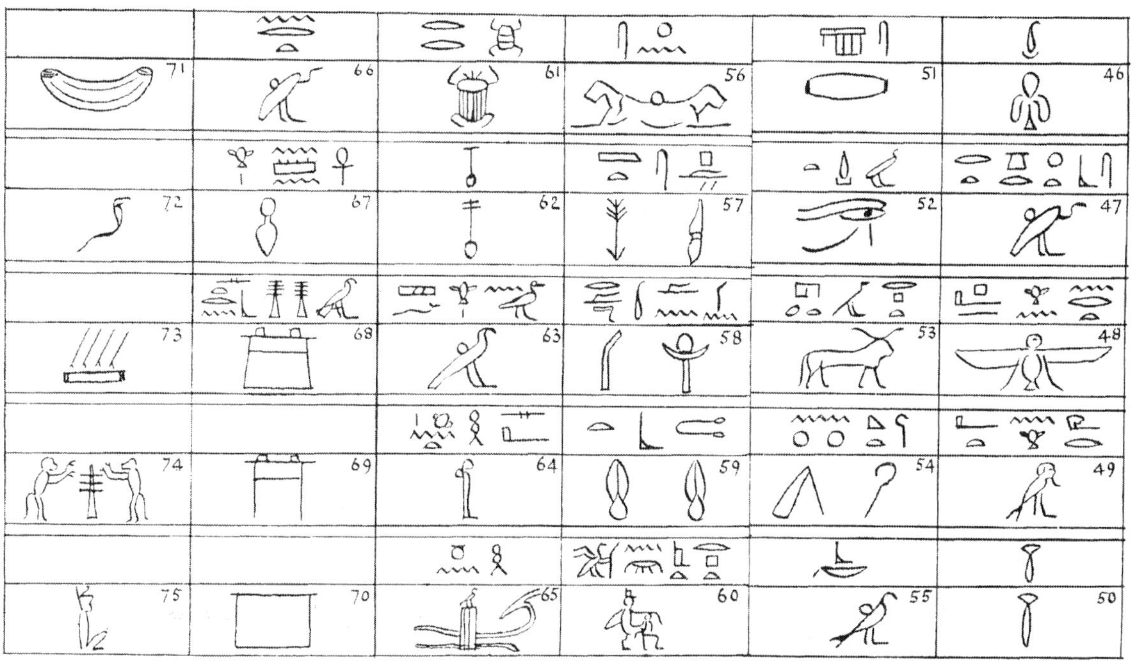

AMULETS OF OSIRIS. DENDEREH, IV, 87.

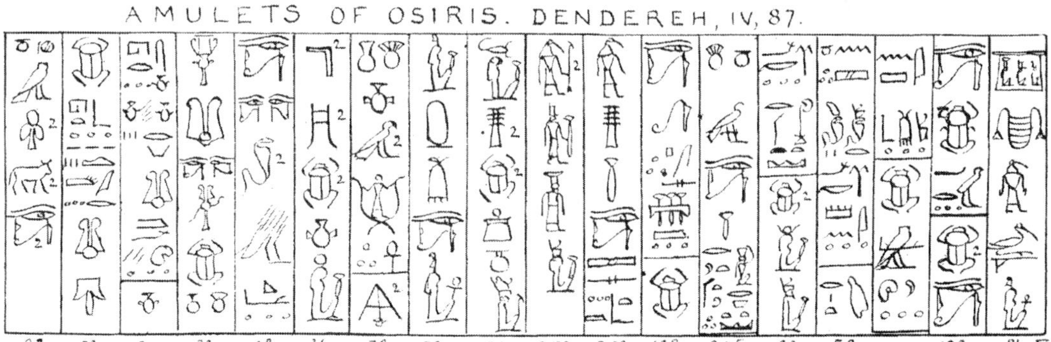

28 208 138	92 39 ?	39 7	32 39 140 92	138 140 58	36 46 92 7 170	70 245 37	172 78 72 138 172	174 35 92 91 164	202 149 154 168	202 35 20 38	138 92	245 139	92 170 168	58 48	92	138 92 92 138	91 71 202 247 172

F.P.

VXA
XVX BA
XAXVX
BAXAΞIXVX

FOUR-
HEADED
RAM

XAB
4 ram-headed
God of North

ΦVΛAΞ
The guardian
Sphinx

PH
ΓOM
Φ

PAY, Ra
4-headed ram
Φ NEC

XHPΦI

ΦWXWC

IAW
I AM and
ΛΛ IΛΛ MA
none else with me.

ABΛANAΘ
ANAΛBA

BES

AΛEΞIM
ANΔPEVΛA
Bark, guardian
of man.

LION
TREADING
ON SKELETON.

AKPAMMAX
Thy most gracious one
AMAPIΞ

HORUS
HOLDING EVILS
STANDING ON
CROCODILES

ABPACAΞ

CABA
Lion

IAW
Yahveh
IHCOVC
Iesus

3 HAWKS
Souls of the Just.
on right
before Horus

3 SCARABS
Triple Creator

3 GOATS, 3 SERPENTS
Souls of the wicked.
on left
behind Horus

3 CROCODILES

IEW BA ΦPEN Yahveh MOUN OΘIA APION EV EA IΦIPK IPA ΘΟ NVOME EPΦ AB WEAI	HORUS ON LOTUS IN BOAT	BPIN TE TI HN	KHNUMU STANDING XNOUBIC XAPNOUC Khnumu the horned.

HORUS-MIN
as Creator

HORUS
as king
with scourge
and tail.

Φ NOEOUOVTI
The God

AP ΠΟ
XNOUΦIC
Horus the Creator

BPIN
TATH
NWΦPI

PWCΘI
ΘVΘ
NEOPTOV

Lion CABA

F. P.

PLANS OF AMULETS ON MUMMIES.

L

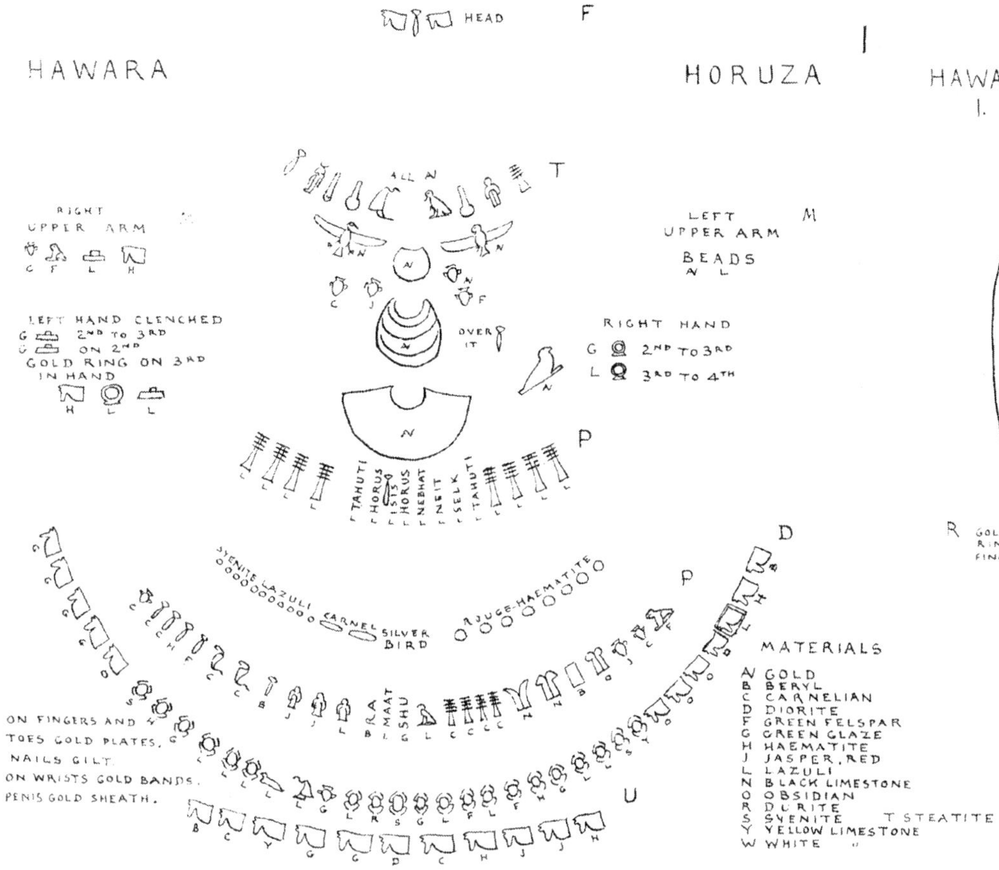

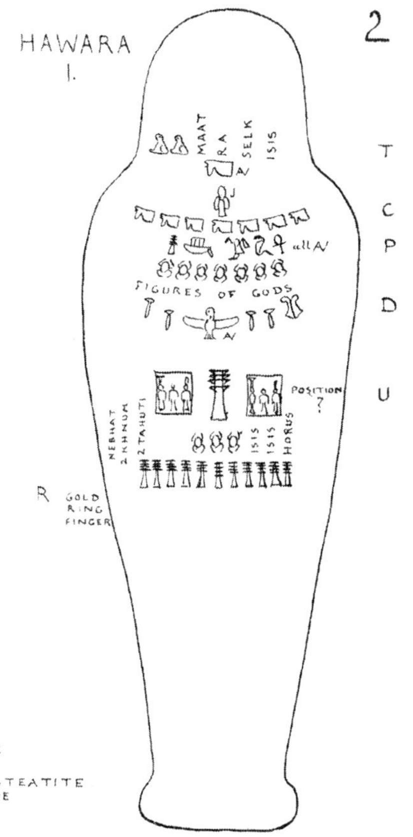

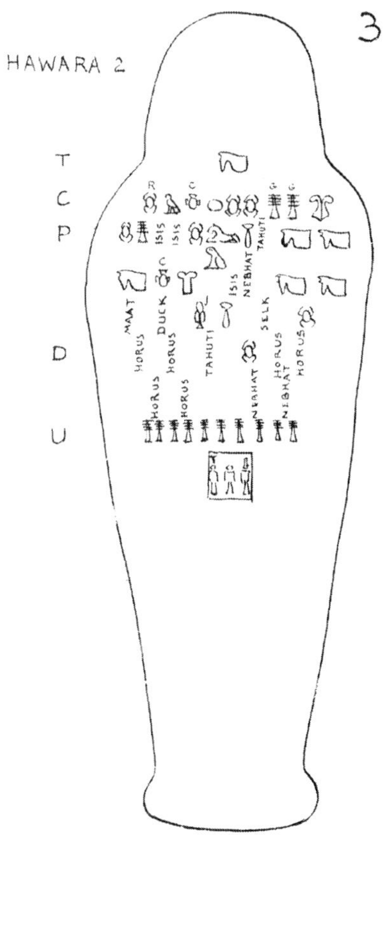

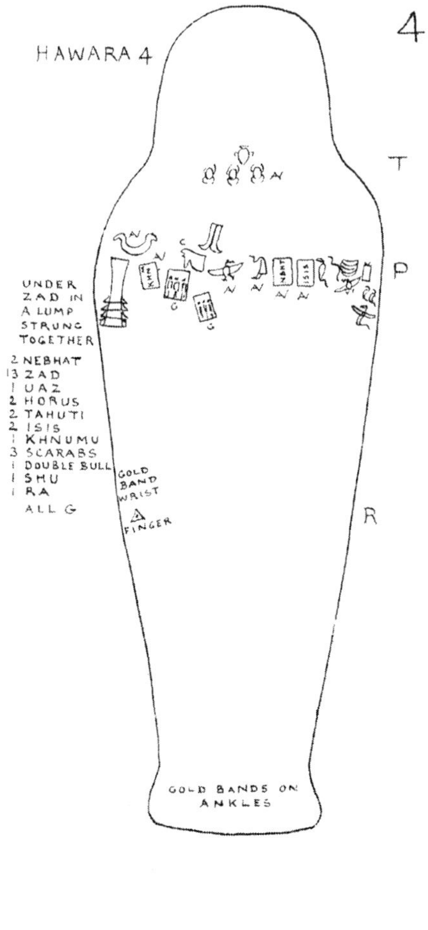

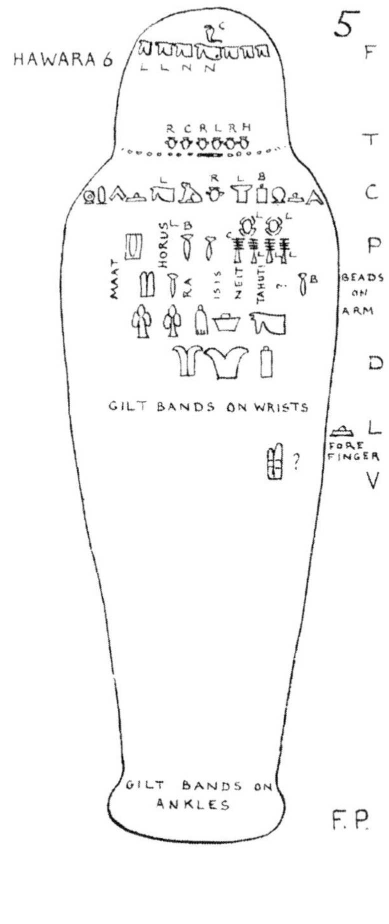

F.P.

6

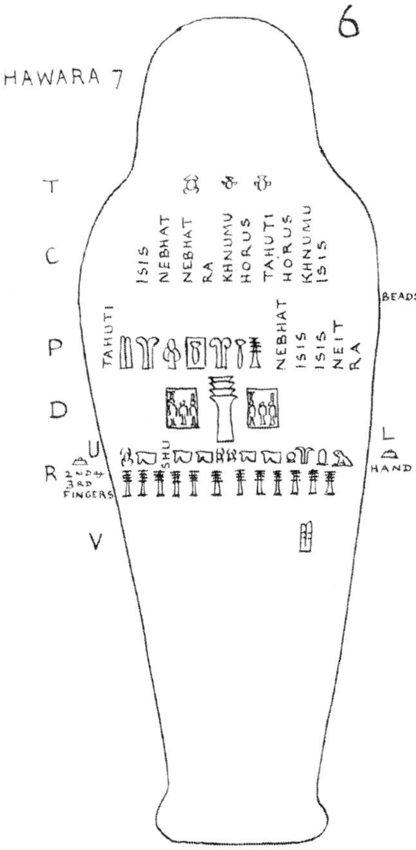
HAWARA 7
T
C
P
D
U
R
V
ISIS
NEBHAT
NEBHAT
RA
KHNUMU
HORUS
TAHUTI
HORUS
KHNUMU
ISIS
BEADS
TAHUTI
NEBHAT
ISIS
ISIS
NEIT
RA
SHU
L
HAND
2ND & 3RD FINGERS

7

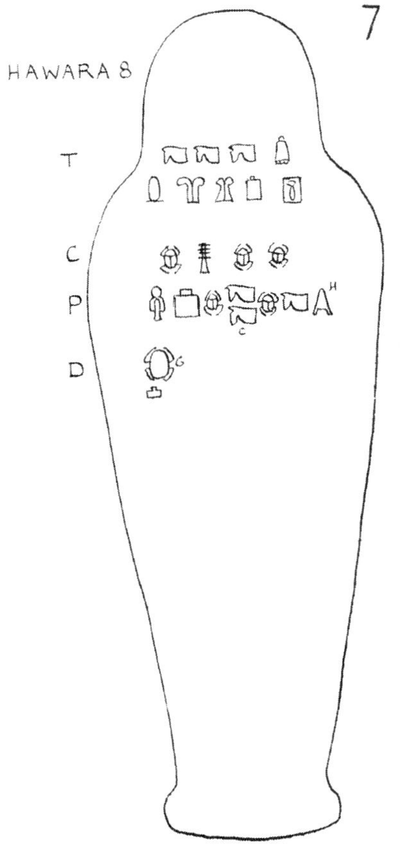
HAWARA 8
T
C
P
D
H
C
G

8

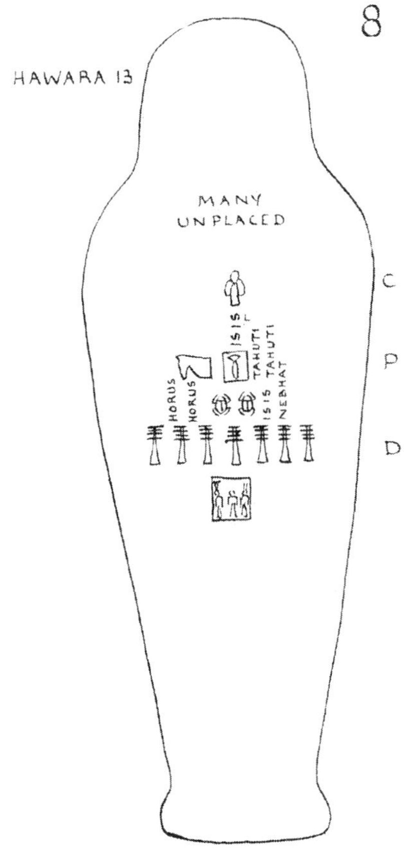
HAWARA 13
MANY UNPLACED
C
P
D
ISIS
TAHUTI
HORUS
HORUS
ISIS
TAHUTI
NEBHAT

9 10

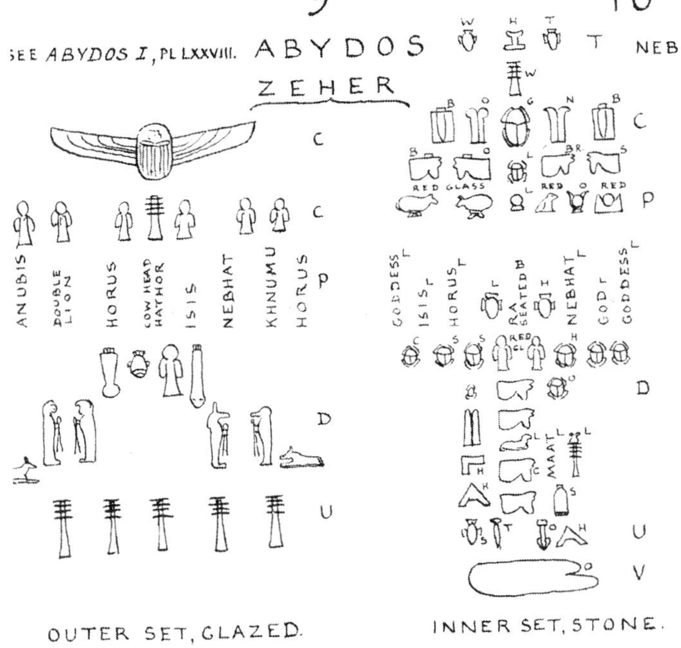
SEE ABYDOS I, PL LXXVIII.
ABYDOS
ZEHER
C
C
P
D
U
ANUBIS
DOUBLE LION
HORUS
COW HEAD HATHOR
ISIS
NEBHAT
KHNUMU
HORUS
OUTER SET, GLAZED.
T
C
P
D
U
V
RED GLASS
RED
RED
GODDESS
ISIS
HORUS
RA SEATED
NEBHAT
GOD
GODDESS
MAAT
INNER SET, STONE.

11

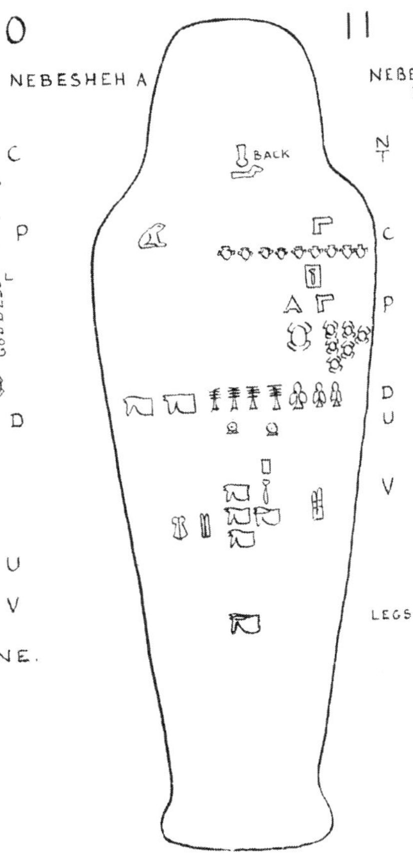
NEBESHEH A
BACK
N
T
C
P
D
U
V
LEGS

12

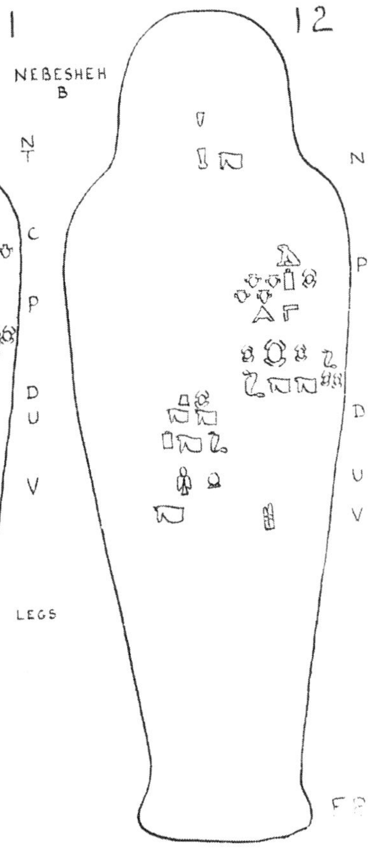
NEBESHEH B
N
P
D
U
V

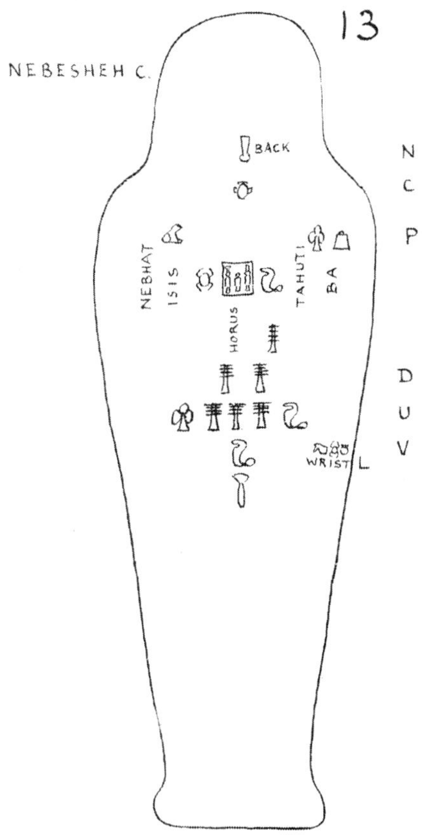
13
NEBESHEH C.
BACK
NEBHAT
ISIS
HORUS
TAHUTI
BA
WRIST
L
N
C
P
D
U
V

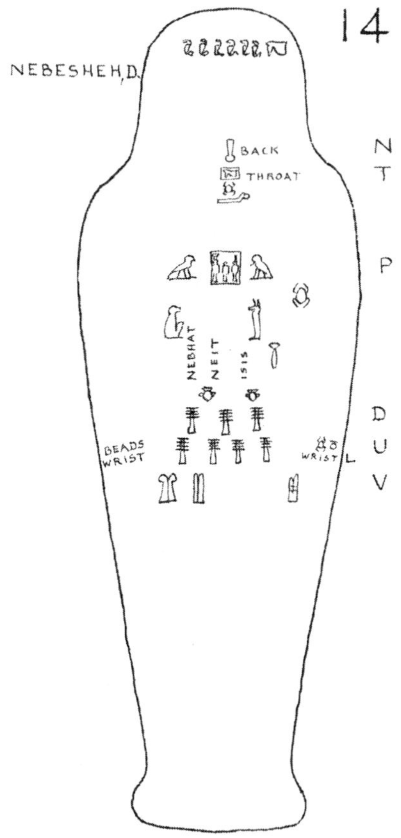
14
NEBESHEH, D.
BACK
THROAT
NEBHAT
NEIT
ISIS
BEADS
WRIST
WRIST
L
N
T
P
D
U
V

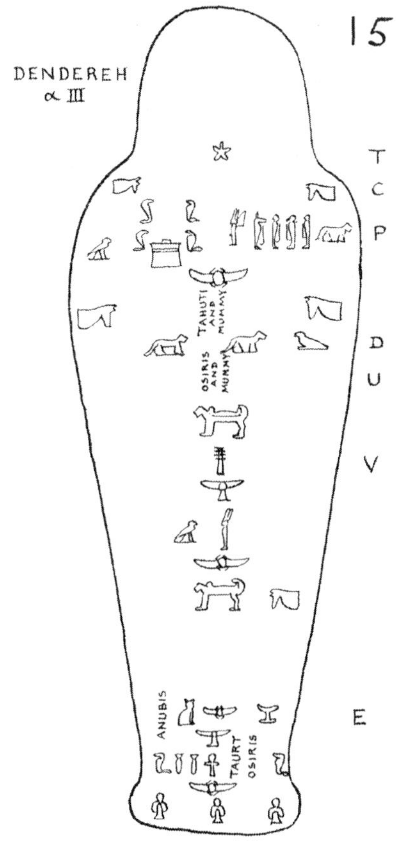
15
DENDEREH
α III
TAHUTI AND MUMMY
OSIRIS AND MUMMY
ANUBIS
TAURT
OSIRIS
T
C
P
D
U
V
E

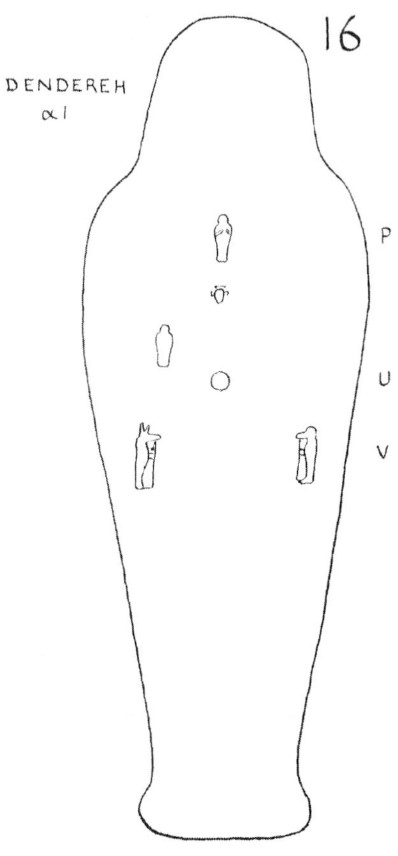
16
DENDEREH
α I
P
U
V

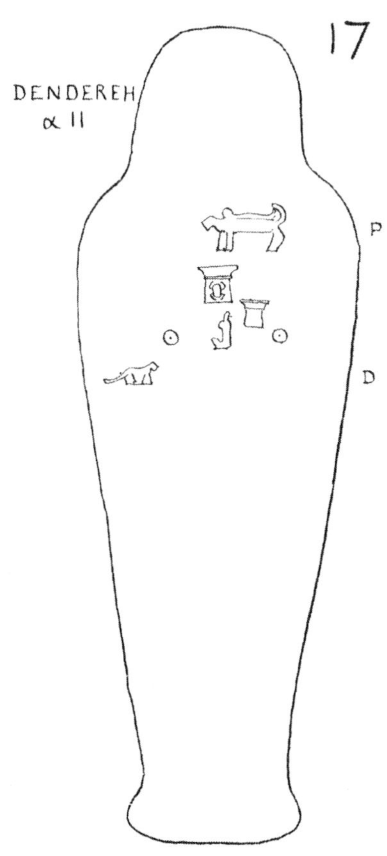
17
DENDEREH
α II
P
D

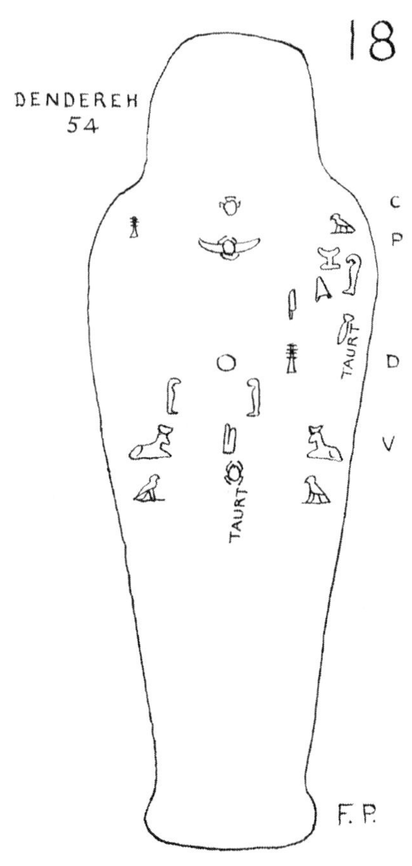
18
DENDEREH
54
TAURT
TAURT
C
P
D
V
F. P.

PLANS OF AMULETS ON MUMMIES.

19

DENDEREH 112

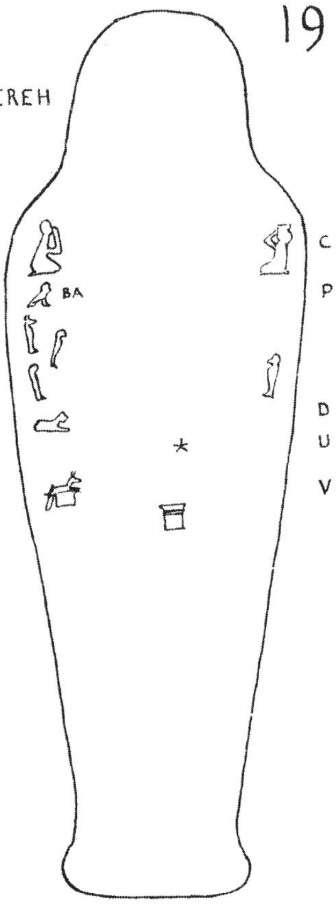

20

DENDEREH 112

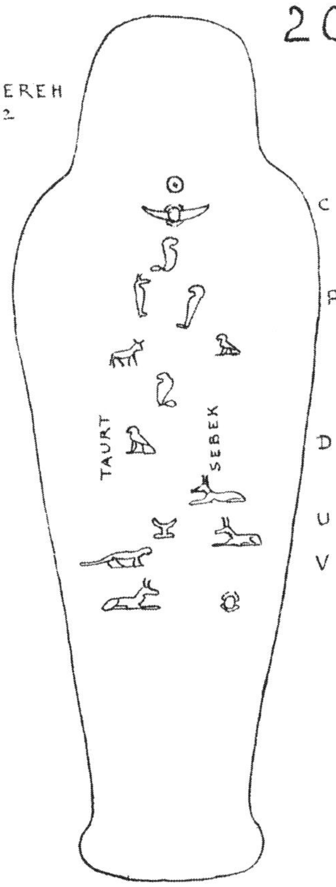

21

DENDEREH 150

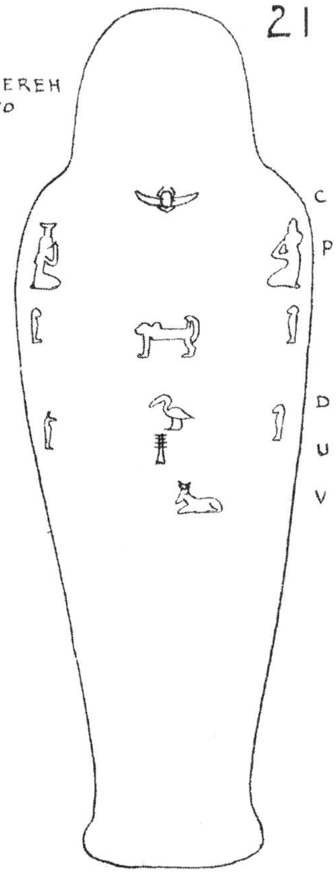

22

DENDEREH 500

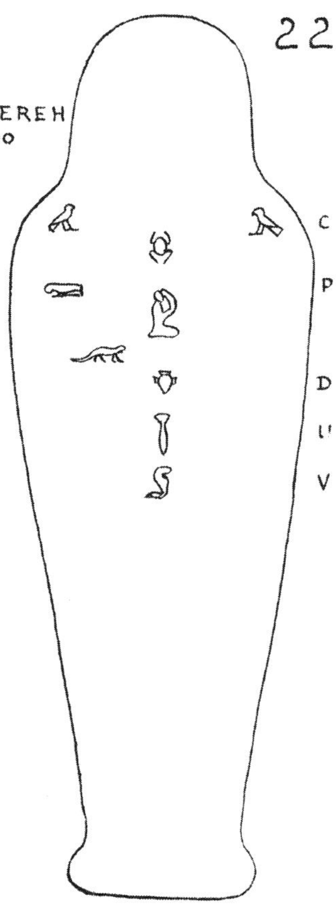

23

DENDEREH

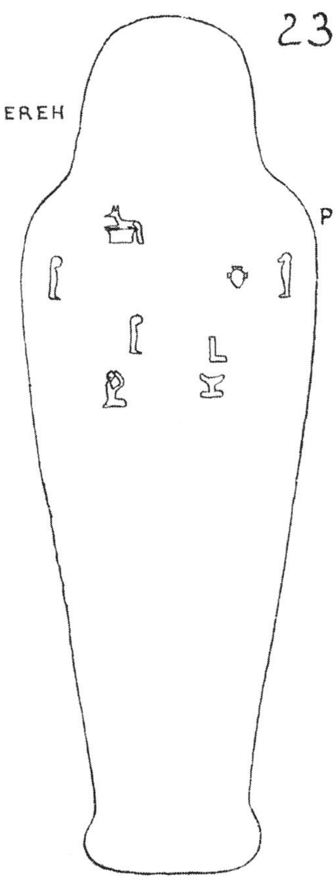

24

DENDEREH α, e.

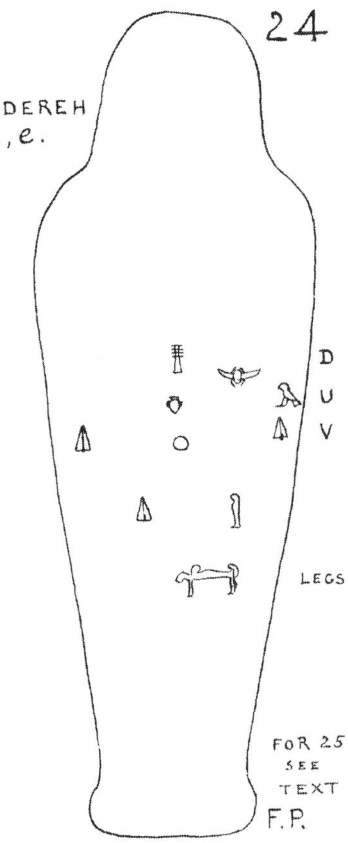

FOR 25 SEE TEXT

F. P.

INDEX TO AMULETS IN POSITION. PLS. L–LIII

POSITIONS

F FOREHEAD
N NAPE OF NECK
T THROAT
C CLAVICLE
P PECTUS
D DIAPHRAGM
U UMBILICUS
V VENTER
M HUMERUS
W WRIST
H HAND
R.L FINGERS, R or L
A ANKLE
E FEET

---

7 HEART. No 1 C,P,D,M. 3C. 4T. 5 T.C. 6 T. 9 P. 10 T.P.U. 11 C. 12 P. 13 C. 14 P. 16 P. 18 C. 22 D. 23 P. 24 U. 25 P.
8. BREAST. 17 P. 18 D? 20 C? 24 V?
17 SMA. 10, U.
18 FROG. 1 P,M. 2 T. 3 P. 5 C. 6 U. 10 P. 11 C. 12 P. 13 P
20 PAPYRUS SCEPTRE. 1 F,T,C,P. 2 D. 3 P. 4 P. 5 P. 6 P. 10 U. 11 V. 13 V. 14 P. 15 E. 18 P. 22 U. 25 P.
21 PAPYRUS PLAQUE. 5 P. 6 P. 7 T. 8 P. 10 C. 11 C.
28 HUMAN-HEADED BIRD. 1 T.C. 2 D. 13 P. 14 P. 19 P
30 MANS GIRDLE-TIE 2 C 15 E
33 COUNTER-POISE 9 P. 11 T. 12 T. 13 N. 14 N
34 HEAD REST 10 T. 15 E. 18 P. 20, U
35 ZAD 1 T,P. 2 C,U 3 C,P,U. 4 P. 5 P. 6 P,D,U. 7 C. 8 D. 9 C,U. 10 T. 11 D. 13 P,D,U. 14 D,U. 15 V. 18 C. 21 U. 24 D. 25 P.
35B 10 D
36 SQUARE 5 C. 10 D. 11 C,P. 12 P. 23 P
37 PLUMMET 5 C. 7 P. 10 D,U. 11 P. 12 P. 18 P. 23 P. 24 V?
38 FORKED LANCE 1 P. 3 P. 4 P. 5 P. 6 P.U. 7 T. 10 C.
39 OSTRICH PLUMES 1 P. 2 D. 3 C. 5 P. 6 P. 7 T. 10 C. 11 V. 14 V.
40C DISC + HORNS 10 P.
41 PAIR OF FEATHERS 3 P. 5 P. 6 P. 10 D. 11 V. 14 V.
42 RISING SUN 10 P
43 DISC OF SUN 5 C. 6 U. 11 U. 12 U. 13 L. 14 L. 16 U
45 BARK 2 C
58 URAEUS 1 P. 2 C. 4 P. 5 F. 12 P,D. 13 P,U,V. 14 F. 15 P,E. 20 C,P. 22 V. 25 T.P.
58D WINGED URAEUS. 4 P.
63 COW, LEGS TIED. 10 P.
66 DUCK. 3 P.
70 VASE. 1, T.
71 COLLAR. 1, C. 4 P.
72 CLOTHING. 5 P. 7 P. 10 D.
76 WRITING TABLET. 1 P. 4 P. 5 C,P. 7 T. 11 V. 12 P,D.
78 CARTOUCHE. 5 C. 6 U. 7 T
79 SEAL. 1 M,L,H. 4 R. 5 C. 6 R,L. 12 D. 13 P.
80 SEAL RING 1 L,R. 2 R. 5 C,L.
81 CIRCLE OF CORD 1, H.
87 MUMMY ON BIER. 15 U,V. 17 P. 21 P. 24 LEGS.
88 GIRDLE OF ISIS 1 T,P. 2 T. 3 P. 5 P. 6 P. 7 P. 8 C. 9 C,P. 10 P. 11 D. 12 U. 13 P,U. 15 E.
91 PECTORAL. 15 P. 17 P. 19 V.
92 SCARAB WITH LEGS. 1 D. 2 P,U. 3 C,P,D. 4 T,P. 5 P. 6 T,U. 7 C,P,D. 8 P. 10 C,P,D. 11 P. 12 P,D. 13 P,L. 14 T,P,L. 18 V. 20 V. 22 C. 25 T,P,U.
92B HAWK-HEADED SCARAB. 1 D. 10 D.
93 SCARAB + WINGS. 9 C. 15 P,V,E. 18 P. 20 C. 21 C. 24 D
93B SAME, ON LEGS. 15 V,E.
94 VULTURE STANDING. 1 T,D. 2 C. 4 P 25 T
95 VULTURE SPREAD 1 C. 4 P.
97 SERPENT HEAD. 1 T. 9 P. 11 T. 14 T.
129 BULLA. 1 C.
138 UZAT 1 F,D,U,M,H. 2 T,C. 3 T,P. 4 P. 5 F,C,P. 6 U. 7 T. 8 P. 10 C,D. 11 D,V, Legs. 12 T,P,D,V. 13 L. 14 F. 15 C,P,V. 25 T,P.
139 UZAT IN SQUARE. 14 T.
149 ISIS. 1 P. 2 T,P,U. 3 P. 4 P. 5 P. 6 C,P. 8 C,P. 9 P. 10 P. 13 P. 14 P.
149B ISIS PLAQUE. 4 P.
150 ISIS MOURNING. 19 C. 21 P. 22 P. 23 P.
152 ISIS, NEBHAT, AND HORUS. 2 U. 3 U. 6 D. 8 D. 13 P. 14 P.
154 NEBHAT. 1 P. 2 P,U. 3 P,D. 4 P. 6 C,P. 8 P. 9 P. 10 P. 13 P. 14 P.
154B NEBHAT PLAQUE. 4 P.
157 OSIRIS 15 V,E.
157D OSIRIS AND MUMMY. 15 U.
161 MIN. 15 P.
167 SHU 1 P. 4 P. 6 U
168 NEIT. 1 P. 2 P. 5 P. 6 P. 14 P.
172 MAOT. 1 P. 2 T,P. 3 P. 5 P. 10 D. 17 P.
174 SELK. 1 P. 2 T,P. 3 P
180 HORUS, HAWK-HEADED. 1 P. 2 P,U. 3 D. 4 P. 5 P. 6 C. 8 P. 9 P. 10 P. 13 P
181 RA. 1 P. 2 T. 2 P. 4 P. 5 P. 6 C,P.
181B RA SEATED. 10 P
182 4 SONS OF RA. 9 D. 15 P. 16 P,V. 18 P,D. 19 P. 20 P. 21 P. 22 P. 23 P. 24 V
186 HATHOR COW-HEADED. 1 T. 9 P
187 KHNUMU. 2 P,U. 4 P. 6 C. 9 P
187B KHNUMU PLAQUE. 4 P.
197 ANPU. 9 P. 14 P.
201 SEBEK. 20 D.
202 TEHUTI. 1 P,U. 3 P,D. 4 P. 5 P. 6 C,P. 8 P. 13 P.
208 HATHOR COW. 18 V. 20 P. 21 V.
219 LION. 3 P. 15 P,D. 17 D. 19 D. 20 V.
220 LIONS FOREPARTS. 9 P. 22 P.
223 BULLS FOREPARTS. 4 P.
224 CAT. 15 E.
231 JACKAL COUCHANT. 9 D. 20 D,U,V.
231B JACKAL ON SHRINE. 19 V. 23 P.
236 TAURT. 15 E. 18 D,V. 20 D.
245 HAWK. 1 P. 3 C. 14 P. 15 P,V. 18 C,V. 20 P,D. 22 C 24 U. 25 C
245E HAWK MUMMY. 1 C. 15 D.
247 IBIS. 21 D.
270 REED. 18 P.
273 TWO FINGERS. 5 V. 6 V. 10 V. 11 V. 12 V. 14 V. 18 V.
275 STAR. 15 T. 19 U.

THE AMULETS ARE SPREAD OUT RATHER TOO LOW IN THE DIAGRAMS IN ORDER TO BE MORE CLEAR. F. P.